HE

Please return or renew this item before the latest date shown below

E.L

Smith

webster

Frost ©

Cuthbertson Ⓝ

Gardiner Ⓔ

Lindsay Ⓙ

Zawada Ⓖ

Mclean

ROBERT GREENFIELD spent years coming to terms with a darkly tragic childhood to become an international fashion designer once dubbed: 'Britain's answer to the Italian Look' by *Men's Wear Magazine.*

He has lived in Florence, New York and Hong Kong, and is now a well-respected interior designer with many successful projects often featured in magazines and the press.

In 2000, Robert and his partner, Michael left London to set up a much-publicised boutique style B&B on the stunning North Norfolk coast. They also run unique holiday-lets along this coastline.

Robert is a keen environmentalist, passionate about animal welfare, a fitness freak, trend geek, and says, and quote, *'Design is my sensitivity!'*

He is currently writing his next book...

www.robertgreenfield.co.uk

Samphire Coast

Robert Greenfield

Samphire Coast

Vanguard Press

VANGUARD PAPERBACK

© Copyright 2011
Robert Greenfield

A CIP catalogue record for this title is
available from the British Library.

ISBN 978 1 84386 917 7

*Vanguard Press is an imprint of
Pegasus Elliot MacKenzie Publishers Ltd.*
www.pegasuspublishers.com

First Published in 2011

**Vanguard Press
Sheraton House Castle Park
Cambridge England**

Printed & Bound in Great Britain

Disclaimer

The publisher and the author have made every effort to contact all persons and public organisations mentioned within this publication. For those wishing to update information mentioned within *Samphire Coast*, contact is welcomed and instructions will be carried out as requested.

Samphire Coast is based upon a true story of the author's first-hand experience in running a B&B business. Consequently all identities of guests have been changed to protect these innocents and sometimes the very guilty. And any guest names portrayed in this book to actual living persons are purely coincidental. Similarly, all guest anecdotes have been recreated to echo real sequential episodes to further disguise all true identities. Dialogue has been compressed in these instances to capture the essence of what occurred some years ago, recorded from the owner's diaries.

Please note that it is not the intention of the publisher or the author to cause offence in publicising this piece of literature.

Special thanks to:

Tony Hall, Walter F. Stowy, Richard Parr, Sarah Hardy, Mark Nicholls, Alec Lom, David Newnham, Justine Hankins, and Marian Pallister.

Mr. Barry Ryan.

The Sunday Times, *Travel*.

The Eastern Daily Press and The *Archant* Group.

The Dereham and Fakenham Times.

The Guardian Newspaper, *Travel*.

Now Magazine.

The Daily Telegraph.

Country Homes and Interiors Magazine.

The Sunday Mirror, *Homes and Holidays*.

For their promotional contribution and assistance in the completion of, and permission to use materials produced and or published within their publications and reproduced within *Samphire Coast*.

Acknowledgments

I am eternally gratefully to Mike's much-cherished mother, Norma for bringing her son into this world to complete my life. *Mike you made it all worthwhile!*

A special heartfelt tribute to my father for being a guiding light from the heavens...

Much gratitude to my surrogate mother, dearest Violet for her understanding and loving support...

A big hug for my bro, Tony for being a dependable rock...

Saluting my stepbrother, Mike, Stateside.

An endearing nod to my cousin Myrna, for always being so wonderful.

I owe a huge debt of gratitude to Teresa, Keith, and Matt Hoddy for bringing the much-beloved (whippet) Barnaby into my life.

A special mention for Carole and Peter Hoare our dear neighbours at Holly Lodge.

A huge thank you to the *East of England Tourist Board (VisitBritain)*, and to the *Automobile Association Hotel Services (AA)* for their fêted recognition of my labour of love.

In heartfelt memory of Paul Ryan, and with sincere thanks to both Paul and Barry Ryan, and their sister, Caroline; cherishing old friendship.

Many thanks to Tony Lawrence for his impeccable timing!

A special thank you to Clay Littlewood. Cheers!

With much appreciation to the very talented Paul Kirk for his brilliant cover design, www.paulkirk-illustration.co.uk.

Thank you to my terrific publishers, Pegasus Elliott MacKenzie Publishers Ltd for producing my debut book.

I want to record a posthumous genuflect to, the late Paul Whittome, founder of the Hoste Arms in Burnham Market; he was the inspiration behind North Norfolk's top place on the map today.

Thanking all of our guests for their custom at Holly Lodge.

Treasuring new Norfolk friends and old townie mates still in my life.

... And most of all, in memory of my mother, Irene, I really wish I'd known you...

For my soul mate Michael.

A WORD ABOUT SAMPHIRE

Samphire (*Salicornia europaea*) also known as sea asparagus rampantly grows over the estuarine marshes and tidal mudflats on the windswept reaches of the North Norfolk Heritage coast.

A seasonal (mid-June until late August) succulent delicacy resembling a forest of miniature cactuses is freely available in abundance to harvest by locals and holidaymakers alike. Or generous bunches can be bought very reasonably at any number of stalls dotted along the A149 coastal road. Paradoxically, marsh samphire *de rigueur* in top London restaurants now commands exorbitant city prices these days. North Norfolk is so blessed...

Always remove the woody stems, and wash the fresh Samphire thoroughly to remove any grit or sand residue... blanch in unsalted (sugar/2 tablespoons) sweetened boiling water 3/4 mins. Drain, and toss with olive oil, knob of butter, and fresh lemon juice. A perfect accompaniment to any fish dish or add as a wonderful garnish to fish pie.

My signature (supper) dish at the Lodge: *dress boneless fresh salmon or tuna cutlets with a little virgin olive oil, sundried tomatoes (paste works well), some fresh basil, roasted pine kernels (handful), and a few diced pitted black olives. Add a dusting of chilli seasoning (sparingly), and a pinch of sea-salt and black pepper as desired. Place in a baking dish (electric: approx. 375°F or 190°C) to bake or grill for about 15 minutes. Any excess jus should be poured over the fish. Serve with fresh tagliatelle or pappardelle tossed in olive oil with garlic and baked cherry vine tomatoes.*

Prepare the Samphire as above (100-200g per person) mix with some grated goats' cheese just prior to serving as an accompaniment for a perfect alfresco summer dish. And oh, don't forget the garlic bread and a green lentil side salad a la Robert mixed with mint leaves and diced red peppers...

Foreword

Fortune favours the brave...

New Year's Eve, 1999, as the clock struck midnight Greenwich Mean Time, would apocalyptic talk of the Millennium Bug become a reality? Lack-lustre fireworks fizzled-out over the Thames in a hapless puff of smoke – cringing Royals linked hands with the smug-faced Blairs under that cursed Dome for a bravado performance of 'Old Acquaintance', and we, two style conscious city boys (an item), were about to embark on a journey beyond our wildest dreams.

The mystery house languishing behind an ancient orchard just beckoned me with a beguiling allure. Was I born to my next calling? Our beloved vintage campervan was packed to the gills in readiness for our furtive escape to a sequestered little hamlet somewhere in North Norfolk.

Who would have believed my story? It became an intense yearning to pen this remarkable roller-coaster adventure in the hope it might inspire others to jump through a window of opportunity and try something different, because a little naïvety can sometimes go a long, long way...

Seven potent years had gone by in a flash in what was to become a pivotal chapter of our lives. There was no going back...

In 2008, Mike and I sealed our relationship formally in a 'Civil Partnership' ceremony at the famous North Norfolk landmark of the Cley Windmill, subsequently embarking on a dreamy (honeymoon) holiday cruise to Venice.

All was well with the world... in fact I felt like the luckiest guy on the planet even reigniting my old career into a new sideline, which was about to take-off big-time on our return...

You see? I had been promised a major contract to interior design a cutting-edge new hotel in a picturesque Suffolk harbour town. Holly Lodge had no doubt provided an impressive track record for my CV!

But life as always is full of capricious (ill) winds. And suddenly that August, the world fell off its booming economic precipice, because as-you-well-know one of the worst recessions ever, took hold. I lost my contract. It was one of life's great disappointments for me at the time...

I dusted myself down in the belief that as one door closes, another one opens... And yep, my *raison d'être* became very apparent from my DNA. The opportunity afforded me the time to write *Samphire Coast*. And I discovered I love to write, but also I found this could be my act of reflection on the human condition...

Subsequently, I started to rummage through a plethora of press cuttings, 'Thank You' cards, comments in our beloved 'Visitors' Book' and reams of scribbled notes in my dog-eared diaries.

I sat at my desk for nigh on a year. I laughed, and I sometimes cried. Mike wondered who the hell I was talking to at times in a variety of cadenced regional accents from across the nation and beyond. Or was I now getting (Norfolk) island fever holed-up in my study...? As I'd act out these scenarios through voyeuristic portals with fond acuity... these little vignettes I simply had to capture into my allegory, as if rescued from some film off the cutting room floor, and now playing in my head like a rolling autobiographic movie.

In all honesty, running an upmarket hotel-type business was never going to be easy, especially for someone of my early morning (lugubrious) disposition. And becoming 'Domestic Gods' was an absolute *must* in a trade that would become such an eye-opener: the hotel inspection rating process, the up-before-god daily breakfast routines, the unexpected (Sod's Law) glitches, the trials and tribulations of it all, and oh yes; **THE GUESTS...** portrayed in *Samphire Coast...*

An unforgettable array of some of my most memorable encounters, a rogue's gallery of errant personas: 'Guests from Hell' sometimes **blacklisted** for wreaking havoc within the sanctuary of our Gothic-esque walls. Thankfully those were in a minority! And most were outwardly genteel types, guests of exemplary calibre; but whose staycation with us inevitably impacted our daily lives as well for all sorts of reasons...

Consequently, in my tribute to them all: I have changed their identities, their names, and recreated similar sequential events echoing these episodes to protect these innocents or occasionally the *very* guilty. And any names created to actual living persons are purely coincidental...

Samphire Coast is my unique trenchant foray into both the light and dark recesses of my over-the-counter view at the Lodge. Often narrated in a candid, heartfelt and sometimes quick-witted regale as believe you me 'A sense of humour was imperative at all times!' Albeit set against the most *bootiful* backdrop on the wilder edge of the North Norfolk Heritage coast.

I sincerely hope you enjoy my debut book as much as I have writing it... Your booking is confirmed! Please step onto the *red carpet...* Welcome to the *real* Holly Lodge (UNLEASHED)...

CHAPTER 1

THE VIEWING

'Country House for sale in Norfolk...'

The words leapt off the page from the minutiae of sales blurbs in the property section of the *London Evening Standard* late that dismal Friday afternoon.

My mobile was low on juice, the traffic was nose to bumper at a standstill, and I'd been sitting in the same lousy jam for what seemed aeons pondering this advertisement, whilst yearning for an escape out of this typical rush-hour scramble for the blessed sanctuary behind my own front door.

Norfolk windmills, scarlet poppy fields, and scented purple lavender projected into my senses as a euphoric recall to a trip long ago. Though that might as well have been in another lifetime... I peered hopelessly through the windscreen at the grey concrete monolith overshadowing my faithful chariot. Faceless hordes of shopaholics poured out of the stores, clutching bulging bags of must-have brands, and flowed like seething oil deep into our dark manmade chasms to lubricate the Underground system: the depths of Hades, and the lifeblood to our metropolis.

A break in the traffic ahead, and I veered over to park, albeit on a double yellow; I could see the warden clock me from a hundred yards away or so, so I knew that time was of the essence as I hastily tapped in the unfamiliar code on my mobile. Call it instinct... This house just beckoned.

A lady answered with a broad regional twang. I asked for particulars to the property, and she launched into her perfunctory sales spiel.

I jotted down the details, while I kept a beady eye on the fearsome parking warden edging perilously closer and closer to my vehicle as he dished out tickets with an evil smarmy grin; a gratifying quota to close his day.

"Tha' is an 18th century farmhouse: five bedrooms, t'ree bathrooms, two large receptions, kitchen, utility, pantry, oover an acre of grounds, an orchard, t'ree self-contained cottages, and oh, a Nissen hut."

"Huh, a Nissen hut...?" My mind raced with the configuration of the particulars, and her lingo.

"Thur owners run Holly Lodge as a Bed and Breakfas', and tha' is located in thur village of Thursford Green near thur North Norfook coas'." Blimey... that accent was thick as it was broad.

I was really enthused, and all for under a quarter of a million pounds...? So I asked by any chance if I could see it the next day at two? She called the owners, it was convenient, and an appointment was set. She would e-mail me the directions that night.

Thursford Green, the name struck a nerve for some odd reason. Visceral curiosity fired my imagination with fanciful images of a mystery house. Perhaps it was a Jacobean manor set in acres of woodland by a lake secretly tucked away from prying eyes? Or an extravagant castellated Gothic mansion: all spires, and turrets, lingering in a solitary nebula as a preserved theatrical set piece; or a handsome Georgian pile with its grand neo classical proportions that would lend itself well to an eclectic mix of today's contemporary interiors.

Ah, a hopeless romantic fantasizing about my hidden passions for fanciful follies, a throwback to my youthful dreams as I sought solace to escape from my dysfunctional family life, but more about that later...

Finally, I arrived home, dashed across the cobbled courtyard, and headed straight for the kitchen to reheat the previous day's cooked pesto-pasta dinner, now languishing in the fridge. I rustled up a hearty salad, and shoved the garlic bread in the oven. The ring tone of my mobile sounded-off, and a text message read '*C-U-in-10-luv-U!*'

I had met Mike on a blind date five years earlier, when I lived in my white minimalist box on Belsize Village, in one of those imposing stucco-fronted buildings. My raised ground floor flat had been a find, and a real steal in the last recession. For three years I had been undergoing a complete cathartic clear out, unloading some messy mental baggage that was cluttering up my life.

Some mutual friends of ours arranged a blind date... Of course I'd always thought these kinds of dates were a long shot, and would never work out into something really special. How wrong was I...?

On 23rd September 1994 at 7pm to be exact, we met up outside 'American Retro' in Old Compton Street in Soho: I was immediately struck by his Nordic good looks. And then we hit it off instantly with a familiarity as if we'd known each other for years.

They say opposites attract... indeed we were both from polar opposite backgrounds; he was from the gritty North East, salt of the earth type of folk who had given him a loving secure upbringing, which was probably responsible for his affable, confident, and sincere demeanour, set off by a sexy fresh-faced, blue-eyed cheeky smile. And in no time I was smitten... (The Robert of old emerged from his chrysalis, and learnt to fly-high with true love.)

That night he came in harassed as per usual from his hectic schedule at the salon. I bet the new temp at the front desk had cocked-up the appointments book yet again, causing untold chaos resulting in impossible schedules. I could sense his frazzled angst. He pecked me on the cheek, dropped his bag, sighed and kicked off...

"Five-thirty... that dragon, Frances Fosdyke wafted in huffing, and puffing, demanding a colour..."

"What foil highlights at that time?"

"She'd been asked at short notice to give a speech on contemporary art forms of species threatened with extinction. Very *Zeitgeist*..."

"What sort of a la Damien Hirst...?"

"Aye! And in some bullshit gallery tonight." He wearily made his way over to the sink.

"She's not exactly your favourite client is she...?"

I served up supper, Mike freshened up, and we sat down to eat.

"No, I could have literally strangled her, there and then, and despatched her offal remains to be sculptured into a ridiculous exhibit for the Tate Modern," he chortled.

"Hey, wouldn't that be ironic...? A star vitrine of a taxidermy Frances Fosdyke an extinct West End cougar, circa 1994: renowned for their fabulous split ends..." I tried to make him see the funny side.

This is what it had become night after night: "Trouble at Mill/Salon."

Don't get me wrong... He was a genius at doing hair, had a real natural flair for it, but the repetitive drudgery of his ever-demanding clients, banging on, day-in day-out about their personal problems, meant not only did he have to make them look as gorgeous as can be, but he had to be an agony aunt to their woes too, which was mentally wearing although he'd go into automatic pilot with most.

Mike had been runner-up to the likes of *Nicky Clarke* and *Charles Worthington* on a number of occasions for *'Hairdresser of the Year'*, so there was no doubt as to his abilities in this field, but his ambition had somehow hit the buffers. By now with a stable of well-known clients, and celebs to his name, it should really have been *his* title in lights above the door; but I guess he just did not want to commit further to a trade that he was fed up to the eyeteeth with. I knew he wanted out, and I just might have the answer...

"Guess what...? We're going to see a country house for sale in Norfolk near the coast tomorrow at two," I said with my usual zeal for house hunting.

"Why Norfolk... huh?" he said quizzically, probing me with his steel-blue eyes.

Often, we'd discuss plans to move to the country, ignited by our many weekends away, so I knew he'd been waiting for me to make waves in this area.

"A good question... well, when I was at Fashion College, about ten of us piled down there to a beach house somewhere near Cromer. I vaguely remember the sharp curvy roads, odd shaped spooky trees, endless beach sands, big, big skies, and that funny old Norfolk lingo. Besides there's a house for sale that I have one of my feelings for..."

His dark mood switched as if a light had gone on. I could see the cartoon caption spring out above his head outlining his thoughts. '*Relocation-Relocation-Relocation*'.

Often on a break away from the Old Smoke, we would jump into our beloved, very retro, pale-blue VW campervan, and head for romantic breaks down to the south coast. Dorset was a particular favourite; we even had our eye on a first floor apartment on the front in Sandbanks overlooking the harbour... Can you imagine? It was going for pittance back then; today it would fetch millions!

The Jurassic coastline was a welcome respite from the intensity of the urban sprawl. Sometimes for a couple of sexy nights we'd end up ensconced in this weird Bed and Breakfast in a fabulously creepy 1930s' house sitting high up on a terraced garden beyond a long wooded drive: it kind of felt like an eyrie. There was a huge life-size Japanese pagoda sitting majestically in the rear garden that would not have been out of place in Kew.

A strange anomaly though was that this guesthouse had no locks on any of the bedroom doors, and the owner, though very accommodating, had something very disturbingly Norman Bates-ish about his persona. He would actually creep into our room while we were sleeping in, first thing, and leave a breakfast tray. It was bizarre! Nevertheless this peaceful retreat became our special place during those early courting days.

One time though we headed over to Rye in East Sussex, and stayed in a picture postcard 'Old Vicarage' overlooking a graveyard in the centre square, serenaded by church bells fortunately at sociable hours. It was very atmospheric...

Curiously the ever-so charming landlady reminded me of one of the *Stepford Wives* running her ship to the utmost perfection; she must have been on robotic autopilot always presenting herself with an immaculate radiant smile at all hours.

Apparently she'd been nominated for 'Landlady of the Year' as indicated by the framed certificate prominently displayed in the front hall. And I naïvely thought it must be a cinch running such an establishment. Perhaps, it was here where the seed was sown somewhere in my psyche. And she was my inspiration...?

However, it was dear old Norfolk in the opposite direction that would become a complete departure from our southern coastal adventures.

That fateful Saturday morning came soon enough. We left early full of *Boy's Own* eagerness to discover what this enigmatic county might have in store.

Once off the motorway, it seemed the traffic became sparser the more we penetrated this verdant lush county, and the land evoked a wilder edge not often seen in the Home Counties.

Suddenly, we found ourselves immersed beneath great Scots Pine trees, and this is the heavily wooded Breckland area or The Brecks, with its mysterious ancient feel rich in rare flora and fauna. I clocked the sign for the 'Iceni Village' home to tragic Queen Boudicca, who must have stomped these grounds two thousand years ago before her humiliated defeat at the hands of her Roman oppressors, cementing her iconic place in East Anglian myth.

A sign ahead indicated we were fast approaching the market town of Swaffham (once a wealthy Georgian bolt-hole), more recently featured in the TV series *Kingdom* starring the omniscient Stephen Fry, with its skyline dominated by a gargantuan eco wind turbine, which seemed to follow us through the town.

Meandering slowly through the town centre, with its Saturday market bustling in full-flow, we glanced across at the packed market stalls, studying their provincial wares curiously as we went. Eventually on leaving, it was as if we passed through an invisible gateway that opened onto another panoramic wilderness of gorse-covered heath-land lined with endless lofty trees en route.

"Perhaps, Swaffham might be the last bastion of civilisation here?" I jested. (But really, I pondered scenes from that morose film *The Witchfinder General*, echoing an insular backward culture stuck in a time warp: loitering indignant wart-faced stereotypes, rampant idiocy, dark family secrets, and gunged trousers – held-up with coarse twine... What!! How sad am I? Or is this really the beginning-of-the-end of my sartorial street-cred?)...

Maybe, it was bad ole King John's fault after all, when he lost the crown jewels somewhere around the Wash, and stigmatised poor Norfolk with England's bitterness for centuries thereafter... No wonder, (bejewelled) Elizabeth I had her duke of *Norfolk* beheaded!

Mike smiled curiously (he could always hear the cogs of my mind grinding with my weird stuff) and handed me some chewy sports mixtures.

"Where in God's heaven are we going...?" He was getting impatient. Although on seeing the beauty of the unspoilt landscape unfold before us, we both swooned at the possibilities...

Deeper and deeper we drove into unknown territory, as we caught another beckoning detour, 'Castle Acre Priory' enticing us for a brief stop to explore its enigmatic ruins – a well-preserved monastic site dating back to 1090.

After a pick-me-up coffee in the grounds of the hallowed Priory, we jumped back into our vehicle, eager to get to our destination, excited at the prospect of this sequestered house. Little did we know then that this was to be the beginning of an amazing adventure that would change our lives forever...

"Fakenham, now that would be very suggestive if the A was dropped in favour of a U! Wonder if it's indicative of its inhabitants?" My sleazy configuration of a town once voted: 'The most boring in Norfolk'. We looked at each other, and sniggered immaturely. As it happened, one day this place would feature prominently in our new lives, becoming a dependable source for stocking up on supplies from its weekly country market – where anything can be purchased from chicken wire fencing to a chateau-chic armoire with a copious range of delicious fare in between. And all produced locally.

It was one o'clock, and we'd just seen the sign for 'Thursford Green' moments away, the excitement was mounting to a crescendo with the prospect of this mystery viewing, however there was still an hour to kill, so we by-passed the little hamlet, and headed up to the coast about six miles away.

Here we found ourselves at Wells-next-the-Sea, where we were confronted by a vast picturesque harbour connected by an estuary, which meandered out for what seemed an eternity to the coast beyond. The sun was high in the dramatic Norfolk sky providing a seamless backdrop to the colourful boats, bobbing on the buoyant dark swell. Some kids were what looked like crab catching on a sea wall as their parents tucked into newspaper-wrapped fish and chips. The entire scene was reminiscent of an old English postcard circa 1956... Making for a vintage hand-painted watercolour catching this traditional utopia in-frame.

As I digested this holiday snapshot, the delicious aromas combining with the pure oxygenated air wafted into our vehicle sending a high-rush of exhilaration throughout my whole being. This was a planet away from the cityscape of our daily grind. We pulled to a stop, and lingered for a while, drinking in the picturesque scene, before Mike broke my reverie announcing it was time to head for Thursford.

Naturally, a secluded hamlet hidden off the motorway would intrigue us. We passed the *Thursford Steam Museum* on our right, and then the small village green on our left, overlooked by a modest Methodist chapel. A charming flint cottage stood on the central reservation, and there were various houses scattered about. But what struck me most was the tranquillity, a peaceful solitude as if we'd been transported to another time... My atavistic instincts were most certainly aroused.

Maybe this was the last unblemished village vis-à-vis a once green and pleasant land... I mused. Then we saw the faded sign for 'Holly Lodge' swinging forlornly in the gentle afternoon breeze; I especially noticed the vacancy sign below, the letters barely legible.

Accidentally I drove past the entrance, and parked on the green verge beneath the great Scots Pine trees lining the boundary to the property like sentinels keeping the world at bay. We were both at fever pitch with the intriguing prospect of our rural idyll as we stole a glance through the magical old orchard that practically screened the entire house save the Georgian bay windows to the lounge.

This fleeting glimpse seduced my heart, which began to race in anticipation of my dreamy fantasy. We looked at each other smugly, smiling with our secret discovery as we reversed to head up the drive.

Slowly, our vehicle emerged onto the forecourt in front of the main building, which was unfolding into the dreariest, plainest, most non-descript property I'd ever seen. My heart sank with heavy disappointment, while the colour drained from Mike's face.

"Let's scarper, turn around quick before they see us, this is not my country idyll at all..." Mike became despondent, and slunk back looking deflated.

"Come on... Er... We've come all this way, I can fix the house, but the setting is beautifully fixed already..." I said enthusiastically. I was putting on a brave face because deep down I was gutted by the dour kerb appeal of what was supposed to be my dream house.

We approached the front door gingerly, ringing the old pull-bell. A matronly woman named Faye, who was one of the owners, opened the door, and ushered us into the front hall, which apparently had once been a dairy. She instigated an official no-nonsense welcome to Holly Lodge, with a curt smile.

Then, the usual pleasantries were exchanged before we were introduced to the curious tripartite collaboration of her husband, Roy, an ex-police officer, a tall retiring type, and their friend, and business partner Charlotte, a gaunt smart lady with a clipped English accent, who also resided there.

Faye, a feisty woman full of bravado showed us around, first through the gloomy dining room, which she explained was where their guests ate breakfast as indicated by the assortment of tables dispersed throughout the room – a room with the only saving grace of having a lovely view out to the front orchard. And then we were led to a large lounge...

Everything was drab, dowdy, and awfully chintzy. Let's just say Laura Ashley had seen better days... This was an untouched 1970s' time warp with so many easy-chairs in the sitting room it kind of reminded me, dare I say of an old people's home. The house was devoid of any interior design, basic, and functional with an overwhelming sense of tiredness; it seemed as if they were trying desperately to hold it all together.

As it turned out they had been at the Lodge for about twelve years, where they'd eked out a half-decent living with their Bed and Breakfast business. And obviously these strong-willed ladies had run the guesthouse with immense vigour, but these period houses are notorious for slurping funds, and along with daily operating expenses in the hospitality business, it must have been tough constantly trying to maintain appearances to placate happy guests.

It was pitiful from room to room. The kitchen was exhausted after years of cooking full English breakfasts; the upstairs bedrooms were truly miserable, with the Spartan master bedroom having a very ominous concave ceiling. I feared for the occupants that slept beneath it.

The master bathroom fared no better. Although huge, it was an interior nightmare, because for me, my pet-hate is 'The corner tub...' And especially the apricot variety with faux gold taps, and to top it all there was one of those dreadful film-star mirrors surrounded by myriad light bulbs (very un-eco today). Please don't think me an *Enfant Terrible*! I was well aware of their predicament, and could see well past these archaic design errors jarring with my keen *decorexic* eye.

"Don't you think the bath is fabulous?" Faye declared proudly.

"Yes, it's delightful..." I replied rather lamely.

"I know you don't like it, it's OK you can be honest. After all you're one of those interior design chaps aren't you? I always watch *Grand Designs* and *Changing Rooms* although some of those schemes are simply airy-fairy-frightening..."

She was standing there with her arms folded glaring at me, and cajoling for a response to her beloved tub. "Well then... out with it!"

"Well, if it were mine, I would distress, and disguise it into a water feature somewhere to be used in the very back of the garden." Crikey... I surprised myself with my almighty gaffe. That's it I thought she's going to throw us out now... Mike scowled at me from over her shoulder.

She burst into rip-roaring laughter. "I never thought of that... Gosh you are imaginative!" She patted me boisterously on my shoulder – she was a tremendous sport about it. Although I felt sick with embarrassment, and I knew Mike wanted to clout me.

Faye led us downstairs, and out into the garden to show us the quaint guest cottages of typical Norfolk flint vernacular like the many enchanting villages we had seen on our way here. Apparently the flint stones indigenous of the region, and once freely available, were a cheaper option than bricks for house building by the denizens, thus providing these romantically appealing façades, which are prevalent throughout Norfolk.

The cottages had been converted from the old stable-block, they were a decent size, had some fetching beams, quirky fireplaces, and rustic charm that would appeal to the townies. But boy not only did they feel fusty, but oh so dreary too – typical of the downbeat accommodation synonymous with the most bog standard Bed and Breakfasts. The wall-mounted televisions looked like they had been there since 'John Logie Baird' had invented them. The beds were covered with ratty frilly throws, but what really astonished me was the centre ceiling light in the middle cottage. It reminded of my childhood bedroom – in the style of a hot-air balloon lampshade attached to a hanging basket – housing a brightly coloured cuddly toy, perhaps a rabbit. I did giggle to myself... What must the guests really think of this? (Hardly the chic interior accessory for today's must-have fashionista...) Come on... I'm not being bitchy: kitsch is back! I'm sure none of their paying guests ever mentioned it for fear of embarrassing their lovely hosts.

The rear of the house fared no better either, with its magnolia pebbledash exterior, and odd shaped ill-conceived sunken terrace. And next we explored the back garden, which was completely enclosed in Government surplus chain-link fencing.

"Probably to keep the inmates from escaping..." I quietly suggested to Mike.

"Aye! Very utilitarian..." I could sense he was not overly enamoured with the place. He became more downbeat.

There it was... the curious Nissen barn-hut that could have housed an entire Spitfire fighter-plane or two, as it was practically the size of an aircraft hangar left over from the war years, I presumed. We opened the creaky doors into the vast space stored with all sorts of grampy-paraphernalia, and numerous wooden crates labelled with all the classic varieties of English apples: 'Pippins, Granny-Smiths, Coxes, Bramleys etc'. I guess all plucked from their very own orchard.

Amongst the dank bric-a-brac there was an old 1960s' lawnmower – very retro... Some beaten-up garden furniture, and a great looking rickety table, that with a bit of tender loving care would grace any farmhouse kitchen admirably. I discovered this was where Roy escaped to, probably for some space from the ladies, becoming his private domain of male preserve to potter around.

The rear garden was a nothingness save the great view out over the farm fields beyond, some more gnarled old apple trees, a gigantic bay tree, a hazelnut tree, some vegetable patches, and a curious tumbledown ruin overgrown with wild flowers. Completely charming... However, it was the horses grazing in the corner field that stole my heart.

As we ambled back into the house, we were greeted with a welcoming afternoon tea in front of the old Inglenook, which was the only redeeming feature in the lounge although it needed some urgent restoring. And pronto!

Faye sat regally in one of those special therapeutic reclining armchairs, but nearly catapulted out of it when she pressed the side-lever. It was comical – echoing the ejector seat of the *007 Aston Martin*... And we had to contain ourselves. However it inspired me with the notion: she was the Queen of this realm on her automated throne...

"What do you think of Holly Lodge then...?" she asked briskly.

"Naturally, there'd be a lot for us to think about here," I replied tactfully, feeling I had been put on the spot.

I gauged Mike's reaction, he straightened his shirt collar looking nonplussed, and I could tell he wanted to make a runner, but of course he was polite, and smiled cordially.

Apparently they'd been seriously let down by two potential buyers over the last year; frustratingly pulling out just prior to exchange of contracts, so it appeared they were now desperate for a sale.

Roy came into the room every inch the former cop brazenly gauging our intentions, while Charlotte was flapping about serving tea; I guess they were curious about us too, but worldly enough not to be fussed about our relationship.

"These fresh eggs are for you..." Charlotte handed me a box.

"Our bantam farm eggs are supplied by a generous neighbour with a small holding nearby in the village," Faye added.

"Oh, thank you... erm – what? Don't they pop out with a sell-by-date already stamped on them...?" I joked.

Mike rolled his eyes. I could tell he was not impressed by my attempt at some humorous banter here; nevertheless they smiled politely just the same.

As we were leaving, and stood in the unassuming hallway I couldn't help commenting on the sound of the loud moos of the cows from the nearby farm.

"Bless, and sweet calves nearby too!"

Faye responded with her school ma'am lesson on rural life. "Oh dear... the young calves have just been despatched to the slaughterhouse, it's killing season you know; but one does get used to the incessant wailing of their bereft mums..."

"Oops..." I was aghast, and felt like such a chump. An ignorant city boy – sheltered from the realisation – that our cling-film-wrapped supermarket meat really is the result of *Kindertransport* despatches to farms with the *Auschwitz* factor. And even more riddled with guilt, because I once used to design heaps of leather apparel. I swore there, and then I would become a vegetarian...

We said our farewells, the front door closed. We stood facing the old orchard filled with all manner of trees laden with fruits. Aside from the copious apple bearers there were Conference pears, Victoria plums, cherries, and a walnut tree – which seemed exotic, as I never knew it grew in this country.

Mike turned to me looking very underwhelmed, whereas I was already visioning that I could create a 'Dream Sanctuary', here. OK, it was all run-down with more than a hint of dearth about its interiors, but what a setting... And those guest cottages were such a bonus; all it needed was an injection of creative genius. I am deft at reinventing things a la mode, these skills had put me in good stead in this rising property market, and culminated in quite a few successes with properties nobody would dare touch. Making them look a million dollars without spending it, that's the trick, and I knew I had it, creating something special everybody would want. The boy was born to his *next* calling...

Naturally this project would be a huge undertaking, but this could be the opportunity of a lifetime in exchange from the sale proceeds of our two bedroom Edwardian garden flat in prime Muswell Hill. And all this could be ours with enough change to develop it into some kind of hotel-deluxe (yep, even manor houses were going for a song back then). Of course it would have to be a viable going concern, there would be no way this could just be a weekend bolthole; it was far too large, and it could make a fine home too. Mike could give up his dreaded schedule at the salon; we'd be living the dream life in the fresh air of the countryside, with our energies concentrated into developing a new business. I just needed to convince Michael...

"How do you feel, about owning, and running the best boutique B&B in Norfolk?" I asked cock-surely.

Mike looked at me incredulously, gasped, then laughed out loud, and replied in a John McEnroe-esque way.

"You can't be serious... you cannot... How can we pull it off?"

"Trust me, Mike... we're young enough to give it a go. Besides with our combined talents I know we'll do wonders with this affordable property. It's scary, but a chance to escape polluted, crime-ridden London. Come on... let's be adventurous – to hell with it!" I said gleefully, justifying the gung-ho spirit of my *derring-do* speech.

He sunk into a deep thoughtful silence as we jumped into our beloved VW.... I revved-up, and our favourite Ella Fitzgerald CD serenaded us as we trundled down the bumpy drive. And me...? I was engulfed with a strange feeling deep down in my gut, a magnetic compulsion that somehow this would be the beginning of the rest of our lives…

CHAPTER 2

DECISIONS DECISIONS

The issue of the day played heavily on our minds. One thing for sure though, was that we relished the idea of moving to the country; deep down it was an aspired dream for us both. I was well, and truly bitten by the bucolic bug, although Mike was not sold on the idea of Holly Lodge as yet. I would have to work on that... I even promised him a dog. He had always wanted a whippet, singing their praises no-end, and one of the greatest prizes of moving to Norfolk would be the addition of our puppy, Barnaby...

It would be bribery on a grand scale...

Back in town, on a glorious autumnal Sunday morning we donned our sports gear, and went for our customary jog through Highgate Woods, our oasis moments from our doorstep at the end of the road.

We trampled the heaps of moist auburn leaves, which glistened in the morning dew, highlighted by the shards of sunlight penetrating through the heavy canopy of the woods; we both felt invigorated, as we slowed to a trot, then down into a gentle stroll. I started harping on about the joys of rural life.

"Hey, can you imagine our little whippet dog at our side now...?"

"Oh, Rob, ever since I'd set eyes on the blue whippets, owned by Mrs Hawkins back in Lune Street as a kid, I knew then that this breed was very special... you wait!"

Mike was already besotted with the idea of a dog, and perhaps intertwined with the concept of a new life, he might just sway now.

After ambling over to the café by the recreation area in the clearing by the woods, we sat down on a bench, to drink our take-away coffees. He looked at me intensely, and a positive smile swept over his face. He held his breath... And then suddenly blurted out...

"OK, OK let's go for it... Call the agents, make a second viewing for next Saturday, and remember you *promised* me that dog..." his overriding caveat as part of the deal.

I was over the moon that we'd be going back to see the place again, for somehow I knew this was to be our destiny. In retrospect it was kind of strange how we never viewed other properties in the area to gauge comparables. Then a string of weird almost celestial coincidences occurred:

Firstly the next morning, while I was training in the weights-room at my health club, I bumped into this chap, whom we both knew from around the Spa. He asked me, "Have you ever been up to the North Norfolk coast?" He'd just been house hunting up there recently. And suggested I take a look, as prices were very reasonable for such a beautiful location. I was flabbergasted...

Secondly that afternoon, while speaking to my dearest cousin, Myrna, I only went and discovered that she had been visiting North Norfolk for years, and often stayed at *The Pilgrim Bureau* in Walsingham just three miles from Thursford. Another coincidence. Perhaps it was meant to be...?

Finally on that very afternoon, Mike subsequently found out, while styling one of his favourite clients, that this fellow had good friends that actually lived in the village of Thursford Green, a stone's throw from Holly Lodge to boot. How mad is that...?

I really believe in a divine preordained fate; maybe these coincidences were all part of some grand master plan? I could feel it deep down in my bones.

That week I met up with my friend Lawrence, a property developer. I had just finished interior designing one of his apartments in the ever-so affluent Hampstead, and now it was being sold for a healthy profit. We were always discussing the pros and cons of when this economic boom would finally turn to bust; this inevitability was never far from our thoughts. But *when* was a good question...

Lawrence was much older than me, a kind of mentor figure, but we became good friends too, although with a somewhat avuncular aspect to our relationship. Sometimes we'd trawl the North London streets looking at prospects to refurbish; so naturally I sought his advice on Holly Lodge too. Little did we know then, that he was to play a pivotal role in the transaction process on our Norfolk house.

This was 1999 there was prodigious talk of the 'Millennium Bug'. Gloomy news reports were ubiquitous daily with apocalyptic pundits predicting a worldwide crash, wholly disrupting the Internet. There would be utter chaos; food and water shortages would ensue as a result. Globally there'd be a massive economic meltdown from the confusion generated by the mass-malfunction of our dependable desk screens – the end was nigh! Even my Chinese-American stepmother, Violet, my father's third wife, kept sending us dire warnings from the United States with detailed instructions to stock-up on reserves. Mike thought it was all ridiculous media scaremongering, until he caught me stock piling our garden shed with crates of bottled water and canned foods. He went ballistic... I felt like such a paranoid *schlemiel* at the time...

With all this doom-mongering nonsense spreading across the nightly news, it's no wonder, my attitude to life as a city dweller came up for question, and perhaps I was spurred on in my quest for another kind of lifestyle greater than this one posed.

The next issue to broach would be our beloved garden-flat, which we would have to put up for sale – or to test the waters at least – prior to our second visit to Norfolk.

I had found the property in leafy Muswell Hill about three years ago, as my pad in Belsize Park would have been too small for both of us to share on a long-term basis now that we had made the decision to move in together. We were incredibly happy in our new home, and I really thought we would live there at least the obligatory seven years as an average occupancy; after all there really was no reason to up sticks, until the discovery of Holly Lodge that is with its beckoning allure. And which for me became all consuming...

I selected a good local agent, and suggested my full asking price that I felt our property should warrant. The reaction from a suspicious estate agent was that no two-bedroom garden flat in Muswell Hill had ever achieved that amount I was suggesting. Ever.

I explained rather cockily: "They may have not seen a garden flat designed quite like this one."

So the next morning Mr Simons came down to take a look.

"Have you shown it to other agents in the area, because we'd love to market it?" he enthused with his predictable schmoozy patter.

"Well, what did I tell you, doesn't it tick all the right boxes...?" I suggested confidently.

"It's worth every penny of the figure you initiated, no doubt there. Wow!" And it was placed on his books immediately.

The house had an impressive Edwardian spec, divided into two separate dwellings; our part stretched over the entire ground floor, and was a split-level maisonette, with dramatic high ceilings, deep light bays at both ends of the two huge reception areas, with rear lounge French doors opening onto a courtyard of sorts.

The rest of the apartment stepped down to ground level, housing the breakfast room, kitchen, hall, and bathroom, all overlooking this central area too. The two rear bedrooms looked out onto a private terraced garden at the back. However the property was very bland when we bought it; little imagination had been spent exploiting its great bones. So as usual I had poured all my skills into redesigning the interiors, starting with sympathetically restoring the stained-glassed windows to both top lights of the bays (the originals had been removed and replaced with plain glass).

I had serendipitously unearthed four-armorial-crested panels in a certain East End reclamation yard that might have come from my Jacobean manor fantasy; these I had reworked to fit, and they looked like they had always belonged. Exquisite... and they set the scene for the interior scheme, a contemporary take on the romantic Gothic-look *de rigueur* during that time.

The original wide oak planked floors, period doors, and window shutters were all restored, everything was revamped paying fine attention to even the smallest details (my trademark). I'd always collected unusual pieces of modern art, so we decided to juxtapose them with our new ecclesiastical finds, which we had both started collecting from our regular outings to antique fairs and auctions. The whole effect created the wonderful ambiance of an 'Urban-chic Castle'. Well, I thought so anyway...

I made play of the entrance by laying a grey-stone cobbled surface to the yard giving it the feel of bona fide *charming* courtyard, maximising the impact of a *Frisia Robinia* tree, established in its centre: the vibrant lime green draping foliage created a dramatic canopy over the space. Potted topiaries were placed in situ. We renamed the flat 'The Courtyard', inscribed in a new slate sign, and *hey presto* a Des Res with the *wow factor* was born...

The following Saturday came soon enough, and we were on the road back to Norfolk once again. This was going to be make or break, for in my heart of hearts, I was praying everything would go right, truly confirming this was to be our destiny.

Essex, Suffolk, and Norfolk, we were counting down the miles on the 150-mile journey that normally takes just under three hours out of North London. Once off the A11, it's amazing how traffic-free it becomes on this stretch to the North Norfolk coast. Now I know why, Norfolk has its arse mockingly facing southern England... a major motorway can never be built through it as it would just hit a dead-end at the North Sea.

On arrival, this time they had laid out an inviting luncheon spread for us in front of the Inglenook with a glorious fire raging in the wood-burning stove. And obviously they were very pleased to see us return for a second viewing.

As we were seated at the table, they milled around us like bees to a honey pot. Charlotte was dressed to the nines as if she had been to some chic luncheon, reeking of *Chanel No.5* Roy entered holding his habitual note pad, ominously disguised with Latin plant names, when really he was about to launch into his Scotland Yard style investigation into our intentions here – and there would be no let-up until we had come clean with the truth... Faye peered at me closely through her specs dangling from their neck-chain looking very regal like a Dowager Duchess about to enter serious negotiations before relinquishing her title to her beloved estate.

Apparently they were keen to emigrate to New Zealand. Roy had had a recent health scare, old age was catching up, and their time was done here. However Charlotte would be remaining in the county – she had her heart set on a little cottage nearby.

The atmosphere became relaxed, and they opened-up revealing certain aspects of their daily routines, day-to-day running schedules, and their lives in Norfolk.

After lunch, they left us to wander around more freely; for us, reality was beginning to bite with the immensity of the daunting task ahead. The costs of a complete refurbishment would be considerable, no doubt... But neither of us had ever run a hotel before, it was a risky new venture, and cash flow would be tight. There would be no going back once we'd signed on the dotted line – the whole experience would have to be worthwhile for the sacrifice of our comfy London lifestyle.

I had already done some homework regarding the local competition, and there seemed to be nothing in the immediate vicinity that screamed... '*Boutique Hotel deluxe*'.

Mike did insist though that the guest accommodation should be contained to the cottages only, and no guests should be allowed to stay in the main house, as this would infringe on our new lifestyle here. I agreed wholeheartedly, although the reality of what it would be like living on the premises running such an establishment would become only too apparent years later.

On this occasion we could not access to view the middle cottage of the three as it was currently occupied. However, we nosed around the other two, and I began to envisage, how each one could be reinvented into something really special; individually designed luxurious suites aimed at the top end of the market, which would then require top-notch ratings from the relevant Tourist Authorities to warrant the higher charges I had planned for our new revamped accommodation.

A fresh new profile would be launched through a spectrum of mediums including a stylish state of the art website portraying an updated image of a more current edge to 'Holly Lodge'. And in the hope to attract trendier upscale clientele... 'Somewhere special', that would bring the epicureans flocking to our enclave.

I became increasingly inspired with how I would conceptualise each cottage in the former stable block, and I devised the names for each one there and then: **Claret**, **Colonial**, and **Country,** from largest to smallest respectively, suddenly I started to rattle-off my intentions, while Mike eagerly listened on.

"We could romanticise that allegedly pilgrims used to stop, and rest here in the stables on their way to nearby Walsingham, known as England's Nazareth, which really is the English equivalent of 'Lourdes' in France. Apparently one of the cottages was once an artist's studio, when a divorcee had moved here for a sojourn from New Hampshire in the 1920s spending her time reclusively painting the filmic North Norfolk scenery. One had been a village games-room, and social hangout during World War II; and an old iron wall-oven ensconced in the other cottage – suggested it might have once been used as a bakery. Each self-contained unit would be crafted into the perfect retreat. We would pamper our guests like no other guesthouse had ever done before, they would be truly amazed at the five star treatment going on six, attention to detail would be second to none, perfection personified in ultra-deluxe surroundings." I talked myself into a frenzy imagining the ultimate escape, and lost in full flow of my fantasy for the Lodge...

"Stop, stop! And how much is it all going to cost? Can we really afford to do it or is it really an impossible *white elephant*?" Mike starkly pointed out stopping me in my tracks with his usual logic.

I crashed back down to earth with an almighty bang from my reverie. We did not have a bottomless pit of gold; I would have to be really creative to give this place that uber-chic verve without ending up in the bankruptcy courts.

Finding ourselves standing on the forecourt by the car park, we noticed some customers step out of the occupied cottage, and approach their vehicle. We exchanged pleasantries, and thought nothing of it (sadly, the consequences of the public crawling all over the premises did not resonate at the time)...

Now back to the main house, which itself has had a chequered, but somewhat interesting past, which I will discuss more in detail later. Subsequently we checked out, the bedrooms, bathrooms, and the all-important suite of rooms that made up the kitchen areas, which we now scrutinised in more thorough detail. There would be no doubt this was going to be a monumental challenge...

Our hosts invited us to join them for a final cuppa before hitting the road. On leaving we decided to suss-out more of the area before we returned home.

First, we headed to the hallowed ground of Walsingham nearby, which once ranked in importance alongside Rome, and Jerusalem, because this is where in the 11th century a nobleman's wife Lady Richeldis had a series of visions of the 'Virgin Mary', and thus a Priory was built on the site. This became the revered focus of mass pilgrimages throughout the ages. And today, the waters from the healing springs of both the Roman Catholic, and Anglican shrines are still much coveted. This unique place has a feel of a great walled-city as you meander along the high walled confines of the original abbey grounds into the main thoroughfare that is quite reminiscent of some medieval French villages. We'd even passed fields of faded sunflowers nearby, quite evocative of Provence...

Driving through in awed respect, admiring the ancient faded charm, we became bewildered by so many shops selling an amazing plethora of religious paraphernalia. But I guess such a place steeped in religious legend carried an epiphanic cachet. And it happened to be on our doorstep. Now that would surely bring in the punters too...

Mike handed me some candles, as we stood in the Slipper Chapel on the outskirts of the village, and I lit them for loved ones, that had passed away. The heavenly room was illuminated with hundreds of tiny candles, which radiated an incredible heat into an ethereal glow. There was a powerful aura that emanated on this sacred ground that was very serene. We lingered for a while before continuing with our little sightseeing tour.

The gentle rolling landscape with that wild unspoilt edge unfolded before us, one flinted village prettier than the next would distract us from our obsessive thoughts of Holly Lodge as we started to lap up the delicious scenery.

Stumbling across The Barshams with that magnificent red brick Tudor manor, a virtual masterpiece nestled on the brow of the hill, apparently once owned by the Bee Gees, and now by the Guinness family. On through Houghton St Giles with its arresting views to the gentle valley below, and finally stopping off for a tea break at Binham Priory. The nave of the church, an important architectural monument, still stands intact defiantly amongst the ancient gaunt ruins of the surrounding cloisters, once a great Benedictine Priory, long since destroyed as a result of Henry VIII's dissolution of the monasteries in 1540.

There are a mysterious nexus of chambers defined by their tumbledown boundary walls, and we sat for a moment near the monks' refectory as indicated by a wall plaque.

Some horses trotted over from the adjacent field, we petted their regal heads, and a lively bay nudged our palms knowingly for the sugar cubes to our tea. It is a very tranquil, and spiritual spot, one that would become a sanctuary sometimes away from our new business.

"This sleepy quintessential village is like stepping into an idealised Victorian painting..." Mike surveyed the picture perfect plot from our vantage point; he became very relaxed, and seemed truly enamoured with the locale.

"Now, wouldn't that be sacrilegious if it were blighted with some soulless housing estate...?" I expressed my topical thoughts on the subject, because it seemed to be going on everywhere willy-nilly, and pained me dreadfully... why don't those blasted quangos responsible for *planning*, think through more carefully about the dire consequences? Instead of off-loading utter shoddy blandness, a mass of *mock* what...? Incongruously marring the once great English landscape...

"Aye, or it could be Wind Farms next!" Mike agreed, as he gazed longingly at the scene.

"Oh, don't get me started on the semantics of Wind Farms," Hmmm, NYMBYISM... aren't we all NYMBYS deep down?

The smart Georgian market town of Holt (Anglo Saxon word meaning a wood or copse) nearby became our next whistle-stop, an eye-opener providing some buzzy café culture to the area with its plethora of antique centres, arty galleries, stylish boutiques, and bountiful delis.

Apparently this well-appointed town is a famous shopping haunt for the Royals too, who spend their annual Christmas at nearby Sandringham, and often the likes of Camilla Parker Bowles can be spotted nosing around the specialist shops here.

Back on the coast for a lasting look at the sea as the orange sun slunk low into the horizon. We caught the looming silhouette of the emblematic landmark of the Cley Windmill punctuating the vast panorama. Flocks of birds took to flight, and swathed in huge numbers across the autumnal sky like a squadron in unison. The twitchers gazed studiously; I expect to catch a glimpse of that rare elusive species that migrate seasonally to these shores...

I loved wandering around the appealing passages of this coastal village with its pretty Dickensian windows filled with all manner of local arts, and crafts, and fine scenic watercolours to entice the visitor as a reminder of their stay in perhaps: one of England's last wildernesses.

Finally we hit the road back to London in complete awe of this new land we had discovered, and seduced in the moment by a *Brave New World* that was called North Norfolk.

I drove transfixed – deep in thought along the dusky roads – the villages flashed by. Should we or shouldn't we take this life-changing plunge...? This could turn out to be a ruinous folly. I gulped with a breathless anxiety I might rue the day I'd ever set eyes on the house in Norfolk.

CHAPTER 3

A TRICKY DEAL

The Courtyard was put up for sale, and our Norfolk friends had accepted our offer by the following Monday evening. It all happened so fast...

But amazingly by Tuesday afternoon back at my home-office I got cold feet. A nook of a room carved-out of the second bedroom, my think-tank HQ, where I plotted, and planned my renovation projects; here I could gaze out over the rear garden with its fine glimpses over to Alexandra Palace, set high-up over this part of North London bohemia.

Despairingly, I stubbed-out my umpteenth cigarette of the day caught up in whether we'd been too rash about moving to Norfolk, and leaving behind our great London lifestyle. After all everything really was hunky-dory, and as the old adage goes: *If it ain't broke don't fix it.* I started to doubt the change, and change after all can be a very frightening thing. I had a responsibility for Mike's future too; what if it all went pear-shaped? I'd surely be culpable.

Basically, I was scarpering for the door, and I was now torn. But it was not too late, I could still pull out with no real harm done, or at least put everything on hold until we were both completely sure. So wrestling in panic mode with my subconscious... I instinctively picked up the phone, and called their agents, profusely apologising and explaining that we needed more time. Next I wrote a heartfelt letter to the Norfolk folk explaining my reasons for my vacillation – for I knew they would be disappointed – and to assure them we were not out of the frame just yet. Lastly I called our estate agents to put all our viewings on hold, just for the time being.

We both seemed relieved for the first few days like a great weight had been lifted off our shoulders, however as the days rolled drudgingly by, and after about a fortnight had passed, the feeling of deflation turned into one of depression; for our aspired plans of a new life in the country had now become scuppered by insecurities.

The days gathered momentum, as the leaves were falling in the full swing of autumn. The silver birch tree marking time outside my window became bare, its white worn speckled bark stood there in all its stark glory – ready to deal with the onslaught of winter. I inhaled deeply on my carcinogenic-straw, thinking if only... I could kick this addiction once and for all... A smokescreen, I often used to quell my inner emotions. The hypocritical health freak, all tanned, and muscled, an epitome of vitality, slowly, but surely killing myself. And now in my fortieth year... I too must undergo a transition and change, whilst time was still (just) lingering on my side.

It's ironic that in the old days a form of punishment was to be beaten with a bundle of birch twigs, it was called 'Birching', and was banned in Britain in 1948, and there I was now absolutely determined to rid myself of this self-imposed purgatory... Oh I did love that tree...

Of course I had tried everything known to man, and woman to kick the blasted habit ranging from aversion therapy, hypnotherapy, courses of acupuncture, patches, gum, to dear old Alan Carr's *'Easyway to Stop Smoking'* course, which sadly did not work either. Now cutting down that was a joke too, and never works if you are an addict. I tell you the games I used to play were pitiful...

One particular night it all came to a head though, after dousing a pack of ten under the tap that very afternoon, removing three to smoke, and binning the rest.

"It's one in the morning, what on earth are you doing?" Mike heard me in the kitchen.

"I was desperate for a smoke..." I replied guiltily. Crikey... I felt like Charles Manson caught red-handed.

"Huh! What's the oven on for at this time?" He wiped his sleepy eyes, and quizzed me.

I had switched the oven onto 5/high... And I tried to explain my way out of why I was baking three soggy Marlboros into the early hours... that's after retrieving them from the bottom of the waste bin, which was no doubt festering with bacteria.

"Boy... Now that's what I call being a slave to your addiction..." he chortled.

I was deeply ashamed at how low I had sunk in order to get my fix. That was a true turning point... And it happened just before the Norfolk idea presented itself.

It was a standing joke – every weekend I was giving up, and every Monday morning I was dying of cancer albeit a paranoid hypochondria... My father, who had died of cancer of the oesophagus as a result of years of the gruesome addiction, had suffered a slow horrific passage to death. It was heartbreaking, I even promised him on his deathbed I would quit, and that was ten years ago.

Although Mike smoked casually, he did want to quit too, so a move to the country would be a catalyst for us both in our resolve to kick the habit.

A window of opportunity for many reasons now to jump through...

'Fortune does favour the brave', a mantra I had long believed in. I had spent my life being bravely adventurous – where was my free spirit now...? The adrenalin was kicking-in as I grabbed my mobile... Mike was at the salon, right in the middle of a cut...

"Norfolk!" I said exuberantly.

"Aye! Rob, you've got my blessing..." I could sense his relief. And I guess the soul searching was over...

So the green-lit button was pushed, and pandemonium broke loose over the next few months with a major upheaval now unleashed on our lives.

I immediately called the Swaffham office to get the deal back on the table by resubmitting our offer, and declared... "This time, our decision is final..."

Strangely the owners of Holly Lodge had shut the house down, and gone abroad on holiday so any viewings had been put on hold, which was fortuitous, although apparently one of the previous applicants, who had pulled out prior to exchange of contracts was now sniffing around once again. This other party owned another guesthouse somewhere nearby, and were considering reinstating their transaction process that had been shelved six months ago.

My dithering had lost me three weeks, however time was now very much of the essence. First I called our estate agents to get those viewings reorganised again for our flat, then I called my trusted broker to get the ball rolling for a mortgage, as currently our invested savings would only stretch to cover the ten per cent deposit. I did not want to wait for the balance of funds from the completion of the sale of the Courtyard as this might inhibit the purchase of Holly Lodge: especially if a race might be on with another buyer in the frame.

The next day Faye had agreed to go with us on the proviso that we completed the purchase by latest/middle of January 2000. I agreed. Now the pressure was on big time...

Our first viewing came along, and in through the front door entered an up and coming young television presenter. He was immediately besotted with the Courtyard, so much so he made me an offer on the spot, albeit about ten thousand below my asking price, and wanted to return the next day with his wife. As it happened that Tuesday there was several appointments lined up, but they came back first thing to strike a deal.

I had always fancied myself as an estate agent – what a cushy number...! So, without any further ado, I proudly led them up the steps into the lounge, where the fire roared vigorously beneath its great mantel, the sun beamed through the stained-glass lights, casting phantasmagorical colours all over the coved walls and ceilings. The view to the Italianate courtyard was resplendent, although the last of the lush-lime-green leaves were hanging on for dear life from the Frisia Robinia tree. And the Courtyard was poised in its final moment of our ownership – I simply had to let go...

He looked at me convincingly sweeping his shock of black tousled hair off his handsome chiselled face, and beseeched me to pull it off the market with an offer for my full asking price, almost begging me in the process in front of his good lady. I agreed to the deal – albeit tinged with an almighty sadness at the prospect of saying goodbye to our beloved home. We shook hands, and it was sold on the spot...

That was that, or so I thought, but just after they left, a flashy black *Porsche* rolled up. A slick-looking city type came running up the path, he hurriedly stubbed out his cigarette into the tub of our Bay tree as he puffed out his name, Theo Hamilton in his plummy public school accent. He was draped in an exquisitely cut suit, probably from *Savile Row* judging by the bespoke hand-finish; and he reeked of city-boy affluence.

I explained to him that I was about to call Mr Simons at the estate agents, as it had just been sold. He did not seem fazed at all, and cannily goaded me into giving him a quick peek at the place. He'd always loved the road, and besides he'd come right across town – all the way over from Canary Wharf.

He was very pushy with his unctuous patter – I weakened... *God I can be such a schmuck at times...* And allowed him in.

He cavorted around assessing the place, and then floored me with an offer of ten grand cash over the full asking price with exchange of contracts guaranteed within fourteen days. I was thrown into a quandary... What if the previous offer was not genuine? But I had to follow my instincts, and not renege on an agreed sale, after all nobody wants to be gazumped... So I thanked him for his most generous offer, and declined.

Now he became even more persistent...

"I tell you what, I'll throw in another five grand on top too for goodwill, how about it... deal of the day?"

He pompously straightened his club-striped tie, and proudly prodded his breast-pocket hanky. He eagerly awaited my response. Then his mobile rang...

"Jason, sell now, if it's 300K. OK! And buy gold at $250 per ounce, sell aluminium, will call you in five." The wheeler-dealer hung up, and glared at me. "Well?"

I asked him, "What would he do if the shoe was on the other foot?"

"Sell to the highest bidder of course, you don't get to be where I am by being a nice guy," he retorted with a laddish guile.

Biting the bullet, and praying for the best I responded on this occasion: "Sorry... erm... it's no deal!" I felt like such a chump, but a paragon of moral virtue at least... albeit a poorer one!

"You'll be sorry..." he smirked. And made a speedy exit in his glossy fuck-mobile, which roared away down the road.

Phew! It just so happened, that the offer for my full asking price broke all records that year for a two-bedroom garden flat in Muswell Hill, so we were thrilled anyway. And thankfully the TV presenter was true to his word, and my decision was vindicated.

Christmas was upon us in no time, and we planned to spend it with Mike's mum in Yorkshire. For me this was always special. Norma, a petite lady with magnetic blue eyes, had the most vivacious smile that would lighten up the darkest of rooms, especially with her irresistible, and ebullient charisma.

We had struck up a great friendship – probably because her Mike was one happy guy in a steady relationship for six years by then. Norma was a diamond in every way... She had a knack of putting me at ease, and made me feel worthy of her much beloved son from the outset. There was no need for any furtive 'La Cages Aux Folles' moments of sweeping away any gay telltale signs under the carpet. She just simply accepted Muscle-Mary-Me, lotions, potions, and all...

I like to think she liked my softy-southern (desert-dry) sense of Essex boy humour; and her raucous giggles were infectious.

Sadly Norma had been plagued with health problems, namely Crohn's disease. Despite her frailty though, she was a tough Yorkshire lass. Mealtimes were always such an issue, because of her condition as she could not stomach most food groups, which would aggravate her system, so it was always awkward to get her to eat enough to sustain her skeletal frame; apart from that major worry we would always have such fun-filled times together.

Days out visiting the insanely beautiful landscape of the heavenly 'Moors National Park' were breathtaking beyond compare. This was 'Herriot' country that I'd longed to explore, and despite my mother being born in Leeds, these were my first experiences of the North East.

I have many fond memories of my times in the North, jaunts to nearby Whitby, indulging our sea-air appetites at probably the best fish and chip eatery in England: '*The Magpie Cafe*' set on the harbour there. Other times exploring the quaint passages around York, and its mesmeric Cathedral, York Minster with its impossible architecture... And of course any excuse sampling those sweet orgasmic confections in the famous *Bettys Cafe Tea Rooms* served by waitresses in black and white frilly pinnies. We'd get a great kick out of seeing Norma enjoy her deluxe high-tea...

In fact the ingenious founder of this genteel establishment, Frederick Beaumont, was so impressed by the splendour of the grand deco interiors of the Queen Mary, after sailing on her maiden voyage in 1936, that he cleverly imitated the ambiance, turning a dilapidated corner shop into one of the most talked about tearooms in England.

Mike's younger brother, Darren, was always such a hoot, a handsome, dapper, and gregarious guy, who has become like a brother to me. He was in the fashion biz back then, and introduced me to those cool specialist boutiques of the North. Big Mistake! 'High maintenance gay guys simply love to shop'. Mike hid my credit cards for days, because now we had Holly Lodge to contend with.

This warm, close-knit family gave me a way of life I'd never known before... A complete antithesis of my own upbringing in the cold empty environment of my dark life in a mansion block on Baker Street...

My mother died when I was barely seven under dubious circumstances – maybe suicide. Unfortunately, I was kept away from her funeral, so as the cliché goes there was no *closure*; she just simply vanished... I have mountains of photographs of my mother, depicting a very beautiful woman, but a complete enigma to me...

About a week before her passing, while she was undergoing what might have been some kind of emotional crisis at home, I had been sent to stay with a very stern uncle, who threatened me nightly with his belt, and indelibly harsh words – as I would cry for my mother way into the early hours, for somehow... I knew then I would never see her again.

There was no doubt that both my father and mother were a golden couple in their heyday, blessed with movie star good looks. My father had grown up in poverty, the youngest of ten brothers, and sisters, enduring a very tough childhood in the East End ghetto of London during the Great Depression.

Dad was a young lad of twenty when he was enlisted; he became a jeep driver in the army, running some very dangerous missions and, most notably, fought at the battles of Dunkirk 1940 and Monte Cassino in Italy 1944. He'd even won medals for his bravery...

Many of his experiences during the turbulent war years are well documented in reams of *mostly* romantic letters from this period, which I have inherited; they are a poignant reminder of my parents' devoted love and painful separations due to my father's military service during World War II.

Curiously, I found in one heartfelt letter, his harrowing account of while en route through Northern Italy, at the time of The Liberation (D-Day): how he witnessed time and again, the nuns freeing Jewish children from their monasteries; that they had furtively rescued from the Nazis. Dad always had a thing about Italy, which I have inherited too...

Hard times must have followed as they struggled through those frugal post war years. Nevertheless, my father sought to give my mother, Irene, a better lifestyle. So through being a steely determined character fortunately blessed with a brilliant, creative, entrepreneurial spirit he set to work on building his empire.

'*Serve the masses to dine with the classes*', was perhaps his greatest mantra; which took him to the upper echelons of society.

He just had a tremendous flair for business. And instigated it with such impeccable timing! Consequently from slavishly toiling as a simple tailor in a sweatshop, he established a flourishing company, which grew to be one of the largest importers into the United Kingdom of prêt-a-porter men's suits, and fashion clothing. And back in the day, I believe he was one of the leading pioneers of this concept.

However, there was a personal price to pay with his demanding schedules, especially overseas, which would have a devastating effect on their marriage, and on my mother's very fragile state of mind; especially as a result of the tragic death of her first born, my sister Maxine.

Mum's sudden death when I was still so young no doubt would have an everlasting impact on me. Dad sold our home shortly after, but just before moving day we became the victims of a devastating burglary while we were over at relatives. Unfortunately, I discovered that my little doggy, Oscar, had been trussed-up and thrown into a wardrobe. Subsequently he died... The loss of the solace of my sweet loving friend ate my heart up for ages thereafter too.

So we left behind the leafy suburbs near Epping Forest, and moved to a smart (of ambassadorial scale) flat in the heart of the West End of London overlooking Baker Street. This was a major lifestyle upheaval as I found myself rattling around a vast gloomy apartment in a fast moving urban sprawl that felt totally alien.

Around my tenth birthday my father was about to embark on his second marriage to a truly unkind woman whom had somehow beguiled him with her wholly fake demeanour, and comely appearance. Brigitte was well educated, could converse in any number of languages, and had cultivated her socialite airs and graces from '*The Lucie Clayton Charm Academy*' (a finishing school for young ladies). Dad must have been initially very impressed...

This for me was a disaster, and one, which would have devastating consequences on my adolescent years. She had a son, Henry, five years younger than me from her previous marriage. My oldest brother Tony was shortly to become a newlywed. And my other older brother, David, had been left mentally handicapped by a botched operation in his infancy. Unfortunately, he was soon to develop severe daily bouts of epilepsy too. I became his caretaker at the age of ten, as my father was predominantly absent.

For about the first year or so of their marriage I was packed off to boarding school, which unbeknown to me might have been my saviour, had it not unexpectedly closed down, and as a result I returned home. Thus the reign of terror truly began...

Mary, an elderly housekeeper, who had been very kind to me, was compromised once Brigitte became the dominant force in the household, and consequently she was dismissed. Which baffled me...

I could not understand through my very young eyes why my new stepmother despised me so much. I would have to endure years of nonsensical accusations, emotional blackmailing, vitriolic verbal abuse, and her strange notions of blaming a little boy for the ills of a disastrous marriage.

Consequently, life at home became an austere vacuum. I turned into a deeply introverted, depressed child hiding myself away, and escaping into my private world of books, model-craft making, and old black and white movies on my portable. Brigitte seemed determined to break my spirit. Moreover, there was never a kind word or a dot of affection... Ever.

I must admit I lived in abject fear of my stepmother. Her penetrating icy stares through her cold dark eyes spoke volumes. Sometimes, she would lash out for what seemed no apparent reason, and taunt my brother David for his disabilities. She was a nasty bully!

Often when my father returned between business trips there would be dramatic rows, sometimes leading to physical attacks on my father, who was not a violent man at all.

Her rages could be terrifying, and one time after such an outburst, she contacted a colleague (legal adviser) of my father's to have me formally evicted from my own home, because apparently I was stealing food from our kitchen, 'food my father had bought, and paid for'. It was very extreme! As was her unstable behaviour... Always.

Shortly after that episode, our flat was engulfed in a catastrophic fire. It was very puzzling why she was found standing safely outside bedecked in her mink coat clutching her jewellery box, while my father, and I only had seconds to spare...

During my mid-teens, I ran away on any number of occasions, frankly, because I just couldn't stand it anymore. And during a particularly low ebb – just after a very foolish failed suicide attempt – to draw attention to my utter desperate plight, of which I am thoroughly ashamed of now, I holed-up in a youth hostel for about six months. It was a welcomed sanctuary...

I know my father became very distraught, and the circumstances drove a great chasm between us. All I wanted was his paternal guidance, protection, and to understand why he had burdened me with this monster, whom he had married.

Behind closed doors, her mental abuse continued for years, but to the outside world, Brigitte purported to be a wonderful socialite, with her spurious affectations, whilst I appeared angst, broody, and a deeply misunderstood teenager throughout those dark harrowing years.

All reigns of terror do come to an end, and my father finally divorced her, when I was twenty... And boy did she get bad karma. Still, she never showed an iota of contrition. Divine culpability seemed to have manifested itself with a subsequent histrionic misfortune for her... Because after receiving her (well-undeserved) settlement, which she squandered with her inimitable extravagance, her vanity became her nemesis, and while under-going a face-lift operation, she suffered a catastrophic stroke.

Consequently her health, and her appearance deteriorated rapidly, and her decadent lifestyle finally caught up with her; as a result one of *Harrods'* most ardent customers succumbed to employment on their multilingual desk... As I discovered many years later when Mike and I were in the store one afternoon.

Now a heavily set, almost unrecognisable harridan, I immediately caught her hard pretentious voice bellowing out across the shop floor in that strong German accent she was so proud of... Mike had to drag me out of the store seething...

The last time I saw her was at my step-brother Henry's funeral, as he had been tragically killed in a car crash at just thirty-six. I was devastated because I considered Henry, a brother, and a great bloke... Actually, it was no secret that he had severed his ties with his mother for a considerable time prior to his death. Apparently, she had allegedly stolen from his trust fund left to him by his dear grandfather... And finally, the last I heard of her was when one of her lovers had died after hanging himself from the ceiling in her bathroom.

Brigitte had the knack of wreaking a path of misery, wherever she trod... And her legacy left a severely fractured family.

Believe you me... I could go on and on recounting more shocking stories from my dysfunctional childhood, but this is not supposed to be a *'Misery Memoir'* about the archetypal wicked stepmother.

Subsequently, I was a deeply troubled pupil all through Grammar school living with my secret frustration of my dark home life, but my salvation came, when I was accepted into the London College of Fashion, and my whole world changed. I discovered my innate artistic abilities, as well as the louche fashion scene of the 1970s. And a newfound burgeoning freedom...

However, maybe I am a chip off the old man's block after all, as like my father I'd also become a consummate survivor. Like him I learned to use my quick wit, and creative will, which after all had catapulted him from zero to hero. Pop's a complex, multi-faceted man, was not without his faults, and paternal failings too. Nevertheless despite everything... he was, and always will be my father, my hero, and my inspiration.

I have finally come to terms with all these early traumas, through years of hard therapy, which have assuaged many of the profound effects that lingered within my adult psyche.

Flash-forward to today though, and my life is blessed in so many ways, and now enriched by the wonderful opportunity with the prospect of this Norfolk adventure, which turned out to be another remarkable period in my life, and for my partner Michael too. But for oh so different reasons...

Millennium Eve was upon us, and we were off to a party at the house of my dear old mate, Marven. Many of our close friends would be attending, so I stuck some photos of Holly Lodge in my jacket to gauge their reaction. Rumours were circulating of our impending departure from London, so obviously I sought their blessing for our new adventure.

At dinner I excitedly passed the pictures about. A glum silence followed, as the photographs of our new life imploded like a lead balloon crashing to the ground.

Myopic comments ensued...

"It just not what we expected."

"It's nothing like I imagined."

"Why...?"

And so it goes... Mike and I looked at each other despondently, and were very disappointed with their reaction to our plans...

"Norfolk is a barren cultural desert, you'll hate it, and be back in town within the year," Josh announced brashly.

I knew he meant well, but I was astonished by his prosaic short-sightedness, and then I launched into an evangelical tirade on why 'Noel Coward' got it so wrong on the entire Norfolk package...

"The North Norfolk coast is like nothing you have ever seen: breathtaking endless skies, infinite possibilities, captivating coastal vistas, verdant rolling pastures to the north. And, no, not pancake-flat like the Fens... Surprising! And some of the most timelessly *filmic* flinty villages you ever did see."

And there endeth my gospel, said the preaching convert to our new land in waiting. I swigged more of my comforting wine.

Then someone commented, "You'll never get accepted into a Norfolk rural community."

I began to feel the effects of the liquor playing evil havoc with my fertile imagination taking me to a place no one wants to go... I visualised angry chargers – heading down our drive at the Lodge – ridden by hooded Klu Klux Klan morons waving flaming crosses – throwing ropes over our loftiest fruit trees. And yelling... "Hang 'em real high!"

Stop! Don't be so ridiculous. I held my breath for a heart-stopping moment, and mulled over my unbidden torments... Besides this was our *dream,* and not theirs. I had pictured it over, and over – how I would reinvent Holly Lodge. And once I had realised my vision, they'd get it...

Little did anyone know that incredibly within the next few years, a coterie of four couples there that night would uproot to relocate to North Norfolk themselves, and within a few miles from our house to boot. This was wholly unimaginable back then.

The fireworks sprayed across the black night sky, I was getting evermore high to lose myself in the moment. And with butterflies in my stomach with how it all might be a year from now.

We all clinked, and chinked our glasses, kissed, and hugged to usher in the dawn of this mysterious new century, a scary new beginning of an epoch about to change us all forever. And with the realisation that we had finally grown up... I hugged Mike closely, we toasted to our future new life, and our adventure into an unchartered territory, a journey into the *unknown*, one that would shape our lives into something beyond our wildest dreams.

Picture key from left to right: My (courting) parents, looking like 1930s film stars in their hey-day; My handsome father, Gerry in the 1940s (Royal Sussex regiment); My beautiful mother, Irene in the 1940s; Me aged 6; The Greenfield family portrait (parents and brothers, Tony and David, and mini-me).

Picture key from left to right: Shortly after Mike and I met over at Roz and Jo's dinner party; Mike's beautiful mother, Norma in the 1950s; Mike aged 11; Mike with his Mother Norma (Right) and her sister (Aunt) Helena (Left).

CHAPTER 4

A NEW LIFE

Moving house is rather like dismantling a life... The New Year had arrived promising our escape from the city. I was busy packing-up: labelling crates, boxes, and thumbing down my endless *must-do* lists when my mobile ringtone rang. It was my mortgage broker...

"I've got some bad news, your application has been denied." His voice quivered with trepidation.

"What...?"

"I'm so sorry, I omitted some key information from the paperwork regarding: *a home versus business*, (Bed & Breakfast can be a grey area with some mortgage providers) and the lender became suspicious."

Blast! And at the eleventh hour too... although he insisted another 'Mortgage Offer' would be on the table shortly. Huh... another four-six weeks at least... Basically, I felt let down – he'd always been so reliable in the past.

This was critical... as I now found myself in a sudden race to exchange contracts, and obliged to complete the transaction on Holly Lodge within the next fortnight. Gutted... I scanned through the digitals on my camera of our Norfolk dream, contemplating my next move. My ringtone rang again...

"Rob, great news! I've just calculated the figures on Steeles Road... Well done!" Lawrence was all chirpy, and upbeat by the results of our recent project.

"Oh, er... that's good."

He immediately knew something was up, by my monotone reply, and I explained my dilemma. He suggested

66

I meet him at his house first thing in the morning – apparently to give me some advice.

I began to feel that at this juncture there was every chance we might not get this property after all. Completion of the sale of the Courtyard was still weeks, and weeks away, and unless there was some kind of bridging-loan in place, Holly Lodge may be lost. Alternately if I delayed the imminent exchange (now slightly overdue) Faye may lose confidence in me, and be bloody-minded enough to exchange contracts with the other buyer, who was now aggressively pursuing the purchase of Holly Lodge:

Life is a game of musical chairs
When the music stops
Don't dare get caught out

I don't know where that came from, but it played in my mind. Panic stations... and I called the Swaffham office.

Uh-oh! More worrying news insofar as I learnt that the solicitor acting for the other buyer had upped the ante. Documents were being finalised, there was talk of an offer increase to outbid me. Moreover, to top it all I heard through the grapevine that Faye was about to sway...

The draw of the Lodge became utterly compelling with my burning desire to own it – now I'd have a fight on my hands.

That night I was like a bear with a sore head. Poor Mike came home to one stressed-out guy. And we discussed the options long into the night.

He was surprisingly blasé, perhaps to soften my distress. Mike could be such an anchor to pigeonhole the dynamics of a disappointment.

"Look it's not the end of the world," he reasoned.

"Mike, I know... But...!" He gave me a big hug, and assured me all would be well.

Finally we crashed out gone two, then I awoke again at four in the still silence – the constant city rumble had subsided – and I began to reflect on a time when it felt like it was the end of my world... after my father's passing.

I simply walked away from a very successful career as an international fashion designer, bereft, and burnt-out; my four-year relationship with a beautiful super model had just come to a turbulent end; besides it was never going to work based on my sexuality anyway! And the country was moving into the throes of a deep recession as the booming Thatcher years were running out of steam.

My father had become guilt-ridden from the *years* of fall-out I had had to endure from his wholly disastrous second marriage. I literally sat at the end of his deathbed for nearly two years watching him waste away, with so little said. Ah, and so much precious time squandered... In hindsight I should have grasped the opportunity, and healed the rift. Profound regrets, and I ran in my subconscious bid to suppress my rancour, and immense anger, that I had laid firmly at his door.

Consequently I isolated myself. I felt the need to cut all family ties... The emotional trauma became crippling. And my lifestyle was about to undergo a dramatic metamorphosis...

A feeling of great emptiness overwhelmed me. I was completely shattered.

So I began my healing sabbatical, entering a 'Twelve-Step' programme using it as my 'Rehab' with thrice weekly group meetings, and regular one-to-one therapy sessions with a counsellor to nail it once and for all.

My mind-altering addictions of my drugs of choice: Marijuana, and nicotine were relinquished. Although, years later only once I had moved to Norfolk did I finally quit the cigarettes completely. Hence the lid was blowing-off the volcano propelling me into new horizons...

During this period some remarkable people crossed my path as different worlds collided... writers, entrepreneurs, dustmen, cab drivers, academics, shop assistants, and a panoply of celebs too; all publicly sharing their troubles in this sacrosanct arena – so many fascinating personas from every walk imaginable. That it was indeed an *education.* Because I discovered I was not alone with my demons, nor indeed was I special or unique in this parallel universe of recovery.

*I began to realise that life does not have to be perfect –
it just has to be lived...*

Paradoxically, I have often found, it seems the people who have suffered the most adversity in their formative years, are the ones that go on to have the most outstanding, and productive lives...

During my early days in recovery, I was introduced by my former fiancée (the model – don't ask) to the pop star twin-brothers, Barry and Paul Ryan, renowned for their world class hit single: *Eloise*. They were the sons of the famous 1950s' singer Marion Ryan, once dubbed the 'Marilyn Monroe of Popular Song', who was married to showbiz impresario Harold Davidson (Frank Sinatra and Judy Garland's UK manager). Actually meeting on Paul's wedding day in Surrey.

The acquaintance soon blossomed into a terrific friendship, because some months later after my father's passing in 1988, these guys showed me great compassion, perhaps saving me from the precipice at the time, by inviting me to accompany them on holiday to the South of France.

An atmospheric shabby-chic villa of faded 1930s' grandeur became my temple of salvation as we were ensconced high up in the *Alps-Maritime* surrounded by the glamorous panoramic French Riviera laid-out below. We had some great times around Cannes. Serendipitously, this was the tonic I needed as my spirits lifted from the mire.

An especially fond memory forever etched on my mind was on one of those delicious-do-nothing azure afternoons by the infinity pool. Paul sat by the edge like a cheeky kid, and pasted his face with layers of vanilla ice cream, but as if missing his mouth accidentally on purpose. He could be a brilliant comic, with the subtlest driest humour at times. And he had me in stitches... Dear Paul.

I adored the twins, and saw them right up until Paul's tragic death from cancer in late November 1992, when he was just forty-four. It was devastating, so unfair, a truly lovely, talented, decent human being tragically taken in his prime, one whom I will always miss.

It's particularly poignant that even way back in those days, we once discussed what it might be like to open a snazzy hotel. And how we would design some very cutting-edge interiors together. Paul did have a terrific eye... And oh, how he would have loved the Lodge...

Sadly somehow Barry and I drifted apart, I just can't explain it... Although it might have been something to do with us withdrawing into our pockets of grief at the time... I had also been very close with their stepsister Caroline, herself a talented singer too, forming a profound friendship with her. She has since gone back to live in the United States, and perhaps if I were not gay, something might have developed on a more romantic level... I am sure!

Another surreal encounter that was evocative of this strange time in my life was an experience that became quite scary in my vulnerable state, but in retrospect could actually be considered a risible drama, although I did not think so at the time...

During my jet-setting days as a fashion designer, I would sometimes go to stay at a very smart Health Farm/Spa for some pampering, and a well-earned rest, although on this occasion, it was on one of my desperate bids to quit smoking. Ho-hum...

I stayed in my usual room, the 'Lord Byron', where I could feel cocooned; but unbeknown to me this would turn into a nigh-on suspense thriller – that almost drove me gaga...

One morning during breakfast, an eccentric looking woman asked if she could join me at my table. Many of the larger tables were often communal, so I thought nothing of it. But when I looked-up I took a double-take...

She was a curvy-forty-something, dressed as if she had stepped off the set of a vintage 1950s' Pinewood classic: bouffant black hair, white-rimmed cat-eye sunglasses, polka dot head scarf, lipstick-red printed frock, and black patent accessories. You get the picture? Great... But just a tad over the top down for an early morning session in a spa retreat, I should say...

Anyway she sat down, there was something unsettling, and rather odd about her demeanour, although I couldn't quite put my finger on it. She chattered pleasantly enough, mainly about our environment, quite mundane really. I finished my tea, we said our farewells, and I went off for a swim, and a steam. And that was that, or so I thought.

Later that day I wandered into the guest lounge for some afternoon tea. And of all people sitting by the fireplace was '*Dame Vera Lynn*', who beckoned me over to join her and her husband (perhaps I must have appeared somewhat forlorn). Of course I was surprised, flattered, and even in awe of this beloved national treasure...

During our delightful natter, the curious lady, who had joined me at breakfast, suddenly entered the room, and made a beeline for me, plonking herself down – aside me on the sofa – and bang opposite Dame Vera. It felt disconcerting, and I appeared somewhat surprised, because in a fit of pique, she took umbrage to my sudden almost knee-jerk reaction, brusquely got up, and swiftly exited the lounge in an almighty huff.

I was bewildered by the tantrum. And I think my legendary lady cottoned on; even so I was chuffed to have had a mind-blowing cuppa with the 'Forces dearest singing sweetheart'... that strange afternoon.

I did my usual stuff that day, went for a long walk, had some treatments, and felt very chilled-out before going down for dinner at eight. Incidentally, as it happened during that unique couple of days, Diana, Princess of Wales was staying at the health farm: often I would get fleeting glimpses of her around the spa areas, with her bodyguards in tow. On a couple of occasions in passing we'd struck up engaging conversations. She seemed so interested in whatever you had to say with her endearing charm, and those captivating eyes. Of course I was completely enchanted by her alluring spell... I was a big fan then, and still am today!

Wow wee... how surreal! Princess Di and *moi* were practically mates with our chitchats of: diet, addiction, and fashion talk in common. Then with all good things – sadly they always have a habit of coming to an untimely end. And so my weekend of terror began...

At around 2.00am there was a sudden knock on my bedroom door. I heard a familiar voice whispering my name, and I nearly jumped out of my skin – jolted from my deep slumbers. I kept silent in the hope of whoever it was would go away, although I had my suspicions whom it might be. This must have gone on for a good fifteen minutes, the knocking persisted, and the voice repeated, "Are you awake my darling...?"

Just as I was about to rush to the door to confront her, she left!

The following day, the ominous woman was ubiquitous – uh-oh... was she stalking me? It became so unsettling that I felt the need to complain to the management. (Remember I had been in withdrawal from cigarettes for three days by now.)

The management kindly arranged to move me to a different location in the building reassuring me that I would not be disturbed. Ironically I was installed in Vera Lynn's suite, as she had left that morning.

I remember settling into my ever so grand, and very blue suite, rest-assured that I could now relax peacefully. And I even hummed myself to sleep to the appropriate tune of the *White Cliffs of Dover*.

Suddenly in the early hours, drifting through my window, which was ajar – I awoke to hear the whispering sound of my name being called over and over. Eerie...

"I must see you now, my darling!" she cooed.

And I completely freaked out!

How the hell did she know I'd been moved to this room? My heart was pounding. I grabbed the bedside phone almost disengaging it from the wall to call down to the night duty manager. He hurriedly went out into the garden to warn her to stop hassling me! And go to bed.

She angrily let rip with, "I deal with you later... Mister!" (Echoes of the film *Play Misty for Me* harrowingly sprang to mind.)

"Robert, I'll get you...!" she screamed up at my window.

"Please... Madam! This is most inappropriate, show some decorum..." The night manager was forthright, and finally she disappeared, although not before cursing him spitefully.

I was at the end of my tether; she was now stalking me with no let up. Perhaps she was some kind of psycho? She certainly looked the part...

Finally, I settled back down again and lulled into a deep sleep.

Then perhaps an hour later, the fire alarm to the building rang – it was truly deafening – this time I damn near had a heart attack from the shock of the cacophony. I dashed to throw my dressing gown on – making for the door.

All the houseguests including the Princess were rushing past me downstairs, it was pandemonium, and everybody was being convened on the lawn.

It transpired that my stalker had smashed the security glass, and pushed the panic-button setting off the house-alarm in some kind of frustrated angst. That's after unsuccessfully trying to gain access to my bedroom.

And then... I became really disturbed when I saw that the lock to my door had been tampered with – evident by the vigorous scratch-marks on the escutcheon plate – obviously instigated by some kind of sharp implement.

Blimey! Perhaps, a narrow escape from the throes of death starring in my own in-house *slasher* movie, eh?

The shenanigans of my stalker had now created a security scare for the Princess too, her heavies were running around looking very concerned with it all; and I believe they all left that morning.

Subsequently, I heard there had been a tussle between the madwoman, and house security, and that she had been carted-out, hysterically screaming my name. Apparently she had duped the management with her booking: after allegedly escaping from some kind of private mental asylum!

The management were profusely apologetic for the incident, which impaired my stay beyond a shadow of a doubt, and they proceeded to compensate me with an entire week free of charge in my hallowed suite. Apropos... I never did quit smoking that time...

Redolent memories stirred: no doubt due to the brink of more great changes playing havoc with my psyche that pivotal night in Muswell Hill. I suddenly awoke as I heard the latch to the front door click into place as Mike went off to work that morning.

I arrived bang on nine to meet Lawrence at his impressive house in Hampstead, which had a John Nash style façade. The imposing architecture of this huge house belied a warm family home. We sat down to some eggs, croissants, and morning lattes in the unassuming kitchen before he launched into his idea to fix my current crisis. And suggested his amazing offer...

"Rob, I can lend you the £210,000 you need to buy Holly Lodge." My jaw dropped, and he continued... "In essence it is known as a 'Legal Charge'."

I couldn't quite believe what I was hearing. Lawrence explained in more detail...

"My name will be temporarily listed as the owner on the Title Deeds until you reimburse me with funds from the sale of the Courtyard. Naturally the title will then be transferred over to your name."

I practically choked on my coffee; it was exceedingly generous of him. It's not every day someone will lend, and trust you with that kind of money in an instant... I was blown away by his support.

"Lawrence, I don't know what to say... you are a star!" I gave him a huge thank you hug, and his wife Laura joined us for coffee.

"Now, take me to see this blasted place in the back and beyond of Norfolk, after all I will be the new owner... Oops!" And we all laughed.

I called our solicitors to push for an exchange of contracts. Then I immediately rang Faye to make an appointment for the next day to show Lawrence the house.

"No! That won't be possible until we exchange contracts, absolutely no!" she retorted tersely.

"Oh! It's just three days overdue!" I explained as much as I dared too, even trying to schmooze her, but she just would not have it. In fact she became so hoity-toity that she began by playing-me-off snidely against the other buyer.

I was furious. And within a hair's breadth of telling her... to stick her house where the sun didn't shine... But undeterred I kept buttoned-up; otherwise I really might have blown the deal.

As it happened Lawrence in curiosity had set up some other house viewings in the area. So we drove up. The weather was atrocious that day; but I showed him Holly Lodge, albeit as a glimpse through the orchard – as unfortunately we were unable to gain access that afternoon because... *The lady was not for turning.* In fact we sat with the torrential rain beating heavily down on his car under the great Scots Pine trees on the boundary. It was ridiculous! And I remember being so mad with Faye, but my dream spurred me on...

We saw a nice barn conversion near Felbrigg, and stopped off at a fantastic fish-eatery called '*Cookies*' in Salthouse, if you are ever in the area... it's a must!

The rest as they say is history; we completed the purchase of Holly Lodge, and were ready to move in January 2000. I paid Lawrence back from the proceeds of the sale of the Courtyard within the month, and all was bliss!

That fateful day arrived. Everything was packed into two large removal vans. One designated for Holly Lodge, whilst the other would carry most of the larger furniture to a storage unit: until the renovation was completed.

The Courtyard became a huge empty void. I wandered around for one last look as my steps echoed over the bare floorboards; and I must confess I almost wept. We had a great life there, and now we'd disappear into its past history, as just a footnote-in-name echoed as previous owners on the deeds.

We found a fine removal service based in King's Lynn. The chap that ran the company told me about six months later, it was as if Mike and I were *pioneers* at the helm of a vast wagon train of relocating migrants from London to the North Norfolk coast: starch collar types, city whizz kids, *Google* gods of the *iPod* nanotech generation, coming of age bohos, newlyweds, copious celebs, and those urban adventurers just seeking a simply better alternative to the inner city blues.

You see we hit it at just the right moment. Pure luck... it just so happened that the spotlight was focusing on this coastline. 'Chelsea-on-Sea' a label branded by travel journalists as the urbanite 4x4s were parking nose-to-bumper on the village Green in gentrified Burnham Market home to the pulsating, and ultra-stylish 'Hoste Arms'. Where you could play spot the celebrity or see a key young royal just hanging-out, or at Blakeney Harbour, another hot spot, where the *Ferraris*, *Aston Martins*, and *Porsches* were mingling along the quayside.

The final sequence to the film *Shakespeare in Love* starring Gwyneth Paltrow had just been shot on the beautiful sands of Holkham Beach. And the TV holiday shows at the time were enthused with features of this coastline *de rigueur*. Fashionistas with their Passionistas were poring over the glossies with their retro-inspired pictorials of this unspoilt utopia.

The trendy movers and shakers were flocking here to be seen, and be seen to chill at boutique deluxe hotels like the newly revamped 'Victoria' a more chic than shabby take on their Brit explorer interiors.

You can forget your Cotswolds, forget your Sandbanks, and your Cornish Riviera because...

North Norfolk was taking-off... And luckily our timing was impeccable...

We hit the Swaffham office full of nervous excitement... Mike dashed in to pick up the keys from the estate agents, and twenty minutes later we were heading up the drive to our new life in the country at Holly Lodge. I drove up to the main entrance – butterflies in my stomach – sincerely hoping all would be well!

I opened the front door. There on the wall opposite hung a large "Welcome Home" sign (a nice gesture!). But as we wandered through the cold, dank, empty house, we both grew overwhelmed with an anticlimax with the reality of how truly dismal the property confronting us really was.

I swallowed with dry disappointment, my heart sank in confusion at the pitiful sight, and I thought... Why had we given up our beautiful home for this? It was a very distressing moment for both of us...

The removal van pulled up with our basic essentials, and we spent the entire day trying to sort ourselves out. Finally they left around eleven that night. Eerily the cottages were left exactly how you'd expect to find Bed and Breakfast accommodation – as if the owners had just popped-out. However the oil tank was stone cold empty... not a drop! Perhaps it was Faye's revenge for the lateness of my contracts... No! She wouldn't surely...?

It was bitterly cold in the cottage, and there was no dry wood for a fire either. This was deep in the depths of winter, so there we were shivering, huddled under a blanket; we ate our garage bought sandwiches; and finally crashed-out.

The first thing I heard the next morning was a cock crowing vigorously...

"What! Is that flipping bird in the room?" I awoke startled.

"I think it must be under the bed..." Mike croaked as he jumped up bleary-eyed.

"Welcome to rural life... Hmmm?" We were feeling knackered. It was an icy morning; in fact so freezing cold that the vapours from my mouth were visible as I exhaled into the room.

Suddenly a car drew up into the drive... the sound of heavy thudding footsteps approached the little door to the cottage.

I could see the shadow of an enormous figure approaching through the blur of the dimple-pane glass in the stable-door. As I opened up, we were confronted with the broad grin of what looked like 'Thor the Thunder God' a dead-ringer for Dolph Lundgren...

"Howdy... Oi am Erik!"

All of him must have been over six and a half foot tall going on seven, built like a brick shithouse with the tanned weathered face of a brutish boxer, and a mane of Viking blond hair (straight-out-of homoerotic *Tom of Finland* books).

I rubbed my morning eyes (perhaps this was all a surreal dream, and my fantasy had arrived!). But of course, not... He was our new builder, whom we had appointed on recommendation of that very, very nice man, who owned the removal company.

I handed him my typed A4/Schedule of Works, which he jammed into his inside jacket pocket. And then we discussed the general state of play regarding the planned refurbishments...

"Erik, I am a stickler for detail... everything must be carried out methodically, and according to spec."

Huh... I discovered these would be my famous last words... as the sequence of events to unfold during the renovations were to become an experience let's say... After all this is the wild north of Norfolk... Yeeha!

"Thur demolition guys will be 'are any minute to star' tearin' the place apar'," he boomed in his local twang. And I gulped to decipher his Norfolk intonation.

"Well, let's get down to it, we have a hotel to open," Mike declared throwing on his warm-winter puffer.

The early morning frosty-haze hung heavily like a blanket over the ancient orchard, shrouding the entire place in a misty isolation, we approached the lack-lustred main building, as its stark exterior languished in the harsh grey-morning light.

I looked up at Erik, and felt dwarfed, although he would prove to be the gentlest of giants, and as soft as s...! Getting things done the Norfolk way though...

"How are you... um – on Grand Designs?" I quizzed him curiously.

"Rob, tha' in' a problem... build 'em every day!" he bellowed.

CHAPTER 5

A STAR IS REBORN

So, here we were in our new abode, not just a holiday sojourn, but serious stuff – building our new life here on Planet Norfolk. We felt totally alone surrounded by an alien wilderness...

We immersed ourselves into our new project with every ounce of energy we could muster. There was no time to waste, the business had to be up and running speedily enough to catch the first fruits of the high summer season.

It became a fascinating learning curve sourcing from local suppliers. I discovered that the county was blessed with some of the finest carpenters money could buy, thankfully most at realistic prices for their outstanding craftsmanship. Although our first experience with a roguish carpenter turned out to be sour grapes.

Fortunately, the house was not Grade-listed; therefore no Planning Permission would be required. Practically everything I wanted to achieve could be done with an intense cosmetic facelift. Usually I am a compulsive architectural freak, and reconstruct my properties from inside out, and top to bottom when needs-must of course... the saving grace with Holly Lodge was that despite its dour appearance the room-layouts flowed well for a Home versus Hotel.

We commandeered all three cottages as our makeshift home, along with our reliable old friend, the VW campervan. Some nights were so bitter, that it was warmer snuggled-up in the vehicle intermittently running the fan-heater.

The Claret cottage became our office and bedroom, The Colonial became our storage room, and the little Country cottage became a kitchenette of sorts, and food store.

I stuck to my original concept with the cottage names that I had created on the forecourt that day of our second viewing. These titles would become eponymous with their inspired themes for each interior. However first on the agenda was to concentrate on getting the main house sorted for habitation.

Many interior design influences abounding at the beginning of the Millennium were based on the nostalgia for everything fashionably romantic in Period. Trend Forecasters were tapping into a retrospective of popular historic themes to inspire new *looks* suitable for today's homes. I guess many of the voguish influences came from the lavish 'Bonnets and Breeches' sagas a la Jane Austen (recently aired in abundance on TV and film). *Elizabeth* with Cate Blanchett was another great example of a visually stunning *Tudor* set piece. And then there were the slew of Gothic-esque fantasy films that resonated too...

Interior and fashion designers often pillage from these types of genres, but of course reinvent them into something palatable for today's lifestyle.

Alternately, the other major trend contender, and popular with my urban clientele of the late 1990s was *Minimalism*: a vogue for the perhaps Freudian, sleek sexy interiors now growing evermore popular to psychologically de-clutter our lives in this ever-complex world. A calming more Spartan style – yet unforgiving: as regimental order reigns supreme to pull it off successfully.

Most designers naturally take all sorts of forecasted trends into account: *one has to have a mind like a sponge to soak it all up, and then rinse out what's not wanted.* The key being is to imbue the scheme with an original stamp that's one's own take on a concept. Moreover a concept that is comfortable to live with.

However I felt that the dreamy location in which Holly Lodge was set should purvey an atmospheric ambiance echoing its past age. Hence my aesthetic for our new *Boutique* sanctuary would evolve into my Gothic fantasy colliding with Global Brit-Explorer in HD (high definition) with an emphasis on heritage colours, textures, and user-friendly finishes of fine quality. And of course paying my trademark special attention to detail...

A scheme that's forever current – a timeless classic that does not quickly morph into yesterday's news; that's the ultimate test...

A contemporary escapist's fantasy meets sumptuous vintage interiors that I knew especially the urbanites would find *simpatico* out here in the wilds of Norfolk.

I always follow my instincts, and am often true to the architecture, which usually sets the guidelines for the interior schemes. Although I remember feeling at this juncture that this would clearly be probably the most awesome makeover challenge of my life to date, and would be pivotal to the future success of the Lodge. And we both knew it! Moreover Mike was counting on me...

However this house was such an anomaly. Even becoming an unbecoming blank canvas of a confection of conflicting periods from its history blurring into nondescript nothingness. Huh? I surmise as a result of its past owners perhaps foolishly eradicating many of its original features from its alleged eight-hundred-year-old history.

Therefore, I planned to sympathetically strip it back to its bare bones, in order to reinstate some much-needed character, something unique, but not a naff pastiche, but something to fill a void that no other guesthouse was catering for at the time in the locale.

Much of the main building dates back to the early 18th century, and one of its many incarnations had been of a schoolhouse allegedly from around the turn of the century, although its roots of origin are firmly based in the 13th century as characterised by a medieval exterior wall jut (known as a Batter) on the kitchen side of the house.

The front hall and pantry had once been used as a dairy especially during its farmhouse life. However the most redeeming feature though, and the main focal point set in the heart of the house was no doubt, the majestic Inglenook in the lounge with its original Bressemer beam of Tudor origins. In fact this part of the house dates mainly from that period. We discovered that Holly Lodge was probably the oldest property in the village of Thursford Green, as it had aptly been numbered 'One' on the main thoroughfare called unassumingly: The Street. And was originally annexed to the estate of Thursford Old Hall.

We'd spend entire days and weeks scouring the reclamation yards of the locale for interesting accessories, and unusual pieces, which we could juxtapose into our new home.

One particular find was a controversial sculpture with an aged patina – an amazing 150-year-old exquisitely carved 'Court Jester' (gargoyle-esque piece) of objet d'art I had bought for Mike as a birthday present; and which he adored! Much commented upon by many of our guests over the coming years... "His eyes sneakily follow you around the room." I feel it's these very quirky 'Statement Pieces' of impact that made our Lodge unique too...

Iconic 20th century (retro) furniture such as: the *Barcelona* chair by Mies van der Rohe, the *Egg* chair by Arne Jacobsen or *cult* pieces by Charles and Ray Eames, Le Corbusier, Eileen Gray, Florence Knoll, or Marcel Breuer will always make a cool statement, add impact, and look especially uber-stylish when juxtaposed with furniture, and schemes from other periods. That's if the budget will stretch of course... Equally an ornate gilt or painted (faux) Louis

XVI piece will sit comfortably in a stark minimal interior. It's all about striking a balance. And for me '*Design is my sensitivity...*'

Here, I must emphasise that the most vital piece of the boutique hotel kit, is no doubt the '*Bed*', which should be very *carefully* cherry-picked as the focal point of each room – to set the scene for the entire décor. And of course will have to endure years of wear and tear.

The roof was leaking badly, especially over the upstairs bedrooms, the windows were mainly rotten, beams woodworm-infested, walls riddled with damp, and the carpeted floors were well past their sell-by-date. And that's just for starters...

Erik, and his team buoyantly got underway. He would practically rewire the electrics to the entire house. Lighting is key to setting the ambiance, and is critical in my mind's eye. Visionary planning is essential for: practical (task) and atmospheric (mood) fittings to make an interior truly sing.

Charlie, the plumber, a charming chap accompanied by his dear little terrier, which we befriended, and wanted to dognap; had embarked on the plumbing modernisation: a major task considering how many bathrooms were remodelled – eight in all. Charlie did a great job in the end, but alas was not the most methodical of types.

One afternoon after all the sanitary ware had arrived I found him in the garage looking somewhat confused, and pacing around quizzically. He had unpacked everything, and somehow mixed-up all the individual packs of accessories I had prearranged for him. Now a mass of confusion reigned: taps, copious showerheads, and endless waste components were strewn all over the place, and not matching their respective sets of appliances. It was a nightmare to reorganise it all... Excruciating! But we did love dear old Charlie!

On the other hand there was the po-faced cowboy carpenter (who is the only carpenter I have ever come across with the misfortune of having a wooden leg). Yes, a wooden leg! Which I would never have mentioned save the fact that he was trying to rip us off big time with his shoddy, outlandishly expensive work, and all delivered with a surly attitude. This chap took an unreasonable instant dislike to us both for no apparent reason, perhaps based on some kind of homophobia... Who knows...? Happily Erik threw him off the job, which led us to discover a real gem near Holt. A very talented local master craftsman of great panache... who bespoke made the internal oak ledge and brace doors, and the authentic hardwood casement windows (neo-Gothic style frames) with external shutters (very French). Later we commissioned a bespoke front door on these lines too. And accessorised it with a rare Georgian forged iron doorknocker found in an Aladdin's cave: the nationally renowned 'Stiffkey Lamp Shop' on the coastal road. Well worth a visit if you are ever in this neck of the woods...

Erik, brought in two brilliant local tradesmen to restore our flagstone floors using simple flagstones, one might find in any hardware store – which we discovered as a cost effective alternative. This comic duo would bicker all day like a pair of pantomimic pantomime dames; but these master craftsmen did an exquisite job giving an outstanding authentic finish. Our guests were duped by our 17th century: 'Ever so original flagstone floors...'

The interior walls looked very drab; circa 1970, smooth magnolia to be exact... But I wanted to recreate an old crooked-house feel with uneven plaster walls giving the house its rightful ancientness. So I asked the plasterer and his mate to go out, and have a blast, the night before they were due to start...

"Guys, please get absolutely hammered, blind-drunk on me. And be *really* slapdash with the plastering."

Naturally they thought I was stark raving mad! Though I did show them a picture of lime-washed old cottage walls that I was hankering after. The result was ingenious.

"What a doddle!" The master plasterer commented as he patted my back. And oh, he thanked me for the extra generous tip for their boozy night out too.

When it came to fixing my aged-old iron wall sconces and dramatic ceiling chandeliers, Erik thought he'd get away with a major discrepancy in the height difference of a pair of wall fittings either side of the fireplace in the dining room that were approximately a four-inch difference north and south off the parallel.

"Heck... No! No!" I retorted when they were supposed to be perfectly balanced. This must be a Norfolk thing... My keen eye can't bear a millimetre of deviation in matching pairs of anything – let alone inches out. I had to be diligently hawkish at all times, when working with a half-blind electrician... Yikes!

One day, as we were leaving for one of our furniture hunting jaunts, a local gardener arrived, who was due to cut the grass. I showed him around, and insisted he pay particular attention to the septic tank overflow rubber hosepipe that ran across the rear garden to the farm fields on the boundary. I could not have emphasised the trail enough...

"Please, this must be avoided at all costs..." I reiterated no end.

Later on our return that afternoon, we just caught him packing up to leave, in rather a rushed sheepish manner as though he was trying to make a sneaky exit to avoid us. Basically he was snookered! So suddenly he came running over, but in great distress...

"Sorry! Sorry! Tha' is really, really, bad back there. Oi am such a lummox..." he cried out as he half-hid his face somewhere in between his Norfolk drawl, and the hood of his parka.

That was no understatement... Oh my God... It was a blinking ecological disaster! Our entire back garden had become a vast boggy quagmire of sewage. And it stank, and I mean really... stank to high heaven!

We were devastated... It took about a week to clear up, and was probably the most unpleasant, and nastiest job I have ever had to encounter in my entire life. The poor bloke never dared to show his face around the Lodge ever again. And we were forced to update the archaic system: or Health and Safety would have shut us down before we even opened.

'WELCOME TO NORFOLK'. From here on then, I learnt to read between the lines...

And then... our beautiful bespoke kitchen arrived. Hey-ho! Designed to a country style spec accented by Gothic inspired panelling, and pewter accessories: all solid wood construction, and hand finished in '*Farrow & Ball*' traditional paint colours (two-toned in lime white and cooking apple-green) with an iroko hardwood work-top. The kitchen had an intended movable-furniture-feel even though it was fitted, and sat splendidly on a grey slate floor.

We were smitten, but, and a very big but... there had been a gross miscalculation by the installer. You see the fire-resistant ceiling height above, the newly sited range in the chimney alcove, contravened Health and Safety regulations – as did the new boiler – now installed in the neighbouring storage room. And to make matters worse a pipe deeply embedded in a concrete wall ran from the boiler behind the newly fitted kitchen. This pipe had an inadequacy in its angle and had to be reinstalled. Uh-oh! A major cock-up...

So, the day we showed some neighbours around for a quick peak, we could have cried our hearts out in frustration because the entire lot had to come out the next day to be readjusted back at the wood-workshops. And it would take another month before it was finally reinstated. In the meantime the wall had to be prised open, causing untold destruction to readjust the bend in the flue to appease regulations.

Norfolk is one step forward, and two steps back more often than not... and here's the thing... everybody knew somebody in their family, who can fix it...

Ultimately though, it all came together beautifully... and proved to be a solid, practical, and rewarding space, an important component in our hospitality factory, where we would spend many a morn producing our special breakfasts.

Of course there were so many things to consider during the renovations, but one unexpected distraction completely threw me off kilter. It happened back when the demolition works began – as the skips were being carted away daily. I made the acquaintance of our resident ghost. Yes you read it right... Our resident ghost!

It was a cold dark Norfolk night... I left Mike all snuggled-up in the cosy cottage in front of the fire. I thought I would have a treat, and take a nice hot relaxing bath in the main house. More fool me...

Erik had thoughtfully left the electrics on, and the boiler running if needed over there. I ambled into the front hall, and placed my torch down in a wall niche. The downstairs was like a building site as I was tripping over piles of rubble, boards, tools, and all sorts. The rafters to the floors above were exposed, cables were hanging precariously, although sealed, and there was one low-wattage light bulb still working – just enough to light my way across the dining room – to access the stairs to the first floor.

I entered the old master bathroom and shut the door. And for some subconscious reason flicked the bolt too. I opened the taps – water gushed into Faye's proud large corner tub. I stepped in, and laid down into the inviting warm water: a saving grace in an icy bathroom.

As I lay there luxuriating for a minute or two, I thought I heard the sound of a bell ringing like the hand ones my teachers used to ring frenetically at my old school to round us up. It was startling to say the least. And the ringing echoed. The ceiling light dimmed and flickered, and I started to get the strong aroma of what I thought smelt like lilac scent. It became intoxicating... and I got the heebie-jeebies. I was infused by the sense of a strange ethereal presence, in effect standing behind me... The notion that I was now not alone in the bathroom became overwhelming.

"What!" I hollered.

The exposed bulb hanging from the ceiling suddenly flickered ominously. I jumped up, and nervously leant over to pull the cord just in reach of that cursed mirror surrounded by the myriad of bulb lights I had so criticised on our first visit. As I pulled it, I must have tripped the power switch, the bulbs flashed blindingly for a split second, and then the room went pitch black.

I remember cursing no end... "Shit! F...!" and so on... Basically I went into a blind panic (I don't do pitch black very well at the best of times), and now my well-oiled imagination was running riot. I was scared witless...

As I leapt out of the bath, I went flying, and crashing into a door, which was to the enclosed linen room. And then I was completely disorientated by the intensity of the total darkness, so typical of a moonless Norfolk night. All the while the pungent aroma of the lilacs permeated throughout the bathroom, and plagued my thoughts for an explanation, which I'm afraid was not forthcoming... "Oh no!"

I tried to fumble my way across the walls to get the hell out of there. Eventually discovering the coat hooks by the main door, which exits to the landing, I grabbed my dressing-gown threw it around my sodden shivering body, and once again fumbled to try and locate the bolt, which had now jammed stuck. It was an effort to slide it out to unlock the door, and in the process, I grazed off half the skin of my knuckle, as I felt the sharp edges of the buckled encasement slice into me.

Finally, I got the darn door open, and made a lightning dash down the stairs to the front door, tripping and stumbling over the works' clutter as I went. I retrieved my torch and made a hasty exit from the house.

When I barged into the cottage, Mike took one look at my shocked pallor, and actually said in jest:

"You look like you have seen a *ghost*, and what the hell has happened to your hand?"

I looked down – it was covered in blood from the gash I had acquired.

"And all I wanted was a nice *hot* bath in freezing-cold Norfolk..." That I'm afraid would have to wait for many more months, as the boiler that ran the three cottages was totally kaput... Cold showers in the height of winter weren't much fun over the next few months...

On another occasion, when the haberdashery lady arrived from the nearby town of Holt, the bizarre sequence of events turned into a day out at 'The Haunted House of Horrors'. She practically ran out of the Lodge screaming!

Jessica had placed her toolbox in the front hall and left her car keys in the ancient wall niche: a perfectly safe place – one might think. We proceeded to show her the windows in question that needed dressing; incidentally no builders were in that day. Oddly when she went to collect her tape measure, she discovered that her tool kit had vanished along with her car keys.

We spent ages searching the entire house. Somehow though her tool kit and car keys magically reappeared later when we all came back downstairs. There was simply no explanation...

Later while she was measuring-up, our postman drove onto the forecourt, and a piece of gravel clipped up from his tyre, with the consequence of hitting and cracking her car windscreen, which exploded into smithereens. Purely by chance one might think. The odds on of a trillion-zillion to one perhaps... An inexplicable freak accident... And then she went to spend a penny in that master-bathroom suite, where I had had my drama a few weeks earlier. But on leaving the room she claimed that the door unexpectedly felt very heavy as though there was a pushing sensation from the landing side – stopping her from exiting. Again mysteriously spooky...

Finally as she was coming down the stairs, she missed the bottom step, went flying, and sprained her ankle; this time she claimed disturbingly, that she felt she had been pushed...

The poor lady did return to finish the job albeit under great duress. But this time she categorically insisted... "For god's sake don't ever leave me alone here!" She was petrified of the place... Apropos her curtains were great!

Sometimes, I'd find things prearranged in a certain order: slices of bread arranged in a perfectly symmetrical circle. Another time, when we had some friends over to dinner, all the CDs were thrown around into disarray in the pantry.

"Sounds like we've got company in the house." Cathy looked startled by the kerfuffle and abruptly jumped up from the table.

"Oh, it's just Mary! (as we called her) playing silly monkeys in the pantry," I shrugged nonchalantly. That's how used to her ubiquitous presence, we'd become.

"Hey! I suspect she's not into your music," Lewis chortled.

Strangely as the film title goes: *There's Something About Mary* which was so unsettling about her disturbances, and choice of times to rant...

Please don't think I am digressing into a 'Ghost Story', but this mischievous presence became very much part of our lives in this enigmatic building. However the shenanigans of our playful poltergeist practically stopped though, hitherto the discovery of a curious *photograph* we found hidden in a secret attic space. This we unearthed once some built-in wardrobes were removed to make way for a home-office. Wow! Our very own Panic Room...

Curiously the cubbyhole space might have once been a 'Priest Hole'. There were some old oak steps inscribed with the name *Tom*, crudely carved in one of the treads with a date of 1610, and there was a old rusty naïve Cross from around that period – which eventually I threw into the old well in the garden for good luck's sake!

The dog-eared sepia photograph depicted a stern looking young couple, standing aside an elderly grey-haired lady all dressed in Edwardian Sunday best. They were standing to a pose in front of the dining room window at Holly Lodge.

Apparently the younger lady in the photo lived at the Lodge to the ripe old age of ninety-nine, and we believe it was her presence that haunted the house, because when we hung up this enigmatic photograph; everything just simply stopped! Strangely, years later I discovered it was her who had planted the seven *lilac* trees in the grounds.

It was now the beginning of April, and the house was morphing from an *Ugly Betty* into a well-fed *Kate Moss*. My dreamy fantasy was coming to fruition, as the property was taking the shape of an alluring period pile. Surely our guests would be seduced at first sight...?

The more the house evolved the more excited we became by the results. It was transforming before our very eyes into something very appealing...

The entrance had been transformed too. Regency inspired black iron railings topped with Arabesque finials were fitted to either side of the front door to create a walkway to the entrance. The nasty hardware store exterior lantern was replaced by a seriously gorgeous fitting with a crenulated crown-like roof, which nestled regally amongst the climbing fragrant tea roses that were now scrambling up the house.

The exterior woodwork was painted in *Lichen* (a period grey-green tone – after all this is '*Farrow & Ball*' country!). Sadly we had to replace the old school doorbell with a reproduction version, but it worked, and looked just the same, and became a charming embellishment to greet our guests as they entered.

A pair of tall cypress (pencil trees) were planted symmetrically either side of the lounge bay window. An old carriage-cart originating from Hungary (found at the Norwich Showground Antique Fair) was placed in situ at the top of the lawn in front of the orchard. This applecart would become synonymous with Holly Lodge, used in many publicity stills.

Inside the house, the beams of galleon-sized proportions were being restored, the walls were being limed a buff white, and then as if it were Christmas, we simply moved in. And all our beloved furniture, and personal belongings finally arrived from the storage depot.

There is no doubt that the Lodge was imbued with an idiosyncratic mix of the *old* and *new* by our eclectic array of collectables: a 1950s' black and white Jean Cocteau vase would somehow sit exquisitely on an Arts & Crafts credenza as if they had once been separated at birth. Or our sumptuous *Knole* sofa (nestled by the Inglenook) upholstered in olive, and red tapestry fabric intricately woven with Tudor-esque mythical griffins would be well at home with a 1920s' Florentine bronze nearby.

A specially commissioned piece, hand painted with a trompe l'oeil of a full-length figure of St Francis of Assisi (very Tuscan monastery), made a dramatic impact in the front hall. The armoire concealed and revealed, shelves and shelves copiously filled with tourism brochures for local must-see attractions (I wanted to keep this type of bumf as discreetly hidden as possible, but of course accessible). And again a contemporary *Barcelona* chair might be juxtaposed nearby.

Another wonderful find came from Bermondsey market in London. A magnificent Tudor 'marriage' chest encrusted with intricate ornate ironwork, and actually had the initials: 'M & R' intertwined on the front, which goaded us into buying it.

We had tremendous fun placing our personal treasures around our new home, but it would take many more trips to the salerooms, antique fairs, and specialist shops which are in abundance in Norfolk to adequately deck the house out to the max. And which nearly bankrupted us in the process.

Once, we had moved into the main house, all our energies would be focused on getting the optimum out of those cottages, it was imperative that they would be drop-dead gorgeous...

The largest 'The Claret Cottage', would be imbued with the *romantic* ambiance, epitomizing a Baroque stately encounter... based around the centrepiece of a grand gilt-edged Gothic four-poster bed (draped with crimson brocaded swags: befitting Empress Josephine). The room would be kitted out with key antiques, oils, and sculptures all complemented by the striking backdrop of the deep Venetian red walls. A dramatic tapestry depicting a scene of *Claret* producing from the French vineyards eponymous with the name – would hang the length of a vast wall – flanked by two pavilion style flame-torch bronze lights (found in Portobello).

A recessed alcove would house a Parian marble bust set on an ebony plinth, and the flagstone flooring would be covered with a huge antique red, orange, and navy crested Bokhara rug, which we had found at the Souk in Marrakesh.

This became our showpiece suite. Very popular with newly-weds... And no wonder!

Walter Stowy of *The Sunday Times (Travel)* wrote, and part quote (17th April 2005):

'The bed had been teleported from the boudoir of an Emperor's concubine. It was a four-poster buried beneath all sorts of pillows, and cushions, and swathed in richly coloured fabrics, the rest of the room called appropriately enough 'Claret Cottage' with wine-red walls, a leather sofa, a classical bust, and even a wire slipper filled with chocolate mints. The décor: exquisite 10/10. A master's degree in interior design.'

Next came the 'Colonial Cottage' suite very reminiscent of the days of the Raj. Pure *escapism* filled with Brit-explorer artefacts from the exotic East. Here the walls were given a *verdigris* hue, and the floors were tiled in Chinese slates. A 1920s' retro fan accented a pair of deco-green velvet armchairs in the sitting area. These we lovingly restored after discovering they had been left to rot in the old barn... what a boon!

We housed our collection of framed Victorian plant lithographs (found in a shop in Camden Passage specialising in antiquarian illustrations), these were mounted along the back wall. An original 18th century map graced the bathroom wall echoing the global trekker's journeys through far-flung lands. And one of my prized possessions (inherited from my father): a contemporary, and beguiling ink-on-watercolour painted by the famous – 7' 1" – basketball star of the American Hall of Fame, Art Beatty, (one of Pop's celebrity friends) hung centre-stage on the main wall. Distressed teak panels were fitted as window shutters echoing the Colonial vibe.

Amidst the imagery of my theme – even a be-turbaned *punkawalla* statuette sat holding a welcome dish (usually replete with homemade Turkish delight).

This room had the option of being a double as the twin-single-beds could be pushed together, zipped and linked into a large king double. And was probably our most commercial suite.

The 'Country Cottage', was Michael's favourite! Best things do come in the smallest packages when staying in this *idyllic* suite. A Tardis full of surprises...

The exposed Norfolk flint walls and rugged beams imbued the atmosphere with a quaint ancient charm. An antique brass bed dressed with an authentic patchwork American prairie style bedspread set the scene. A native homespun feel 'New England meets Old England' enhanced by our collection of antique Samplers (embroidered needlework from the 18th and 19th centuries). Windsor chairs, an old chest, naïve farm tools, a dairy stool, and 1960s' Cornish earthenware pieces played heavily on that rustic charm. There was a quirky Victoriana rocking-toy set on a ledge (an amusing piece of vintage ephemera). And guests' coats could be draped around an old tailor's dummy that used to belong in my atelier.

This cottage became a firm favourite with older guests, and younger trendier couples alike.

Each suite would be kitted-out with up-to-date gizmos: CD music, and DVD film libraries, state-of-the-art *BOSE* sound systems, *iPod* docking facilities, and Internet connections – discreet mini-fridges loaded with complimentary drinks – and luxurious tea-coffee trays offering a wide range of goodies. Each bathroom would be filled with an abundance of every size of fluffy towels, voluminous (monogrammed) dressing gowns, with matching slippers. And those wonderful '*Molton Brown*' toiletries everybody ran-off with!

Attention to detail was paramount!

We found a terrific graphic design company in Cromer run by a savvy young couple: David and Amy whom have since become dear friends. They produced an exquisite A5/eight page brochure – all beautifully photographed by David himself – a very talented photographer – and computer whiz kid.

My literature and website was highlighted with key buzzwords as descriptive elements to the accommodation: *Ambient – Deluxe – Escapism – Idyllic – Romantic –*

Tranquillity. This was my conceptual message depicting a staycation at...

'A not so faraway getaway named Holly Lodge'.

Finally, after a long hard slog the major first stage of the refurbishments were completed, and Erik with his merry band of men were packing up to leave. I never imagined I'd be sorry to say goodbye to a bunch of builders, but they turned out to be very good company, and through all the trials and tribulations did an outstanding job in the end.

Now we were on our tod to organise and prepare for the impending opening of our new business. Scary to say the least; but we were refreshed with the confidence of a stunning new residence about to open its doors to the public.

This was a defining moment, when we threw away our very last cigarettes.

"That's my last smoke ever!" I said triumphantly with my newfound strength.

"Me too, yuck! No more poisoning ourselves in this fresh air..." Mike was committed.

Norfolk finally brought me freedom with conviction... And I can happily report that I have not so much as touched one in over ten years now. "Yippee!"

I received a timely e-mail from Violet, Dad's third wife (American Mom), who I mentioned previously, and whom I truly adore, announcing her forthcoming visit. Naturally, who would be better to road test our new establishment? Americans are sometimes so notorious for being pedantically fastidious with their creature comforts abroad. Hey... especially when it comes to water pressure...

"How many times have you heard an American comment on this topic – especially in the UK? Some treat it as a sport!" I suggested to Mike...

"Oh, I remember when Vi lambasted that hotel bathroom in London..." Mike had reminded me of her trip two years ago, when she stayed in that gruesome overpriced pile deep in the West End. "She was scathing about it!" he continued.

"Oh yeah! I remember it well. Blimey! I hope she will approve of our efforts," I gulped.

"OK, Rob, checklist," Mike advised. It was now 1am on the morning of her arrival.

"State-of-the-art water-pumps. Check! Hand safety controls. Check! Massage jet options. Check! Soap dispensers. Check! Hang-on..." I was winding-down.

"Shall we go all 1970s, and shock them all with soap-on-the-rope. Huhhhhh," Mike cackled.

"Oh my God, a kitschy-camp revival of '*Brut*'," I grimaced.

"Coffee... size zero latte – skinny latte – fatty latte – and xxx fatty super latte." Mike was now in fits. "Hey, how about naming our coffees after celebrities from: *Posh Spice* to *Dawn French*?"

"Clever clogs... You forgot cappuccino, with or without *Cocoa Chanel*..." I chortled.

"Corny..."

"It's no use, we'll get slaughtered by those meany-mouthed nannying lefties – for not being PC," I feared.

"Okay, eggs, sunny side up, easy-over, poached, blah, blah, blah... and then there's organic, corn-fed, but no way am I having battery farmed eggs..." I rambled as my mind jumped about.

"Battery farmed! Are we talking fucking all singing all dancing digital eggs here?" he wisecracked.

"You're terrible..."

"Firm mattresses – touch lighting – cleanliness not a speckle of..." now I was exhausted with it all. "Vi will be the perfect critique to road-test the whole darn caboodle," I muttered, sighed, and then finally crashed-out.

My father's marriage to Vi, as I affectionately called her, was truly seminal, and a complete antithesis of his erstwhile marriage to the Teutonic Brigitte.

Vi was devoted, kind, loving, and very beautiful, a Chinese version of Faye Dunaway I kid you not! But most importantly of all, she managed to heal some of the severe damage that dad's former wife had wreaked on our family.

He became a changed man in many ways during his relationship with her, and although their marriage lasted just shy of ten years, only to be parted by his passing, I knew these were his happiest in latter life. She was no doubt a godsend!

I had first met her in Hong Kong when I was nearly twenty-one, and on one of those rare father-son occasions, when we actually travelled together, him on one of his usual business trips, and me assembling one of my earliest menswear collections in a factory in Kowloon. My father had been introduced to Vi by one of his business partners, and unbeknown to me, a dinner party had been arranged in one of those humongous, Chinese eating-houses; always bustling to the gills, where a private room downstairs had been booked for the occasion.

On our first meeting she was so utterly engaging, and her dazzling Oriental beauty just floored me... However, it was her sincere demeanour that shone through. And I was immediately won over! The great irony is that we immediately became great friends unlike my relationship with mother-number-two. And I know she considers me to be one of her boys, as she has two sons from a previous marriage to a Texan, and two daughters from her first marriage to a doctor back in China.

Vi has had the most fascinating life, and narrowly escaped from Shanghai during the Great Revolution in China of 1949, a harrowing story in itself... After years of hardship, she eventually settled in the former British Colony of Hong Kong. Here she built up a successful Import-Export agency – trading to Europe and the United States.

Hence, she met my father through this medium, and they dated, just after his divorce was finalised. She settled with him in London, where she afforded me generously much of her time, becoming a key figure in helping me establish my own career. Her extensive business knowledge, and astute acumen were highly beneficial to a struggling young fashion designer trying to become independent, and establish his own way.

My father's relationship with me had become purely cerebral on a work-only basis, blanking out all else that had gone before. It was his deal with me – a shield of denial perhaps...? So be it. And I was driven...

Vi worked tirelessly with me from the beginning as we schlepped my design samples around in the back of my beaten-up old Honda, knocking on doors to gain an audience with crucial retail buyers. And the day we broke '*Harrods*' was a day like no other... (I knew *Pops* would be very impressed – even proud!). This remarkable lady's presence provided a hugely positive impact on my life. On one level she helped me, and my father connect, assuaging our often terse, and sometimes hostile meetings: especially during my twenties.

My design label using my middle name *Maxwell* was launched, and doors opened. Chic boutiques of the day like: '*Ebony*' in South Molton Street, '*Jones*' of Covent Garden and King's Road, became stockists of my clothing designs, then other exclusive outlets throughout the UK ensued. The glitterati of the day were sporting my leather jacket designs too: *George Michael, Spandau Ballet, Duran Duran, Yazz, Sir Elton John, Shakin' Stephens, Rod Stewar*t to name-drop just a few... And my showroom in Islington became inundated.

Hence, my career was launched, coinciding with London's return to prominence as a *cool* fashion centre in the 1980s.

Can you imagine in those days, I was dubbed by *'Men's Wear' magazine* as 'Britain's answer to the Italian Look' and the likes of *Giorgio Armani* etc (my idol).

Basically I had produced my top end gear on home turf, exclusively in England. Originally, in a very small way in a London workshop – working with a genius sample maker: Mr Willie Blum, who would realise my creations. And in doing so, my specialised collections of the finest quality filled a void as a direct competitor to some of the leading Italian fashion designers of the day who were cornering the British market. These high fashion leatherwear, and knitwear ranges were more competitively priced too; hence they became a big hit...

Demand grew and grew for greater production levels especially as a result of my order books being copiously filled during the London and Paris trade shows from season to season. My exhibition stand was regularly swamped with buyers from all over the world. Consequently my lines were sold in many outlets throughout the major capitals of Europe, Japan, and America. Features ensued in an internationally celebrated *'Fashion Bible'*, *Sportswear International,* and *The New York Times* etc.

Then, somehow I managed to pull off an even greater coup, and got accepted to exhibit at the 'New York Designers' Collective' – a very prestigious fashion show, where there would be hundreds of applicants vying for membership, but with just a mere handful chosen on merit each year.

Hence, I became a relevant player amongst a prodigious new breed waving the *Cool Britannia* flag overseas; like the incomparable *Paul Smith*, chic *Mulberry*, and *Browns* such a class act, controversial, ground-breaking *Katharine Hamnett*, multi-talented *Paul Costelloe*, and even the iconic *Vivienne Westwood*.

This arena, Stateside, was an amazing platform for my work, and then as if it could not have got any better, I was head-hunted by a large American corporation, after they spotted my jackets in *Harrods*, and *Barneys* exclusive department store on Madison Avenue, New York.

They made me an irresistible offer to come and live in the Big Apple (the stuff of dreams). I would design for their company, whilst they marketed my name as their exclusive in-house designer. And with the bonus of creating a new diffusion label *'Maxwear'* showcasing my work – and extending into all areas of men's clothing under an exciting new brand. Thus marketed at first from coast-to-coast in the United States, then internationally, enabled with their large production facilities in the Orient. It was a mind-blowing opportunity. And I did relish living in the most exciting city on the planet...

I'll never forget, when I first arrived at New York Kennedy Airport, still in my early twenties, bright-eyed, and keen to get on... A chauffeur had been sent to pick me up in one of those huge white stretch limos courtesy of Elliot and Richard my new American backers. I was wooed... And the *stretch* was at my disposal thereafter! They treated me like a *star* to be wined, and dined no end at the most swankiest, and hippest places in Manhattan. But what really stood out was dinner with Elliot's parents on my first night in town.

They lived in a magnificent duplex atop The United Nations Plaza. The elevator was like an eternal ride to the heavens. I lost count of the number of floors, and boy the view from their spectacular white marble encased penthouse was impossibly breathtaking beyond any cityscape view I'd ever seen before.

The gleaming impressive monoliths of the New York skyline were stacked as far as the eye could see down to the Hudson, night-lit with a zillion bulbs. I felt I could almost touch the iconic Chrysler skyscraper – shimmering in all its silver-clad deco glory.

I was set up in a hip loft apartment on Columbus Avenue overlooking the Lincoln Centre. Hence I became a 'N' Yarker'. And my pace of life became even faster in the city that never sleeps. I guess that's why they named it twice – because every day seemed like living forty-eight hours! The sidewalks bubble with an undercurrent to fire even the weariest of souls. I was down the gym at six, or busting an Olympian jog in Central Park before I broached the longest day every day.

I'd love to mooch around Greenwich, and West Village, with its great buzzy bars, and eateries or ebullient, and very bohemian SoHo, where the esoteric shops are unique with great élan.

I'd spend months on end designing copious collections from my garret. More often than not, stoned with a spliff on the go, and burning the midnight oil... Boy, I worked very hard. And made sure they got nothing less than the best from me.

Weekends would be a manic round of clubbing, and hobnobbing with the trendsetters at in-places like the *Limelight* (a former church converted into a madcap nightclub on Sixth Avenue), or even mingling with star-studded-guests during the final days of *Studio 54*.

Of course the international travelling intensified too. I would have to spend many long months in the Far East assembling my collections in their factories. Luxurious hotels became transient homes like the grand dame of the Orient, *The Peninsula* in Hong Kong or sometimes a stopover at *The New World Hotel*. Now that was epic... Where one morning the blasted lever got stuck on my toaster in the room, while I was taking a shower, and smoke poured through into the hotel corridors setting off the fire alarms.

Can you imagine? How embarrassing it was being dragged naked out of my shower... by the hotel staff, as I had been oblivious to the pandemonium caused. Phew!

After some years Stateside, my glamorous lifestyle finally caught up with me, and in many ways it had become a very lonely existence. I often awoke in a different hotel room in a different country through season-to-season, almost losing sight of who I was anymore. And one time in Hong Kong I became so worn down physically, that I ended up contracting a dreadful bout of bronchitis made worse by the incessant air-conditioning, as the island is stifling... It was a deeply depressing eight weeks that made me terribly surly. And I just wanted to go home, but I wasn't sure where home was anymore.

There'd be multiple fabric-buying trips to Europe, with whistle-stops in Barcelona, Paris, Milan, and my favourite place on Mother Earth: Florence. In fact I once lived with a family there for six months, when just out of college. They owned a factory in the hills near Montecatini, and that's where I produced my very first commercially successful collection. And fell madly in love with Italy. But that's another story...

I lived the life of a jet-setter, hobnobbing at some of the world's finest hotels: The arty *Mondrian*, the glamorous (Art Deco) *Sunset Tower Hotel*, in Los Angeles; stylish *Morgans*, and the iconic *Hotel Chelsea* in New York (before I moved to my loft apartment on Columbus Avenue) – all became familiar places to lay my hat. And then there were the many charming little boutique Bed and Breakfasts set in quaint pretty shuttered townhouses on the Left Bank in Paris too.

The American thing lasted a fair while. Until Elliot, and Richard, who really were aficionados in their field now offered me the deal of a lifetime... There is no doubt, what with their financial clout, that they would have made me a *household* name – it was on the cards. But I dithered hopelessly with my youthful, and fragile insecurities, and was swayed by some poisonous bad advice from my then, partner. Somehow I foolishly let it all fall apart...

Regretfully, I returned to London. Though keeping on good terms with the guys in New York, even still sending designs over on a freelance basis, but sadly it all just slipped away with the passage of time. I later realised I had really blown a golden opportunity, which I naïvely did not grasp at that pivotal moment in my life.

However, back in town I set up a new studio. And went on to have a modicum of success, but not under my own label anymore; so my design name sank into obscurity over time, and I became like a ghost-designer behind the scenes for the next few years. I diversified more into commercial casual-wear, and sportswear. Designing ranges for major high street brands, and mega sportswear giants: *Adidas*, *Converse*, *Puma*, *Reebok*, and *Hummel* where I was involved at the forefront of the *Lycra* body-conscious revolution – aerodynamic fashions of the 1990s, and new technological advances in graphic design, and logo imagery. And oops, please forgive me, but I was even partly responsible for the resurgence of the chavvy shell suit...

Wimbledon stars and sporting heroes were wearing my designs, but sadly my name was now nowhere to be seen...

Finally disheartened, and burnt-out, I simply walked, and vanished off the radar... The years that followed were lean, even despairing at times, but gave me the space to look inwards, grieve, and come to terms with my inner turmoil, and eventually to start afresh.

Those sure were heady days, a far cry from Thursford Green in Norfolk, but that's where I wanted to be right now, a more settled way of life with my soul mate Michael.

I could harness an amalgamation of those amazing global adventures, and travels to far-flung exotic places, having experienced a wide range of establishments in all their cultural diversity.

And together, we could imbue our technique into a cohesive, relevant new *Sanctuary* par excellence, while I could have a more anchored existence, if all went according to plan...

Mens Wear

British answer to Italian look

ROBBIE MAXWELL

PUTTING BRITISH LEATHER ON THE MAP

An editorial in *Men's Wear magazine*, 1985

That's what they used to call me…

Robert, Boca Raton, Florida on New Year's Eve 1983.

One of my big winners sold worldwide.

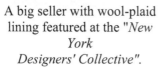

A big seller with wool-plaid lining featured at the "*New York Designers' Collective*".

Paris Trade Show "Sehm" in the mid-1980s.

CHAPTER 6

THE OPENING

The one o'clock train from London to Norwich was imminent. Vi, accompanied by my stepbrother, Michael, would finally be visiting us for their first foray to Norfolk.

It had been quite some time since I had last seen my beloved-bro Michael. I had heard that he had tired of life as a struggling actor in Los Angeles, and had moved back to Austin, Texas to pursue his new career as Venture Capitalist – and that a certain southern belle had stolen his heart.

Actually my first meeting with Michael was way back in the day, when I dropped out for a couple of months just before my career became an all-consuming: 24/7/365. Taking my meagre savings, I just took off with my backpack, and got my first taste of America.

A naïve young lad, full of wanderlust hit the Pacific West Coast. I hired a low budget Japanese car, in fact the last forlorn vehicle left on the lot that day at the hire company in San Diego. Michael worked at the Sheraton Hotel on the marina, and that's where we first met. In fact brotherly love was immediately sealed... because he helped me out with free room and board at the hotel, as nothing had been pre-booked.

Memorable days were had in this dreamy location. And we even slipped over the border to visit Tijuana in Mexico. A dodgy prospect at the time, which I soon discovered after some sinister-looking *banditos* followed us around town. That's after spotting us alight from his American registered *Ford Mustang* (tourists back then could be rich-pickings). Nevertheless after some canny ducking and diving we shook them off our trail, and got safely back over the border. Phew!

Michael advised me to be very cautious as I set off on my journey up the Californian coast. I would be travelling a great distance alone.

Little did I know, that my spontaneous solo trip would evolve into one of the most awe-inspiring journeys of my life to date...

I first holed-up in a Bed and Breakfast, practically right on the sun-kissed beach of Santa Barbara, a gorgeous town revelling in its CV of much Spanish Heritage. Solvang, a town (Daned-up to the hilt) was an interesting anomaly on my next whistle stop, and a mooch around San Luis Obispo charmed me with its name alone.

The Pacific coastal 'Highway 1 or 101' spans from glam, smoggy Los Angeles to San Francisco, and has to be one of the most gripping, and thrilling scenic drives ever. The road meanders perilously between jagged cliff-faced sheer drops into the Pacific shore-side, and mountainous giant redwood groves on the inland side.

An unforgiving route, that becomes a struggle not to ignore the spectacular ocean vistas revealed around every hairy-twisting-bend as I followed in the riveting path probably taken by thousands of 1960s' hippies – in search of that *Californian Dreamin'* utopia.

Here's the thing. Petrol stations are few and far between rather like North Norfolk, and these were the days before our precious *Sat Nav*, and more often than not I'd limp into the next whistle stop café, dangerously low on fuel with my heart in my mouth. I arrived in 'Big Sur' one public holiday weekend. And typically all the Lodges were darn full. Oh...

So I was forced to bunk-down in my car on the outskirts of the dense forests in a campsite of the State Country Park.

I sampled a famous 'Ambrosia burger' which really hit the spot, before I ensconced myself inside my sleeping bag, on the front seat. I lulled into a deep penetrating sleep, serenaded by the allure of Mother Nature at her finest, blanketing my senses with the false security of her whispering coastal breezes, and comforting ocean swells.

"Oh my God!" I yelped as I awoke, startled by a ferocious growl... There peering at me through the windscreen was a darn cougar (mountain lion)... Our eyes locked in bewilderment that seemed to last aeons. The great cat clawed precariously into the gap of my window. And a fierce swipe narrowly missed my head... No doubt he was on the prowl for breakfast, and was lingering over the prospect of moi!

Instinct took hold, and I clobbered his paw with a rolled-up magazine in what became a terrifying tussle. Seconds seemed like minutes... but somehow I managed to wind up the window, honk the horn and send the magnificent creature bolting back into the thicket.

My sabbatical continued...

Sometimes, I drove through the night guided only by the crashing waves of the Pacific spray glistening in the moonlight. Scary, but oh so enthralling!

I crossed the awesome Bixby Bridge where the purple mountains drop dramatically into the sea, forming sequestered bluffs. Built during the Great Depression to open the route north, and here I discovered a slow puncture, but thankfully just reached historic Carmel in the nick of time. Clint Eastwood was once Mayor of this elegant town on the Monterey peninsula.

There are not enough superlatives to do the setting justice, where the sun shimmered off the glistening ocean through the Monterey pines. Fast Forward to Norfolk years later to the sea glimpses lashing the white sands of Holkham through the Pinewoods at Wells – so reminiscent of these Californian vistas through my mind's eye.

I arrived at the neighbouring town of Monterey: John Steinbeck's setting for his thought-provoking novel *Cannery Row*. Though more casual than Carmel pervading a more lived-in feel, I loved it just the same especially for its compelling views, and authenticity. And where I was lucky enough to spot a posse of whales surfing the inky waters.

I could wax lyrical singing the joys of this entire experience, but one place for me that left such an indelible impression has to be the inimitable '*San Simeon*' set on what is known as 'The Enchanted Hill' (*La Cuesta Encantada*) as it's known in Spanish.

The fabled castellated citadel of mega-publishing magnet, William Randolph Hearst, married to silent screen siren Marion Davies spent thirty years passionately building his sublime behemoth. Now a State monument, and museum housing his priceless, and eclectic collections – scavenged from the finest art vaults of history.

The Great and the Good of the day would party around the much photographed 'Neptune Pool' echoing the days of the Roman empire, and Hollywood's golden era. The outrageous audacity of this whimsical confection, and fantastical monstrosity – beggars belief!

Finally, I reached the fabulous, and very *cool* city of San Francisco basking in its most European disposition. Here I blew my last few dollars on some much-needed *decent* accommodation on Fisherman's Wharf. And the rest I will leave up to your imagination…

I set out on a three-week break, and stayed thankfully ten carefree weeks bumming around the Golden State until I was flat broke. Consequently I had to return home to start earning a serious living back at my atelier in a warehouse in Islington. And that is how I first met my new brother Michael and a bro'mance was born.

Back in Norwich station as the passengers rolled out through the exit barriers, I was surprised not to see them disembark. Naturally I thought they'd be on the next one in, due at two, so I waited.

Again no-show… this time, I called Vi. She asked me, "Where was I hiding in the crowds at the station?" I was curiously dumfounded; as Norwich station was practically deserted as we spoke. Then it dawned on me, "Huh?" They must be at the wrong destination…

Indeed, they were. As it turned out they were right across the other side of the country in Warwick near Birmingham. Vi, bless her, had stated that…

"We are in **Wowich**!"

"Wowich, where the hell is that?" I queried. Of course... it was that Oriental thing, as the R was dropped out of the spelling of Norwich, and the N mistaken for a W in the pronunciation as she repeated my instructions to her son Michael the night before.

It was always frustrating to say the least, this little language nuance that would make such a crucial difference to everyday details. And then typically in American fashion, I was told...

"No problem, we'll get a cab to Norfolk..."

Which horrified me, as they were about three, and half hours away, roughly one hundred, and fifty miles across central England, and it would cost a mint!

Naturally, I insisted I'd return to meet them at the station later that day, but Vi opted to take a taxi all the way to Holly Lodge. Here's the thing. America being such a vast continent distances like that become inconsequential, whereas they'd be considered awesome to us Brits. Another diverse cultural nuance that's so intriguing! Mind you one time, after I made some serious greenbacks during my life Stateside... I extravagantly hired a Cadillac limousine, driving from Los Angeles to the hipper-than-thou resort of Palm Springs about two hours away. After spending a few days there, luxuriating in a swish desert Inn, I hired another stretch limo to take me across the desert to Las Vegas in Nevada another one hundred and eighty miles away (five hours' drive). Hey, I hold my hands up too...

They finally arrived later that night. To top it all, their taxi driver got lost too. What a fiasco... Bless.

Michael, her son, is a strikingly handsome six foot-five, and built like an American pro-soccer player. A product of his Texan roots, blue-eyed, yet with his mother's Far Eastern features creating a fascinating exotic mix to his bone structure. Fortunately he has inherited her sunny and, adorable nature, but with a seductive Texan drawl.

Her other younger son Danny, is deep, sensitive, and artistic... *my default setting mode*. Although on every other level we are entirely different. Thank goodness!

Rakish Danny became a big hit on the London scene, cutting a devilish dash with the chicks. At one point though he had to hightail it fast out of London with a bevy of babes in hot pursuit. And a posse of disgruntled gangster rappers too...

'Munkberrys' in Mayfair was a particularly favourite haunt of ours. A secret world of make-believe revealed through a discreet basement door – evocative of a forbidden Speakeasy. And where the club music, and the outré fashionista crowd were the coolest of them all.

Those were the self-absorbed days of my reckless youth on the louche clubby-circuit, when I was a hot name in the fashion biz, and my world was pretty glitzy. I was chummy with the outrageous, and waspishly lovable Philip Salon, the renowned bizarre eccentric: he of the inner sanctum of the Boy George entourage. And a time when the 'New Romantics' ruled the roost...

Unfortunately it's been many years since I last saw bro' Danny, himself a very talented artist. We'd spend hours burning the midnight oil, stoned, and entranced by soul-jazz-funk vinyl classics on the stereo – sketching our latest creations into next season's winners. He is now living, and working in deepest China. Perhaps paying some kind of penance...?

Pops left a legacy of a very internationally based family. Special occasions evolved into a United Nations shindig. Believe you me...

Well, I was proved right insofar of my Chinese-American side of the family being the perfect critiques. Each suite was tried and tested with a few minor details adjusted in accordance with their constructive criticisms.

And thank heavens those darn power showers impressed them... In fact they were really taken by the black-pepper body wash too – said to increase circulation – soothe the skin, and be somewhat of an aphrodisiac. Vi loved the décor, and ambiance created throughout, then of course she would be my biggest fan.

After some memorable days, and donning my tourist guide hat, we sadly dropped them off at Norwich for the next stage of their European trip. Boohoo!

I will never forget the thoughtfulness, and kind welcome from the people of Thursford wishing us well in our new venture. There was a dapper gentleman, named Dick, whom we likened to a *Colonel*: a requisite fixture for every quintessentially English village. Eh! Our lovely neighbours Carole and Peter, a wonderfully genial couple who have turned out to be the greatest of friends to this day, and not forgetting Ross, their cuter, than cute Jack Russell terrier. In fact one day he'd become our dog's best pal. And then there was that blessed Millennium barn barbeque...

Tony and Wendy had a smallholding nearby, where the barbeque was held for all the villagers.

We discovered we weren't '*The only gays in the village*', to coin a familiar catchphrase made famous by the television show, *Little Britain*. And then again why should we be; even in this remote locale. Actually the village was hardly parochial, in fact bursting with arty Bohemian types, designers, TV soap writers, a revered horticulturist, the odd grandee... in fact all sorts from all walks, escapees migrating to this side of the M25: evangelical converts from Greater London to the far-flung sticks. Thursford must number amongst many villages as a contemporary snapshot of the changing rural (Britscape) of the Noughties. Where have all the indigenous folk gone...?

Though, sometimes little vignettes would play-out with more than just a lingering whiff of the black-and-white (camp-comedy) years of Ealing Studios a la Margaret Rutherford, and gang. And then there was *us* adding our colourful new edge inevitably to create such a stir in this little hamlet with our own 'Passport to Pimlico' cor blimey... I mean the nouveau principality of (Thursford)...

What was most amusing though, is that local newspaperman insisted forevermore that Mike and I were... Err *brothers*. And even 'Confirmed Bachelors'... Hah! His *un-closeted* denial bemused us forever more.

I decided to do a Hygiene Course as recommended by somebody up at one of the big Tourist Boards, because the qualification would add credibility to our establishment. OK... It was informative, mostly stuff I already knew, although there were some eye-openers, things we normally take for granted, where extra vigilance and common sense is required. Mind you, what with Health and Safety gone mad these days, I think they may have preferred we served breakfast in surgical gowns, masks, latex gloves and Perspex goggles for heaven's sake... And insist our guests disinfect themselves on entry from a dirty world of unbidden bacteria. Good grief!

However, I received a certificate for my earnest efforts... The first official framed *something*... to be proudly hung in the front hall.

Everything was now just about in place for the opening: cannily we had sifted through the box files – left behind in the attic. I think we must have mailed out around 500 or so new brochures hoping to snare some of these former guests with our enticing modernisation.

The Lodge was decked out with seasonal flowers, usually there would be about eight vases doted around. The flowers, and foliage would either be sourced from Fakenham market (Thursdays) or from our garden. I prefer naturalistic rather than pretentious grand rigid arrangements. And work the colours to coordinate with the scheme of a particular room for best effect. Lilies with their aromatic fragrance were always a showstopper, and great for longevity, as are sophisticated tulips – very stylish en masse in the one colour-way. But, hey I love to experiment with all varieties...

It was the beginning of June. And with no grand fanfare, no drum-rolls or fancy red carpet rolled out, we just simply opened our doors... **'Welcome to Holly Lodge...'**

Up first were Jake and Becky Turner rolling up in their 1950s' dark-green Morris Minor, those classic ones with the ash-framed-trim, and uber-retro-trendy this time around.

Naturally, we were anxious, and full of eager anticipation, because this was the real McCoy... everything we had invested was now loaded into the Lodge, there was no going back it would have to pay off...

We watched them approach the front entrance, clutching one of our brochures, so we immediately assumed they'd been previous guests at the Lodge. Actually as it turned out Becky's mother had given her daughter our literature as she thought the new makeover to Holly Lodge looked inviting, and this was to be a birthday surprise break for her boyfriend, Jake.

I welcomed the attractive young couple in. These were the vibrant *hip* types I had in mind for our new boutique niche... although ultimately, it would appeal commercially right across the board.

They seemed heartily enthused with the stylised interiors, and the overall feel of the place. She was a gamine, fresh-faced pretty thing with a black bob, dressed in vintage chic from head to foot; while fresh-faced Jake with his college cut was all preppy in a tan, grey and white plaid shirt, jeans, and buck-skin hiking boots. After checking in, I showed them through to the lounge. Soft classical music permeated throughout the circulation areas, and the scent of the fresh tiger lilies immersed amongst the branches of eucalyptus wafted seductively around the room.

Imagine... These were our very first guests, beaming away at us, seemingly delighted with their choice of destination. They sat buoyantly chatting, sipping afternoon tea, and enjoying our homemade apple and cinnamon cakes. Mike and I were relieved as we caught each other's smug faces. It was all going great guns; and then the doorbell rang. It was the next arrivals due...

I left Mike to show the couple to their room, and I sprang with a spring in my step to the front door.

A distraught tweedy lady with a Sloaney accent introduced herself as Arabella. She informed me that her mother had been booked in to the Lodge today. Apparently her husband had point blank refused to have this woman in her house ever again; so to stave off a family domestic, the arrangement had thus been made. She assured me, she had been instructed to be on her best behaviour, as she could be rather formidable depending on her mood swings.

"By the way, the place looks terrific... Jolly well done! And oh good luck!" she said rather ominously.

Moments later, an elegant burgundy *Bentley Continental*, with white-walled tyres rolled up, this classic beauty must have cost a king's ransom ... It was pure old money. And it was the Parkers... Um? The elderly gentlemen alighted, decked-out in county tweeds probably from fine gentlemen's outfitters; he was sporting a distinct silver-white handlebar moustache. The only time I can ever remember seeing one of those would have been down a Leather Bar in Earls Court (not that I was regular let's get that ironed-out...).

Obviously he was the real deal... His wife peered at me from the back seat of the impressive car. I was almost expecting a grand royal wave; maybe they were done for tea with Lilibet at nearby Sandringham?

He handed me a portable wooden step, as we gently helped his spouse step out of the car (rather grandly). I collected their luggage: an entire set of *Louis Vuitton* no less... Perhaps they would be sailing on the Queen Mary next?

They entered the house (regally) to register. She must have been seventy-odd, of foreboding demeanour, a perfect purple-rinsed coiffure framing her florid complexion, and tightly pursed lips. Her ladyship might have been applicable to her title, very la-di-dah, I mulled. She was fittingly attired in an elegant hounds-tooth suit with suede trim (hunting style on the top collar,) a *Hermes* scarf accessorised, and a string of fine pearls with an unmistakable *Cartier* clasp adorned her plum cashmere turtleneck.

They were a dying breed... 'Old Empire' sprang to mind, shame they weren't in the Colonial Cottage... All of a sudden... Mrs Parker quizzed me on the age of our house in a cut-glass crystal tone – her accentuated vowels ripped through me like a piercing staccato...

"The Lodge is predominately early 18th century," I replied politely, and then she cut me to the quick explaining hers preceded ours by several hundred years in the main. And she strutted into the lounge, with her husband in tow (as well as her airs and graces) – looking down her nose as she went.

"Is that a Queen Anne winged-back chair I spy over there in the corner?" she said stroking its studded-leather upholstery. She peered at it closely through her *Poirot*-esque pince-nez.

"Actually it's a good Victorian copy, rather authentic – don't you think?" I replied gingerly.

"Urrgh, how dreadful! One should never buy a copy of anything," she retorted. She eyed-me-over disdainfully, and scrutinised my classic tan brogues. And then she sniffed snidely…

Crikey! That was tantamount to an insult – a blatant slight, if ever I'd heard one… I had to keep a stiff upper lip in front of this crowd, or I would flip. My alarm bells were ringing: '*KEEP CALM AND CARRY ON*'.

Mrs Parker cavorted around the room, examining piece after piece. Our personal treasures were criticised in a very blasé and condescending manner. And Mr Parker just stood there like a schmuck, letting her act-out her embarrassing tirade.

One snarky comment after another ensued, I was aghast by her blatant turgid audacity. And lack of etiquette! Her ostensibly upper-crust appearance was coming more into question by the minute…

Finally, I led them over to the Claret room before offering *Madam* tea. She was beginning to remind me of my *very* affected Germanic stepmother.

"Tea for two. Piping-hot. Loose-leafed. And oh, some homemade Madeira cake… I can't abide those plastic supermarket confections…" She reeled-out her orders acerbically not even with a pretty please. "And be a good boy, and close the door gently behind you; I can feel one of my headaches coming on…"

116

Who the hell does she think she is...? Are we her hoi polloi? And I was seething.

I caught up with Mike in the kitchen, and sounded off about the *dragon* now installed in the Claret. Mike assuaged my doubts in handling her, and not to let her get to me on our first day of trading. Of course he'd experienced some pretty awful types during his years at the salon too. I was peeved with that Arabella woman. Why had she dumped 'Mommie Dearest' on us at our launch? Although would this *be* a true test...

Later, I collected the tea tray while the 'Nosy Parkers' were wandering around the garden. And the next arrival at five were a lovely couple from Bury, down for the horse races at Fakenham.

Breakfast was served in the main dining room between 8am-10am unless otherwise prearranged. There was a wide selection of dishes for our guests to choose from on the in-room menu cards. Ideally, they would be asked to preselect their choices, the day before to minimise food wastage. Either, I would collect the menus or they could slip them in the allocated drop-box by the entrance – preferably by noon each day.

There was the all-important 'Full English', which I was to develop into something very special. They could customise this dish as they pleased, too. However when served with my trademark creamy scrambled eggs, topped with garden fresh parsley, dressed with a small triangular fried bread wafer (think wafer nestled in circular mound of eggs like ice cream visually), they became an enormous hit, and were ordered daily. My method is to keep the eggs moving continuously in the pan with a wooden spatula, and just before serving add a dash of cream with a smidgen of runny *honey* – always remove from the hob a tad undercooked; and then whisk them rapidly in a hot pan just before serving onto a warm plate.

The accompaniment consisted of: crown-cut tomatoes, locally produced bacon – grilled, apple sage or spiced sausages from a terrific artisan food supplier nearby, sautéed chestnut mushrooms, and house hash browns. And oh, black pudding, too, a la Mike.

Alternative main courses were either: smoked salmon with scrambled-eggs on bagel (dressed with seasonal samphire), a 'House Special', which became exceedingly popular; basically a fluffy croissant was delicately filled with scrambled eggs, diced mushrooms, cheese, basil, and optional Parma ham, set off by an accompaniment of honey dew melon. Of course egg dishes could be prepared any which way as desired. Then there were fresh kippers, a couple of hot vegetarian options, an array of pancake dishes and kedgeree.

The buffet table would be laid-out with a copious array of starters, such as Greek yogurt, oats'n almonds and honey in a glass (think healthy *Champneys*), a wide range of cereals, delicious homemade breads, and jams, fresh fruits – usually seasonal (many from our own orchard), squeezed juices, and early-riser smoothies.

Mike's mother, and his Aunt Helena had given us a beautiful fine set of Regency bone china as a house-warming gift; so all the above fare would be presented on this porcelain edged in gilt, and red banding. And complemented by silver cutlery in the style of '*Dubarry*' which we had scrimped, and saved for.

The large refectory style dining table was in fact an old monastery door inlaid with wrought-iron work, which we had reworked into a table – always a conversational piece at breakfast. Every day became a major production: fresh white starched linen napkins were made into origami wonders, inherited Italianate candelabras lit the table like a shimmering palazzo, scented seasonal flowers were arranged as a centrepiece, and classic music was cued in the background. And there was a Pembroke table set up by the French doors overlooking the garden for intimate dining.

A suit of armour affectionately named 'Dudley', sat proudly on the mezzanine landing presiding over the proceedings – he became a firm favourite with our visitors. A 17th century portrait of silver bewigged 'Bonnie Prince Charlie' resplendent in chest armour hung on a main wall (a nod to my Jacobean Manor fantasy), while a large studded leather shield excavated from ancient Persia hung dramatically over the fireplace.

The guests were seated at the table on carved-oak-turned high-backed dining chairs that sat proudly in unison on our 'ever so original flagstone floors'. Padded regal-crested tasselled cushions were added for comfort, and co-ordinated with the rich hues of the crimson damask drapes. The beamed room was filled with treasured pieces, and quirky theatrical artefacts. In fact for us every object was heady with familiarity. Hence all in all pervading an atmosphere of Baronial splendour for their sumptuous breakfast banquet... "Who could ask for anything more?"

The next morning was to be our first debut breakfast. Initially everything was *swellegant,* if there is such a word, until Mrs Parker entered. She arrived at ten-thirty unfashionably out of breakfast serving time, and not prearranged as House Rules (remember: boldly stated in information folders and menu cards). Madam was never going to play ball anyway...

Mike and I were in the kitchen clearing up, when suddenly taken by surprise Mrs Parker banged fiercely on the door, and hollered at the top of her voice:

"Urrgh... the service is absolutely dreadful here... Waiter. Waiter. Waiter...?" And so it goes...

Mike went out to calm her down.

Fortunately the Turners and the other guests had left for the morning. The Parkers sat down. Her husband cowered in silence – I suspect he'd become an emasculated schlemiel in her presence...

Mrs Parker stared into space as she caustically reeled-off her order...

"Organic lime-blossom tea, boiled duck-eggs **precisely** three minutes, cocoa pops, and marmite spread on pumpernickel bread," she enunciated like an echo of Maggie Smith in *The Prime of Miss Jean Brodie.*

"What!" I mulled, but I smiled politely through tightly gritted teeth, and beat a hasty retreat to the kitchen. Now I wanted to frigging strangle her.

There was every variety of tea, breakfast cereal, and jam imaginable in our pantry – except the ones Mrs Parker had so impolitely ordered. And blasted duck eggs were not on the menu either!

I needed to chill because I could have been driven beyond distraction... So I sent Mike out to see her. Naturally I expected truculent tantrums.

Strangely though there was a still silence. Mike marched back into the kitchen with her revised order: lemon balm tea, organic chicken eggs *precisely*...three minutes, lemon curd, and muesli, and Oh... the pumpernickel is to be diced into soldiers buttered with (margarine), which as she has pointed out was not on the table.

Mike said the offered alternatives were accepted reluctantly, and incidentally she hiccupped profusely throughout the order as she snuck her mini silver flask back into her handbag.

Ah ha! I thought I detected alcohol on her breath when they arrived.

Later that day, I brought them a tray, with a summery jug of fruity *Pimm's*; something we did (complimentary) for all our guests during the summer months. She had the gall to ask for a second jug about an hour later. And I never saw them till breakfast the next morning.

Blimey here's one for my diary... that sequel breakfast. What a fiasco that became...

It was a full house, the dining room was buzzing with the most congenial company that morning. Until that is... at 10.45am, the unfashionably late Mrs Parker swept in as the 'Wicked Witch of the West'.

The atmosphere suddenly became charged. Uh-oh... She swayed precariously, her husband tried to steady her as she clumsily slunk into the chair. The table shook violently, and a vase nearly toppled over in the kerfuffle.

Everybody bless them, tried to go on as normal, but the pervading atmosphere became very awkward, as she slurred her words, and dribbled pitifully down her blouse.

Mike and I though, utterly perplexed continued the rounds of coffee refills. An impasse ensued for the next few *tortuous* minutes... whilst she carried on arranging herself making loud sighs, and the most hideous inebriated burps.

We just smiled convivially through the painful ordeal. And then all hell broke loose. In a sudden invective outburst she shrieked...

"Go on... the lot of ya! Look real 'ard, er... erm... at real money, it don't buy happi' happi' 'appiness...!"

We were mortified. She collapsed back into a dribbling heap. The room fell silent, you could have heard a pin drop. Our guests seemed to hold their breath with arched eyebrows raised in unison.

And then... Mr Parker, finally, *finally* got off his tardy arse, gripped his unruly wife by the arm and pulled her too. She yelped with a hiccup. "Home James..." and the poor man frogmarched her out of the room, through the hall, and out the front door.

Another stunned silence ensued for a moment, and then we all carried on our business as best we could, forgiven the circumstances.

Oh god! It was an awfully ugly scene – selfishly blighting our guests' enjoyment of their breakfast. We were both gutted.

Mr Parker came to the door about an hour later to settle up, and a few words were exchanged frankly. I handed him a silver flask belonging to his wretched wife – another boozy container found this time on the circular garden seat under an apple tree.

He must have felt awkward, but unfortunately he did not even have the common decency to apologise on her behalf at all. He just turned on his heel to exit – back shouted "Tallyho," and whistled-away in some kind of irritating denial. I bit my tongue.

He approached that fabulous *Bentley Continental*, sitting proudly on the forecourt... now in my mind's eye: a carriage of abject despair a glossy glamorous veneer concealing a woeful life.

Just two days open, and sadly they became the first names to go on our: '**BLACKLIST**'.

"Phew, what an ordeal!"

Mike felt my utter disappointment – what with our debut opening being almost wrecked beyond the pale.

This had indeed been a true test for me, especially when embroiled with *'Public Enemy No.1'*. (The Mrs Parkers of this world.) Mike just took it in his stride, of course he was not happy about it, but was able to move swiftly on.

But for me... How do I behave like a professional hotelier at all times? Unperturbed when this stuff happens on my home turf. Because I did not want to turn into a grotesque sycophant, obsequiously serving my guests, and kow-towing to their capricious mood swings. Only time will tell... eh?

However on the upside (after that squalid affair) – the next day Jake and Becky came bursting into the hall to actually re-book for next year. They were full of praise for all our efforts, and informed us that they would recommend Holly Lodge to their friends. In essence, a palliative that immediately put the *feel-good* factor back on the table, and most certainly ameliorated the bad taste left by the Parkers. I could now move on!

Guests came and went over the next few months, the pace became intense as the days rolled into one, July, August, and then it was late September. The leaves were tumbling thick, and fast, now exhausted by the end of the summer season, as we too had felt the hot flurry of our first full-on summer at Holly Lodge.

Now we must prepare for the next big challenge of having the dreaded inspectors over to rate the place, the chaps from the major *Tourist Authorities: The East of England Tourist Board*, and the *Automobile Association (The AA hotel services)*. My resolve in turning our little known Bed and Breakfast into the *finest* in the county was now: 'GAME ON!'

CHAPTER 7

AN INSPECTOR CALLS

I was always filled with such dread and trepidation, especially in our early days of trading, when an inspector from one of the two major Tourist Boards would descend upon us. In those days we were allocated with a *Diamond* rating, however the equivalent that is currently set in place today is the *Star* rating for Bed & Breakfasts; therefore I will refer to the 'Star' definition as I describe how it really was...

Truthfully, it is a fascinating, and thoroughly rigorous assessment of the quality, and standard of accommodation on offer. Holly Lodge would be microscopically examined taking into account every aspect of the service, ambiance, hospitality, accommodation, facilities, the all-important housekeeping, and the location.

A scoring system based on the number of points obtained would be factored for each of these specific categories having been broken down into minutiae for analysis; with the consequence of an overall score given, which was key in determining the number of stars to be awarded to an establishment.

However if worthy, and an establishment has that something extra, *extra* special, the bonus of a Silver or Gold Award, or in the *AA's* case, *Red Stars* would be attributed: adding a tremendous cachet to one's residence.

The inspectors not only visually assess the accommodation, but also with a hands-on approach using a fine toothcomb, are even kitted-out with *white* gloves, to monitor dust levels – say at the top of a wardrobe, or high shelf – difficult areas to reach that may be overlooked occasionally. Alternately, comparable to the science of forensics, apparently, I've heard some inspectors carry a small state of the art device, which electronically detects levels of bacteria. This contraption responds to surfaces touched by its sensitive swab giving a numerical reading level on a monitor, and suggests accurately whether these levels are indeed acceptable.

Therefore, evidence is gathered, sometimes to pin a missed opportunity onto an unsuspecting proprietor. Consequently a star could be dropped, because their points might not have made the grade on their current inspection. A devastating faux pas...

I know for a fact, that they even move all the furniture around to check if the floor has been vacuumed, or washed underneath – they don't miss a trick!

The serious scrutiny pans like a camera lens over such things as: How was the bill presented? On making their reservation was the telephone answered within five rings? Was any form of refreshment offered on arrival? Were there any outside disturbance noises to the bedroom? Was breakfast served at the correct temperature? Was there any peeling paintwork on the external windows? Was there mould on the tiles in the bathroom? Was the car park free from litter? Were management, and or staff, clean, well attired, pleasant, and helpful at all times? I could go on and on...

The list of requirements by the Tourist Authorities in adhering to their standards of quality was copiously lengthy. A standard template had been created to provide a benchmark guideline to accommodation providers, and without doubt played an integral part in our future successes at the Lodge.

We would maintain our quality efficiently through sheer attentive hard work, but would raise the bar each time to benefit more from the system ultimately to gain greater, and greater recognition. Therefore we endeavoured to surpass all the necessary standards needed for an assessment. And went above, and beyond this call of duty with our extra-deluxe embellishments to make a guest experience truly memorable with us.

Framed certificates, and door plaques of the current rating would then ensue. Remember this current rating standard would be transferred to all one's promotional literature, and website etc. Clarifying our shop window to the niche market, we were aspiring to attract.

However, now I can honestly say, that in my opinion there was one predictable flaw that we discovered in the almost perfect system, by that I mean, we would always suspect when an 'Inspector was calling', and whom he was, when he or she arrived.

And so it transpired... You see none of our other guests would turn up for a stay in the country looking like a grey-suited and booted bank manager, carrying a briefcase and laptop; and for the most part single bookings were usually rarer. Inevitably, one particular inspector would call us regularly from his mobile – practically from the end of our drive to announce his impending arrival. Which just would not happen with other guests... Consequently a kind of predictable game-format would play out to test *our* hospitality processes.

The inspector would leave his room for a meal out around six, in which time I would be expected to access the room, turn the bed back, plump up the pillows (finish with a placed wrapped chocolate), switch on a lamp, refresh the towels, general tidy up, perhaps a squirt of aromatic room-spray, and play some relaxing mood music – low for their welcome on return. This attentive service without doubt would gain extra *brownie* points.

By the next morning, I would have received the ticked menu card prefilled with his order usually requesting a plate of 'Full English' as expected... although our 'House Special' (my signature dish) would sometimes be tested as an alternate experience of my culinary skills. However instead of eating the usual plateful like most guests, more often than not only fifty percent of each portion would have been sampled. 'A dead-giveaway!'

The game continued...

And when all the guests had exited the dining room, he would introduce himself, present us with his business card, whereon, we would be expected to react in complete surprise of our supposedly, unexpected visitor.

One particular inspector had a distinct Gaelic accent, immediately familiar, as he'd become almost a regular on alternate visits (don't ask). On making his reservation, he'd confirm a different name, and address for the confirmation details to be sent. Consequently suspicions were nearly always aroused by their style of booking, which screamed 'Tourist Board!'

Many guesthouses in the area echoed these obvious nuances and sometimes notes would be compared with a giggle. However I must point out that these inspectors would get no preferential treatment over our other paying guests. And I must also emphasise that the job these men and women (we never had a female inspector at the Lodge) do is crucial to the hospitality business, and ultimately to the paying public, whom naturally expect a certain level of quality from their hospitality provider.

A curious situation arose on our very first rating though. Trust us to cause a frisson of contretemps between the two major Tourist Authorities... There was a contradiction in our rating. One Board had awarded us four stars, which we were initially thrilled with, while the other in contrast had awarded us five stars; which changed our whole perspective – especially as they announced it was very well deserved. Subsequently after a week's reanalysis by an arbitration tribunal, the stars were tallied in unison, and agreed by both Authorities at a 'Five Star' rating to be awarded to Holly Lodge conclusively.

Naturally we were ecstatic, as we had taken this tired old establishment from two stars to five within a few months of opening. This was very encouraging, as it authenticated our provenance to cater for the upper-end of the luxury market. Nevertheless on each *inspection* I would always be filled with tentative *terror* in anticipation of the outcome... "The stars my dear, the stars!"

We seemed to evolve into a daily routine, conducive to each of our individual strengths: shopping for household goods, head chef duties, meet and greet, registration, and general hospitality were my department, including all official paperwork involved in the day to day running of Holly Lodge. While Michael, expertly took care of housekeeping, laundry, and waiter service, although sometimes we'd share this, and many other duties too.

We had no staff initially for the first few years, our days started at dawn, and finished quite often after dusk. Many of our urbanite friends really thought we had semi-retired to the country finishing our working day by noon. "That could not have been further from the truth..."

We began to perfect our regime, becoming an all smiling all performing double-act, always well turned out, even if one felt like crap! Portraying the perfect proprietors: the nouveau 'Stepford Husbands', summed-up our inhabited roles.

Sometimes to escape the confines of our duties, we would explore the wonderful diversity of oceanic pleasures that our region has to offer, and realise we had definitely made the right choice of moving to North Norfolk.

The wide-open expanses of the breathtaking coastline deemed an 'Area of Outstanding Natural Beauty', a backdrop for providing seasonal habitats for a vast array of migratory birds to and from these shores: '*A wilderness to rival the plains of Africa in our own back yard*' – now that's worth working for!

Catching a glimpse of the deserted reaches of the 'Titchwell Nature Reserve', where flocks of thousands of pink-footed migrating geese take to the vast skies might echo a scene from the magical 'Serengeti'.

A stroll around picture-postcard Blakeney harbour, up its steep quaint cobbled passages reminiscent of any Cornish fishing village worth its salt, where in summer the lofty hollyhocks are so abundantly splendid – they beggar belief! These passages lead to tiny choc-box enclaves tucked away off the high street with its dramatic view down to the quay: '*No wonder Londoners go mad for the place!*' And are keen to pay exorbitant prices for a two-up-two-down holiday cottage – albeit with bags of period charm.

Near the Blakeney Hotel there is a plaque depicting the tidal marks of the Great Flood of 1953, epitomizing the fragility of this coastline. A rare treat is a boat trip up to Blakeney Point to see the seals at a real life *Disney Sea World* a la Norfolk. Hundreds of Common and Grey Seals often bask on the sandbanks and swim up to the boats dog-like in their curiosity. Off-season is the time to spot the pups born around November-December.

Another favourite '*Boy's Own*' haunt of wonderment, and evocative of the thrilling Erskine Childers' 1903 novel of *Riddle in the Sands* is the very captivating Stiffkey Creek. Here we'd navigate the winding canals between the slippery creeks of the salt marshes seasonally covered in bountiful sea-asparagus known as samphire (*Salicornia europaea*). A local delicacy resembling swathes of blanketed forests of miniature cactuses, though without the prickly spines: a perfect accompaniment to any fish dish. (Top-tip: boil in sweetened water for a few minutes, and drizzle with olive oil and lemon – *no* salt.)

This sequestered cove on a mesmerising, and very emerald **Samphire Coast**, with a rickety jetty where the boats shelter covertly amongst the tall reeds could well be part of the stunning setting for the aforementioned stylish espionage story. Perhaps Mike, and I would portray the modern day protagonists ducking and diving in a satirical North Norfolk version, with the 'New Labour Government' of the day as the evil oppressive enemy! This riveting spot is a water-colourist's dream.

Likewise, a sail to Scolt Island Nature Reserve composed of sand dunes, salt marshes, and a shingle ridge is another sequestered location to view nesting colonies of birds: Arctic and Sandwich terns, oystercatchers, waders, and black-headed gulls amongst many species. This precious wilderness is the land that time forgot...!

Over to Brancaster pervading a jolly nautical feel where the sea on the sandy shoreline is more accessible, and forever Enid Blyton. A hot-spot for some serious kite surfing, as on a breezy day the sky is illuminated with garish coloured sails bobbing frantically over the mysterious wreck stranded offshore.

In contrast, we'd head over to the pebbly rugged cove at Weybourne, set beneath the jagged chalk cliffs winding their way east to the distant clifftop gardens, and promenades of the faded grandeur of Cromer, with its traditional 'Seaside Special' pier. The once glorious bow-fronted period terraces of the Edwardian grand dame now languish lacklustre with a beckoning vibe awaiting urgent regeneration from the salty erosion of years of neglect. Be patient... and one day this time-forgotten gem will sparkle more brightly than ever, in North Norfolk's gleaming tiara. Mark my words!

But be warned though: sensible walking shoes or waterproof boots, a map, tide-timetable, binoculars, camera, bottled water, picnic rug, and mobile phone *perhaps* are essential prerequisites for any of the above hikes. And oh, don't forget the dog...

Après walk. And repair oneself with a Cromer crab sandwich garnished with samphire of course, and good ole Norfolk ale or cider at any number of terrific pub-eateries dotted along this coastline: '*The White Horse*' at Brancaster Staithe with its far-reaching views is especially tasty. That's my tip... And loving it!

And then there's the steamy, emblematic '*Poppyline*', a vintage train ride ploughing through purple heath-land, and glimpsing spectacular sea views from gentrified Holt, to retirement-town-Sheringham nestling under heavily wooded uplands by the coast. A Norfolk 'Orientated Express' pervading the authentic charm of a bygone era of the *Dad's Army* years, and where an episode of the show was actually filmed on location at Weybourne station.

A particular favourite outing is to spend a day at Blickling Hall. Once owned by the Boleyn family between 1499-1505, and where arguably it is said Anne Boleyn was born, although more than likely it would have been Hever Castle in Kent in 1507. A statue and portrait of the doomed Queen proudly live in the hall today. And on the anniversary of her death, her headless apparition is said to haunt her ancestral residence, as testified by numerous witnesses over the years. Subsequently the Hobart family became the new owners in 1616. They remodelled the hall imitating Hatfield House. The magnificent Long Gallery measures 123 feet, and is one of the finest of its type with a sublime ornate plaster ceiling. Bon vivant, Charles II visited the Hall amongst many other illustrious royal visitors.

Blickling a crafted gabled-masterpiece nestles majestically framed by great clipped box hedges, and via its front aspect is a vision to behold exquisitely composed as if it were an organic Dutch old master.

Another relaxing spot, where we would sometimes picnic would be at the gaunt ruins of Baconsthorpe Castle set tranquilly by a lake. And where I'd half expect Excalibur to rise from the still waters in this fairy tale setting. The fortified manor house once belonged to the prominent Norfolk based Heydon family in the mid-15th century, and they were actually related to the Boleyns by marriage. However when their fortunes started to wane, the house eventually became abandoned. There is a legend that a tunnel ran from beneath the house all the way to the Guildhall at Blakeney harbour, perhaps created as an emergency escape-route from the volatile whims of Henry VIII.

Often, a stroll along Holkham beach would blast out the cobwebs, which without doubt, must be ranked amongst the top three best beaches in the country for sheer unspoilt breathtaking beauty. On occasion a real treat would be catching sight of the thirty or so galloping horsemen of The Blues and Royals – the Queen's Household Cavalry pounding the surf – an arresting spectacle evocative of an epic motion picture.

If 50,000 sunbathers were placed on this beach, one could still find a peaceful spot. Please don't all rush here at once!

Hey, if you get really lucky you might even come across some 'Baltic amber' (perhaps fossilised with an in-bedded insect or plant) washed up anywhere along this shoreline. Geographically and geologically this is a result of the 'Eocene' period as amber the fossilised resin from amber bearing trees of Scandinavian forests, floated down rivers into the Baltic, and inevitably to the North Sea shores of North Norfolk – due to the great push of glaciations from the north. One can find all manner of stuff beachcombing, and some local artists like the inimitable Andrew Ruffhead, ingeniously turn flotsam and jetsam into a creative panoply of artworks and sculptures echoing imagery of the region...

For some city culture, we'd drive to fine historic Norwich; where it is said there is a church for every day of the year (about fifty minutes away). It has become our substitute London, and offers a great variety of all that is expected of the capital of Norfolk.

One morning on a rare day off, we visited the 'Old Vicarage' at East Ruston, a mesmeric thirty-acre tropical coastal garden; a cleverly landscaped plot, designed by the two owners, Alan Gray, a regular on BBC's *Gardeners' World* and his partner Graham Robeson. Their Arts & Crafts house is nestled in the midst of an exotic paradise that they have created, and toiled over here in Norfolk.

The feast of formal and theatrical exuberance, combined with brilliant innovative planting provides an exciting journey through the eyes of its creators. Borrowed landscapes from beyond are incorporated with eye-catching vistas, such as the enchanting view of a 'Lighthouse' in the distance caught through a porthole window creatively carved through a hedge. Brilliantly conceptualised this unique garden gives the visitor a lush taste of an ebullient global exotica belying its quintessential English setting.

When I returned to Holly Lodge, after a day at these subliminal gardens, as I wandered through our bland nondescript back plot, 'I wanted to cry in abject despair...' because I was so inspired by what I had seen at East Ruston... that there, and then I decided we too would one day have a stunning back garden for all to enjoy. Although festering in my mind was the burning desire to build a glass Orangery too – as an annexe to be used as a guest lounge in the future. However right now we were spent-up, and I would have to be patient with the completion of my vision for Holly Lodge; and besides Mike would kill me if I spent a penny more...

Although the one little addition I was planning on providing was that *dog*, I had so promised him back in Muswell Hill. He'd been hinting recently, and I heartily began my quest for our little whippet puppy...

That autumn some of our London friends visited our new abode for the first time. They immediately became converts, and were dead envious of our new life in our hidden bucolic setting away from the grimy urban rat race. Hitherto the changes made from the photographs they had seen of the Lodge, which clearly unimpressed them, that Millennium eve, but they now wholeheartedly grasped why we had embraced our new life in this house – in this county. We could tell they were itching to imitate us, and inevitably a couple of new guesthouses would spring up nearby – owned by our mates from the city.

They were tickled-pink by the van that parked at the end of our drive every Wednesday evening: selling fish and chips to the villagers of Thursford Green. A mobile library and fishmonger came by weekly too – those oldie-world customs hanging-in-there from a dying era.

Occasionally, Charlotte, the third ex-partner of the Lodge, who eventually found her cottage in the locale, would drop by, and was the first to embrace the changes to her former home, in fact so much so she became a proud tour guide showing her friends around the place. She was always on tap for some friendly advice.

One time, I went to visit a lady who ran an established Bed and Breakfast, she was supposed to give me information, and guidelines for running our business.

Thank the Lord I did not take her advice. She suggested we offer a range of cuddly toys and weird dolls for our guests to take to bed with them for good company, as evident by the hundreds she had on display on her landing, which could be misconstrued as rather kinky in my opinion; judging by what was on offer. Um...? And dusty dried flowers were not my cup of tea, either.

I informed her that we were putting together more of a boutique style operation... She just glared at me myopically with saucer-size eyes that gave me the collywobbles...

I discovered a coterie of local guesthouse proprietors, who used to meet up regularly. Perhaps they were akin to *Salem's Lot...* well we were new in Norfolk... Eh? They produced a monthly paper on the subject. However, when we received our 5-Star rating there was never even the slightest mention of our achievement in their local paper. For some reason these cronies seemed to take umbrage with us – maybe out radical style upset the old applecart!

During our very first autumn, some Japanese tourists descended upon us. These neat pocket-sized people stood up to their courteous reputation admirably, I have never bowed so much in my entire life, so much so, that after three days with them, I aggravated an old injury, and was laid up for days with chronic backache. The things we did to satisfy our beloved guests...

Stereotypically, they photographed just about everything on the premises, then one morning after breakfast one of them inquired: "If any English Queens had visited the Lodge...?" Naturally I was tempted to respond with the usual "Of course Elizabeth I had slept here," as apparently she had practically stayed at every Inn in the country – not!

So, with my usual humour, that would sometimes irritate the hell out of Mike, my riposte was...

"Actually as we speak there are a couple of very nice Queens in residence – today!"

"Arrrgh so! ... Arrrgh so!" they giggled euphorically as they continued blinding us with their flash photography, while we stood posed at the Inglenook.

Anyway, a couple of days later, on checking out, they presented us with a gift-wrapped box, which they said we were not to open until after their departure.

As their coach was heading out of the drive, we discovered to our surprise a beautiful pair of sterling silver chopsticks thoughtfully engraved with our names. Also a framed photograph of the pair of us standing by the Inglenook, cleverly doctored by computer generated imagery... so now we appeared resplendent in royal paraphernalia... bedecked in robes, sceptre, and the campest sparkly crowns on our heads. The cheeky... How they'd found time to do it, I'll never know, as they just about did every tourist attraction imaginable during their short stay.

The generousness of some of our guests in this department was very touching. We'd receive many wonderful gifts over the years to come, as a thoughtful gesture of appreciation of their enjoyment of Holly Lodge, although we did not expect to receive such gestures. I have many fond memories of some truly lovely people, their 'Thank You' cards and heartfelt letters are still treasured: safely kept in my favourite Georgian rosewood box. This for us was extremely gratifying...

Another reminder of where we had landed came in the form of trying to order a taxi for some guests for dinner at eight. The local minicab firm informed me that they could only supply a taxi for the following night at eight. Would that do? Blimey, will I ever get used to these funny old Norfolk ways?

That autumn, we planted thousands of daffodil bulbs, and crocuses along the front boundary to the village, and throughout the orchard. The one thing we did splash out on though was a large snazzy new sign at the front gate. 'Holly

Lodge' in White Times Roman, on a country green satin background.

There would still be many pieces of the jigsaw to fit together before my *dream sanctuary* was complete...

One morning, at an unearthly hour, armed with my garden tools and sack of bulbs, I strolled bleary-eyed out to the orchard. And there to my surprise were four wild Roe, or Muntjac deer reaching into the branches to eat our juicy ripe apples.

I stood transfixed. And then two sweet fawns tentatively stepped out of the scrub. So fine and fresh in the first light – little droplets of dew trickled off their moist noses as they foraged beneath the fallen leaves in search of sustenance.

I must have spied my doe-eyed visitors for a good five minutes or so until a farm tractor came hurtling out of the blue – instantly they became startled, casting a fearful glance – before nervously stampeding out of the grounds. Their enigmatic appearances became a fairly common occurrence at the Lodge...

Actually, I have always revered these ethereal creatures, and for that reason I just could never eat venison, although a very popular delicacy in Norfolk.

Mike and I would often visit Holkham Hall nearby, which is host to the rare herds of hundreds of white Fallow deer roaming freely on this magnificent vast estate on the coast.

It has the energy of a sweeping safari park, teaming with creatures gambolling in its verdant pastures; and on a drive in to the estate they are usually to be seen just within a few feet from the car.

The great Estate is owned by the Earl of Leicester, (Viscount Coke), and his family; their ancestral home was built by the first Earl between 1734-1764. An early imposing Palladian Mansion appearing as a subliminal Italianate Villa on the windswept coast here. And is no doubt a much-prized jewel in Norfolk's Crown – a location much sought after for still photography and filming.

More recently in 2008 key scenes were shot in the magnificence of the 'Marble Hall' with its stunning alabaster colonnade for the film *The Duchess*, starring Keira Knightley, and Ralph Fiennes. The Hall has a fascinating plethora of staterooms, and suites filled with treasures echoing the days of the 'Grand Tour'.

This tremendous must-see attraction has copious treats such as a Bygones Museum nostalgically exhibiting an insight into the farming history of Holkham. And a slew of other attractions including an Art Gallery, Tearooms and Gift shops displaying locally made wares – ranging from their specialist pottery, traditional linseed paints, sensational ice-cream, confectionery, and all sorts of fine fares: all under the Holkham banner.

There's the joy too of the annual Holkham Country Fair, where thousands descend from far and wide, and then of course there's the wonderful outdoor concerts where world-class superstars perform in the gorgeous setting of the park. Not-to-mention the outstanding Holkham Nature Reserve a mile's walk down Lady Anne's Drive from the uber-chic Victoria Hotel, which the Earl's son (the next in line), and his wife, Polly, have recreated with great panache. Today though they are the new incumbents of the great hall, as the seventh Earl retired in 2007.

One day our little Lodge would be featured alongside this formidable modern day *Camelot*, in a way back then we never thought possible... But hey, I am getting ahead of myself...!

Our very first Christmas season was fast approaching at an alarming rate, but luckily the books were healthily full. We'd gathered up most of the fruits of the orchard in preparation: slavishly making homemade jams and compotes from the Victoria plums, pears, wide variety of apples, cherries, and blueberries to add to our *smorgasboard* of delights for the morning buffet. In fact we had so much fruit, we'd joke, "If all else fails at least we could set up a market stall selling the darn stuff." Scrumping was very much encouraged...

London now seemed a million miles away as we became totally immersed in our new venture – we were well and truly on the way to fulfilling our destiny in this idyllic little hamlet.

CHAPTER 8

FIRST CHRISTMAS

People would say Holly Lodge was a Christmas house, and indeed it really was... Our home was imbued with a richness of furnishings such as the deep lush colours of the red and olive tapestry fabric of our beloved *Knole* sofa, that we had raced to claim in a sale at *Liberty* on Regent Street, one snowy Boxing Day years earlier.

A luxuriant array of jewel coloured cushions bedecked the faded grandeur of the Jacobethan settee now ensconced on the garnet hues of an antique *Bokhara* rug – invitingly set to cosy in front of the flickering embers of the Inglenook.

An Arts & Crafts grandfather clock chimed on the hour announcing the passage of time, standing proudly at the entrance to the dining hall. And so the beamed, sumptuously filled rooms became an opulent set for our Christmas decorations to adorn the Lodge.

Pine garlands would be draped overhanging the fireplaces, complemented by naïve woven-willow sleigh bells tied in the centre by gingham ribbons. The Christmas tree would sit in the front bay of the lounge, shimmering like a magnificent jewel casting myriad prism-like reflections into the room.

Mystical glinting suns, half-moons, planets, stars, and winged angels dangled amongst the branches, offset by gleaming crystal rubies, home-spun carved reindeers, miniature toy-rocking horses, tin-soldiers and folkloric mythical figures whisking me into a grainy snapshot evocative of when I was aged just six...

My earliest recollection of the Yuletide was back in my boyhood days, when I attended Richmond House Primary School on The Ridgeway in Chingford. Somehow I had managed with the assistance of my art's class teacher to abscond with various ornaments and lamps from our lounge at home to use as props for the stage set of the Christmas production that year. As the curtain lifted, my parents seated out front, were aghast to see half the contents of their living room adorning Pontius Pilate's drawing room. My first artistic inclinations decadently evident, no doubt...

'Shame on me, a nice Jewish boy decorating a heathen's palace'.

The Lodge would be illuminated with Moorish lanterns, and beeswax altar candles warmly glowing throughout the season. The living spaces were infused with the fragrances of: frankincense, cinnamon, rosemary and pine; and a homemade eucalyptus wreath, entwined with red berries would dress the front door to welcome our guests. The boughs of the cypresses sparkled with icy glistening berry lights as a seductive beacon at the top of our drive, to invite our arriving patrons to come inside... *The Christmassy Lodge nestling warmly in the magical snow-globe of universal childhood memories.*

Each guest cottage would be meticulously decorated with seasonal arrangements echoing the style of the room; we'd spend days and days in preparation for our festive season...

On arrival, we'd offer home-baked mince pies sprinkled with snowy frosting sugar and edible red berries, dressed with holly synonymous with the name of course, and snipped from the three variegated holly trees at the bottom of our drive. My special brew of Mulled wine served in Moroccan tea-glasses always went down a treat – probably too well given the extra hit of brandy! At breakfast we'd add extra touches: such as sprigs of rosemary aside the Full English, even edible gold dust was lovingly sprinkled onto cereals and yogurts nearer the big day. And special seasonal loafs like cinnamon flavoured granary, and fruit and nut breads were produced in our ovens. Classical carols played in the background, however the more monastic feel of Gregorian chants would be my preference, for a serene sanctuary of spiritual ambiance that many of our city visitors would love to chill out to.

On departure each guest would be presented with a personalised photographic Christmas card, which each year depicted a scene carefully sourced from a wealth of vistas at the Lodge. And a hand-tied box of homemade chocolate truffles would enchant the ladies as a parting gift... It's the attention to *detail* that makes for a memorable experience!

Thursford is home to a museum, eponymous with its village name. This gem was instrumental into luring thousands of visitors to our tiny hamlet each Christmas season for their spectacular shows held from November through to the *23rd December*.

The owner, John, is the boy genius son of the founder of the *Thursford Steam Museum*, George Cushing – a dear man, whom had planted the great Scots Pines along the boundary of Holly Lodge, seventy years earlier. Each year John Cushing would create a cavernous *Disney*-esque grotto in the auditorium. And where he'd present, a no-expense spared, lavish extravaganza. The cream of the crop of talented dancers, singers and choreographers were cherry-picked from the theatre-land of London's West End – all to stage his amazing production in our little backwater.

This unique show is based on a melange of snippets and sequences from well-known musicals of stage and screen. Yes it could be construed as undeniably camp... But nevertheless it has to be the *very* best Christmas show of its type in the entire country – testified too, by the relentless coach loads of thousands of visitors that come from far and wide to be enraptured by the twice-daily performances. My favourite moment is show-stopping as the cast members immerse themselves into the audience; pouring through the aisles, singing enchanting gospel-like carols, and carrying tall-lit church candles. It really touches the soul with the *spirit* of Christmas.

For Holly Lodge this was such a boon. We'd be inundated with bookings for the neighbouring spectacular.

Sometimes I wished we had twenty bedrooms – they'd be filled solidly for the six-week season: no doubt!

Apropos, the museum is renowned for its displays of magnificent restored steam engines. Sometimes remodelled from Cushing's collection of old rusty wonders that he had saved from the scrap heap, and stored on a pocket of land, discreetly hidden in a field adjacent to Holly Lodge. This collection is an insight into the living past of the mechanical world.

Hence our first Christmas was full to the rafters. Although some of the erstwhile regulars, who had rebooked would either adore the changes we'd made and become our faithful clients too, while others would fall away, their spaces quickly to be filled by newcomers appreciating that the higher tariffs now in place were representative, and more-in-line with the superior quality of accommodation now offered.

Once they realised that Holly Lodge was now not just a bed for the night, they'd make a complete break out of it, ensuring to book up for two nights or more on subsequent visits. Also making sure to take in the delights of the fine town of Holt nearby a bustling cornucopia, and huge attraction at Christmas.

Visitors from all over gather here to admire the charming Georgian doorways and windows festooned with glistening icicle lights en masse – creating more than just a lingering whiff of Christmas... illuminating throughout December, and beyond.

We were truly blessed at this time year with the special attractions of our locale...

In my zeal, I had overbooked the Lodge. And heaven forefend we had to utilise the 'Oak Room' as it was called in the main house. A more contemporary suite, with a large picture window that had the best views out over the garden to the farm fields beyond. This was our back-up emergency room that if ever there were a problem with one of the guest cottages, it would always be ready for occupation at a moment's notice.

Yep! You have guessed my acquiescence. But the infringement was sometimes unavoidable when faced with the potential of extra income. And boy how we needed the cash flow...

Now this brings me onto some remarkable visitors, who descended upon us that very first Christmas season...

One Friday afternoon I checked in an engaging, bubbly pair of Mockney (middle-class Cockney) movers and shakers from Clerkenwell. They regaled fascinating stories of renovating 'Fincas' on the trendier-than-thou pleasure island of Ibiza. However with their foresighted interest now diverted into the fashionable rise of the North Norfolk coast, they had come here to bag a bargain-priced beach hut. And wait for it... at a knock down, thirty-five thousand pounds on Holkham Beach at Wells-next-to-the-Sea. What you might say is that about...? And heaven knows... but these pretty pastel painted garden sheds, set-on-stilts, with no fuel or electricity supply from the mains, have been known to fetch outrageous sums of even fifty-sixty thousand pounds or more. I kid you not... and they rarely come up for sale, proudly kept in the same families for years.

These beach hut icons are a throwback to the Victorian-Edwardian days, originally used as changing rooms on wheels, or dare I say bonking rooms – pardon me for being so glib, but all those tight corsets, and pretty petticoats...

Seriously though, the big attraction must be their frontline positions, nestling on the sand dunes at the foot of the Pine Forests – offering stunning sea views. A glorified garden shed, prized for its premium *Location, Location, Location...*

So the couple off the rave-floor from the *Ministry of Sound* had become the new incumbents of jade and turquoise beach hut number...? No! I wouldn't give that away. But they were dead famous!

Shortly after their departure we had the most curious visitor arriving within a party of three. The couple were just a regular looking pair, around fortyish, dressed conservatively with no outstanding characteristics, however their more conspicuous travelling companion was let's say rather striking. Mariella as she was known was much younger and dressed to the nines, in a navy and white trimmed *Gucci* suit, *Versace* neck scarf, and she flouted those distinguishable double-C gold logos of the unmistakable *Chanel*, which accessorised her patent waist-belt, and chichi clip-on earrings. And oh, she carried a large *Birkin* (the-*it*-bag) – you know... the ones that need a mortgage! Mariella would have been at well at home sashaying down the boulevards of Saint-Germain on the Left Bank...

Her brunette hair was tied back in a classic chignon, finished with a soft fringe framing her sad doe eyes, but, and a very big but... set in a strong face with a cleft chin, which was gloriously caked in pan-stick!

I welcomed them in the usual manner, however I sensed an air of tension as if there had been a row, it was etched on their faces as they tried to be courteous with each other.

I did suspect though that all was not well with this tripartite arrangement. They had told me they were down for a spot of retail therapy in Holt, and might try to catch a Christmas performance at the Museum, which was highly unlikely as it was booked up for many months in advance quite often years, although to be fair cancellations were a possibility.

The next morning at breakfast, the atmosphere could have been cut with a knife. Prosaic conversation was delivered with curt smiles and a restrained politeness: subtly disguising the underlying tensions between the lugubrious Mariella, and her companions. The other guests in that morning seemed to be riveted to our alluring visitor, although they tried their best not to make it blatantly obvious. However all eyes were unmistakably glued to this creature... A demure persona emanated, and with her large masculine hands more befitting a labourer, that really did not help this protagonist portray the sophisticated woman she was trying to purport, although in every other aspect she almost pulled it off... You may have guessed by now, where this is leading?

That afternoon I went to collect the used tea trays around five. As I knocked on the door to the Country Cottage a husky voice beckoned me to enter.

Mariella appeared in one of our robes topped with a white-towelled head-turban; she stood at the entrance to the bathroom, as if she were *Lana Turner* in that unforgettable scene from the film noir classic *The Postman Always Rings Twice*. Mariella, although a striking vision likewise was albeit a more distressed one.

Her doe eyes were bloodshot, as if she had been crying for hours, and she was trembling nervously.

She sat down by the dressing table. I clocked her wig half-concealed by a silky *Versace* scarf, which was resting on top of my beloved tailor's dummy by the door. At first, she calmly asked about Mike, probing how long we'd been together? Were we accepted in the village, and so on...? And then she surprisingly let rip...

"I am about to undergo the final stages of a sex-change operation, sorry to spring this on you..."

"Oh!" I felt a little uncomfortable with her very *personal* proclamation, but she needed to talk to someone about it. I guess.

She continued... that she had endured years of agonising mental cruelty from her domineering father, who had now ostracised her, for her sins... as she claimed! There would be no way that although being the rightful scion, would she be allowed to inherit the titled Country Seat unless she amended her fixation with her lifestyle. Everything would be passed onto her younger sibling: the spare to the heir... Her ailing mother was non compos mentis, and therefore completely oblivious to her child's plight, because she was suffering from the final stages of Alzheimer's. And now poor mama was more than indisposed, and holed-up in the West Wing with private 24/7 medical care.

I listened with interest, as I began to get drawn into her tale.

"Pater, was awful to me, he cursed me no end, and said some unspeakable things, and I stormed out in a blaze of a

144

row…" She welled-up and a pear-drop tear ran down her cheek like a tramline.

"I am so sorry, it must have been very tough on you?" I handed her a (man-size) tissue, and she dabbed her streaked-cheeks.

"So, I ran away and found myself in Suffolk, travelling aimlessly until I met the couple I arrived here with, one night in a pub."

Apparently she was now almost broke and the couple offered her what seemed a lifeline at that pivotal, and most dire moment for her.

It just so happened that they were scouting for suitable candidates for their fly-on-the-wall documentary programme, which they were producing on the subject of *Transgender Sex Changes*. Their independent film company offered her a contract on the spot. Sequences were to be filmed following her through pre and post operation stages.

Hence in desperate need of some funds she signed their contract to receive a healthy, and very handy deposit cheque. Although deep down she knew full well this was an almighty blunder, realizing they had taken full advantage of her fragile state of mind. And the other thing of course was their fascination with her upper-crust background thrown into the mix. What a boon that would be for their viewers…

Mariella was due to receive funds from her grandmother's trust to be bequeathed to her for when she turned thirty, which was now imminent. Solicitors were preparing the necessary documentation for the substantial sum of her pending inheritance. Holly Lodge was to be a base, while they went roundabouts for some location filming for the next few days. However now in acuity with a complete change of heart, she wanted to terminate the agreement with these vultures as she put it… And to make a clean break – head for the overseas clinic – and start a new life abroad.

Tears cascaded in full flow… She obviously needed a confidant, as she seemed so alone with her dilemma. I felt touched by her troubles. I'd only known full well what that was like in my own darkest hour of isolated despair when I had nobody to turn to... I needed to think quickly to ameliorate her situation, as there always has to be a solution. And I had an idea...! But I needed to run it by Mike...

And so this is how it played out... It became a very cloak and dagger affair...

They all went out for a meal that evening returning to their rooms around ten; at around eleven-thirty I quietly knocked on her door. It was so silent that night you could have heard a pin drop. And the lamps to the neighbouring cottage where her companions were ensconced, still lit.

"Mariella, are you ready, the car is waiting..." I whispered.

She emerged tentatively pushing the door to, and handed her bags to us one by one. Out she stepped as a dazzling paradigm of Pussy Galore in a clingy zip-fronted black cat suit. Oh boy...

Suddenly the curtains to the next cottage were pulled to, and we all held our breath for a harrowing moment as a figure appeared at the window...

"Come, quickly it's parked outside the main gate," Mike said in hushed voice.

We made our way down the long drive. She did make me smile though as she cursed her high heels as a wrong choice of footwear for the occasion. She hobbled, stumbled and clicked the gravel as she went...

"Oh heck! I shouldn't have packed my thigh-high boots."

"Shush... keep it down," I implored.

"Sorry... it's these blasted sling-backs," she huffed, and removed them. Thus lumbering out the front gate barefooted.

The driver took her bags, and I confirmed to him her destination, "Applegate House, hurry!" This was a temporary safe house we'd prearranged for her, to give her time to take stock.

She became tearful again, hugging, kissing and thanking us no end for all the help. And in haste, she literally fell into the back of the cab ass over tit. Bless.

Mariella waved goodbye and blew a Monroe-esque kiss as the car stealthily drove off into the night.

Mike and I stood there gaping at each other...

"Can you believe it?" he said.

"Let's hope all will be well with her..." And I mulled whatever next...?

The next morning at around eight there was a sturdy knock on the front door. And as expected the dubious couple had come looking for her. I handed them a brown envelope. They just gawped in disbelief...

And then aggressively tore it open on the doorstep. It was their *contract* ripped in half, with a cheque for the refunded deposit. They were seething, and cursing, and proceeded to try and prise any information from me regarding her current whereabouts. I just informed them that she had to leave unexpectedly – pleading ignorance! They immediately checked out in a terrible huff, I guess in search of Mariella.

I spoke to her by phone a couple of times that week. She informed me that a flight abroad was booked with an operation at the clinic scheduled for early January – it was now or never...! She seemed much happier with her decision, and again thanked me for all our help.

About a month later on Christmas Eve, a large wooden silk-lined crate arrived, containing the most amazing pair of vintage bottles of wine, labelled remarkably: '*Château Lafite Rothschild 1962*'. A lovely heartfelt handwritten card full of gratitude was found inside the straw. Mariella stated she was doing fine, the operation was a success, and now she would be living permanently in Switzerland. Unfortunately there was no contact address. And that is the last we heard of Mariella ever again.

Fast forward to years later... We'd often wonder how it all turned out for her. The precious bottles had been stored away at the correct temperature only to be brought out for something really special... that my dear readers, turned out to be the occasion of our own Civil Partnership about eight years on from this event. And as we raised our glasses to toast each other and our guests at the luncheon, we both gave a sly smile thinking of Mariella in her new life. End of.

In complete contrast that first December, a young Muslim couple arrived for a stay in the Claret Cottage.

Nabil and Baha had booked Holly Lodge for their romantic liaison unbeknown to their strict orthodox parents. Baha had made the reservation expressly requesting the room with the *Gothic* four-poster bed. I checked them in, and nothing seemed untoward, in fact they seemed an adorable couple obviously very much in love.

The next morning after breakfast events unfolded into a shocker... Mike came hurtling into the kitchen...

"We've been burgled!"

"What?"

And we dashed over to the Claret Cottage.

Well, when I walked into the room, I felt my stress levels soar through the roof, and beyond. To my utter horror, I was confronted by the bare emptiness of our beloved prized room. I gulped in dismay. All the pictures had gone from the walls, and every piece of objet d'art had vanished. Bizarrely though, the television was sitting on top of the dressing table stool, and perched precariously above a chest of drawers at the foot of the bed. Why...?

This was very alarming to say the least! The cottage had been lovingly filled with some of our personal treasures, and even a much-prized 16th century Russian Icon too. We stood there gutted...

Pacing around the room, I instinctively decided to call the young couple first for an explanation, before I rang the police. Baha picked up... as Mike checked out the room more thoroughly.

"Baha, what the hell is going on?" I asked furiously.

"Robert, sorry! But..."

"Hold on a second..." Just then, Mike opened the door to the large closet, and before our very eyes, and to my utter amazement. I saw that all the paintings had been crammed, one against the other on the floor at the back, and all the shelves had been stacked with our artefacts languishing amongst their clothing. I implored her for an explanation, and suggested it better be good...!

And this was her tentative reply...

"Robert, I am very sorry for the inconvenience caused, but it was all those eerie faces in the portraits staring out at me from their ruffled collars, I was terrified in the night..."

"Um. What...?" I looked over at Mike, who was now standing there with his arms folded glaring at me impatiently waiting for an explanation.

"And all those ecclesiastical religious pieces, we are *Muslim* you know! So we hid everything visible that we just could not get along with." Her voice quivered.

My mind raced with visions of wailing minarets, golden-domed mosques, and now Islamophobic being stamped on us in our back-of-beyond backwater. And the next thing... would be a trajectory, courtesy of Osama Bin Laden sending an unfortunate airliner slamming into our roof. Oh my god! And I am on a mobile too...

I reasoned with her that she had especially asked for the room with the Gothic bed, and *Gothic* style usually spelt *Christian* influenced art. And if that did not bother me, and I am *Jewish*, then take it as 'Art for art's sake', get over the symbolism, and just be open minded enough to enjoy the decoration for crying out loud...!

"And what the hell happened to the television...?"

"Nabil had forgotten his glasses, we were watching an in-house movie, and decided to remove the flat-screen TV from the wall, and rest it on the displaced furniture nearer to the bed.

"Baha, if these so-called offending pieces bothered you so much, then on arrival you should have come to ask our permission for their removal, and as for the TV, that's ludicrous... Huh!" What chutzpah...

"I am so sorry! You're right, it was very inconsiderate, even rude, and oh please don't tell my parents...!" she apologised profusely, and I told her we would see them later.

Everything was reinstated, and we decided to move their belongings to the Oak Room in the main house, insofar that the neo-contemporary surroundings might be more suitable.

They returned late that afternoon, and sheepishly came to our door.

"Chaps, we can't begin to tell you how sorry we are... please accept this token as a gesture of our profound apology."

They both looked so contrite, and stood there forlorn holding a large gift-wrapped potted palm tree waiting anxiously for a response.

Naturally a redeeming gesture to schmooze us, and of course the impertinence was well out of order... However no real damage was done. Ah... so young, and we all make mistakes. All was forgiven. Consequently the Christian, the Jew, and the Muslims all shook hands on it, and peace ensued... Thought-provoking eh? In fact they came back year after year, and became familiar regulars at the Lodge.

I tell you the experiences that unfolded over the coming years could be astounding at times. There was no discrimination between class, creed, or race when it came to bare-all eccentricities – personal revelations blatantly exposed – creating a fascinating repertoire of visitors passing through our doors.

How do you tell an erstwhile Member of Parliament that he should not be putting his grubby hands down the blouse of his weekend-bit-of-totty at the breakfast table? Thank the lord... the other guests had left, when I caught them at it. I just nodded my head, and clouted my hand down onto the table in a *Basil Fawlty*-esque stance of defiance, "No! No! Not here!" Do you know...? Not a word was said; they just looked at me coyly, and sheepishly left the dining room. Mind you, I shouldn't have been surprised, judging the way some clumsy politicians behave nowadays. And perhaps, a booking claimed on MP expenses courtesy of taxpayers' money... Who knows?

On another occasion a Public School old queen touched me up, by the breakfast table. When I admonished him for his sordid indelicacy, he then in blatant disregard, proposed for my services to be extended for his sexual pleasure within the privacy of his bedroom. And I believe the traditional punishment of *spanking* was one of his predilections... In fact he was a complete pest to both of us for the duration of his stay, so much so I nearly contacted '*Gaydar*' to cater for his needs. And one time, I stumbled upon a certain soap actress giving, dare I say most crudely, a blowjob to her horny tryst on the sundeck by the pond. The paparazzi would have killed for a shot of that peccadillo...

Probably about ninety-five per cent of our visitors over the coming years were extremely well behaved courteous model guests of exemplary calibre, but there were a minority of errant personas that seemed to indulge in taking great pleasure for paying for the privilege of abusing our hospitality. Mike was more tolerant than me, but some blatant indiscretions would make my blood boil to be quite honest. And very occasionally I would be forced to let my guard slip with these bad mannered individuals. Call it unprofessional... but if you were standing in my well-worn shoes on your own home turf – you might just do the same!

And then, flipping heck... The things one does for an extra buck I tell you, but the Lodge had drunk most of our capital. And desperate times call for desperate measures...

The doors were thrown wide open to an audacious bunch of lewd revellers for a three-day all-inclusive Christmas break. A party of six commandeered all three cottages.

They all arrived promptly at teatime, but I must point out here, that this arrival thing was a huge *bugbear;* resulting in a major downside to the business, which I am sure most guesthouse proprietors will agree with... In fact it became the bane of my life at the Lodge...

The booking confirmation forms clearly state as part of our policy, that check in times are between 2pm-7pm, unless otherwise prearranged. Fine! So when a guest turns up at ten at night say, without considerately informing us of their late arrival time, then I'd be driven to distraction having to wait around dressed up at all hours – not knowing when they are going to arrive.

OK, if it's an 'Act of God' then fair enough... However some folk assumed we were like a twenty-four hour metropolitan hotel, with night duty staff, and did not care to understand the personal nature of our type of establishment. Consequently we'd be on call twenty-four hours a day, disrupting our daily routines, and playing havoc with our sleep patterns, especially when some arrived at one or two in the morning. Totally unacceptable!

For crying out loud! I had to get that off my chest... Now on with the festive celebrations of our six visitors from the Welsh valleys... A lively group that were in and out of each other's cottages all night long, doors slamming, music blaring, and I think a bit of my old favourite, smoking pot, as even after ten years off the stuff, I can smell it a mile off.

I did not condone it at the Lodge, and sometimes rebuked the more blatant residents for their conspicuous habit, but this lot were sixty-somethings probably a throwback to their misspent youths.

Lunch on Christmas Day became a very laboured affair, and they certainly milked us for all that it was worth, but the main thing of course was that they enjoyed everything, and would come again. Perhaps...?

We prepared a special traditional luncheon with a contemporary twist, naturally served up with our trademark sartorial elegance. And we even presented them with some super complimentary gifts sourced from local artisan specialists to remind them of their stay in Norfolk. But hey, they had other things – more pressing on their minds...

After lunch, they plied themselves with brandy and port in front of the roaring fire in the Inglenook. And gifts were passed around.

Suddenly in the heightened boozy atmosphere, they all loosened up into a frenzy of shenanigans... Sexual innuendos were abounding and partners were canoodling with other partners out of wedlock. What...? And at one point I thought we were in for a full-blown orgy – a real eye-popper – even to my liberal eyes. Because Dai and Gwen, Reece and Bronwyn, Owen and Megan were in actual fact 'Open-Swingers...'

"So this is what they get up to in the Vall...eeys!" I regaled to Mike in the kitchen.

"Oh well... they seem to be enjoying Christmas Day at the Lodge. Whatever!" We resigned ourselves. And rinsed the endless glasses and used plates etc, etc, etc. Mine hosts were compliantly at the beck and call in the name of... Dosh!

My head; finally touched the pillow around two in the morning on Boxing Day. We were both utterly annihilated... However, they left full of praise though for our relentless hospitality, and even tipped us *most* generously. Tips were something I found very amusing, as hitherto this guesthouse experience I'd never been tipped in my entire life before, but when they were that generous into the hundreds of pounds, my bemusement turned to gratitude – believe you me...

We were learning thick and fast what it was like to be an hotelier, but just when you think you have seen it all...

Yet another torrid instalment of life's soap opera makes its way to our little enclave; another bizarre foray that could be easily portrayed in some top shelf trashy gossip mag! Each remarkable encounter would become another entry into my log.

I would learn that the strangest thing happens to *some* people when staying, straying, and playing away from home. I was almost very temped to provide my own welcome mantra as a standard greeting to new arrivals...

"*Good afternoon and welcome to Holly Lodge... Before I check you in, are there any interesting little foibles you care to share with me, or curious unpalatable habits I should know about...?*" **Just another day at the Lodge**...

CHAPTER 9

LUCKY MASCOT

The storm clouds were gathering over our first full year at Holly Lodge in 2001. The spectre of widespread disruption by the striking fuel tanker drivers threatened critical shortages of the precious commodity, the Foot and Mouth crisis enveloping vast areas of the countryside, and the worst floods to hit the United Kingdom in years were portents casting a huge shadow over our prospects.

The British Tourism industry was preparing for the worst, teetering on the precipice from the inevitable repercussions from the looming national disasters.

Every cloud does have a silver lining though – our little whippet puppy arrived that May...

Throughout the bleak winter months, I had scoured the Internet, researching breeders of whippets as I tried to find the one with the right specifications, which matched Mike's dream wish list: fawn, with a white neck blaze, and white socks; the sex did not matter, but if possible a loving, gentle, bright temperament would be a bonus! I put the word about with various breeders in the East of England.

One afternoon an angry lady called me, perhaps from The East Anglia Whippet Club, on hearing of my search suggested: I go to a department store, and buy a designer *Haute Couture* fur. Oops!

Then a young chap called Matt, sent me an e-mail out of the blue to inform me that there might be a chance of a fawn whippet coming back to his mother, who is a reputable breeder living in Newmarket. She had supplied the dog to a couple that were now in the throes of divorcing, and therefore could no longer care for the six-month-old puppy. As I inquired further about the dog, the more he talked about him the more it became joy to my ears with the notion, that this might be the one...! Matt said he would contact me in due course regarding any further developments. I kept the little secret to myself, sincerely hoping I could now fulfil my votive to Mike.

Spring was stirring, and the scent of the lilac trees was always heady at the Lodge. Bountiful blooms of white, and purple were draped heavenly atop the drive framing the house, and cosseting it with the hope that a new season brings. Blankets of crocuses and daffodils wove a carnival of colour throughout the orchard. The pastel blossoms of the fruit trees provided an arresting canopy that stretched marquee-like to the great pines on the boundary beyond. Against the dichotomy of the doom and gloom reported daily in the news: the restricted movement and mass culling of farm animals – which made for depressive reading...

A double whammy would be generated for many farmers, and locals alike, whose incomes were supplemented from holiday accommodation-lets during the crucial summer months of the tourist high season. Vast swathes of countryside from Devon to Cumbria were deemed no-go areas. The Government had ordered many country footpaths to be closed in an effort to curb the epidemic, and disinfect diseased zones. Bookings were down for home trade, and to exasperate matters: overseas tourism had dramatically escalated as reported by many travel operators.

The constant news footage was disheartening... And severe storms caused havoc flooding many counties. Now our very own coastline was on high alert too...

A news flash came up on the TV that night that is so redolent in my memory, evocative of that harrowing seven days, which I am sure, you will remember when the country came precariously close to being brought to its knees... It announced that if last-ditch talks with the unions were not successful the United Kingdom would be paralysed, and therefore go into meltdown.

"Bloody hell! There's panic buying in the supermarkets now... and look at the queues on the forecourts escalating by the second." Our spirits were dampened as we looked on helplessly.

"Who in hell will want to come here with all this going on? No petrol, no food, no holiday... Eh?" Mike was beside himself with all the bad news being pumped-out constantly.

And then to our horror report after report showed heaps of dead livestock being dumped and their carcasses burned smouldering on live TV broadcasts bringing home the calamity that indeed beset the nation. The epidemic truly worsened in many quarters. Our hearts went out to the farmers faced with ruin, and naturally we felt sick for the poor animals.

Those compelling calamities tormented us... Imagine having to close in our first year of trading, it will all have been futile...

"Don't worry Rob, if it doesn't work out I'll go back to hairdressing." Mike was hovering somewhere between despair and martyrdom. Of course he was trying to comfort me with all the worry ensuing.

I tried to keep a brave face though. But he knew me too well. Although the bottom line was... I'd already begun searching for options...

However despite the parlous state of affairs, some holidaymakers did venture our way during these turbulent times, so we had to buckle down and make the best out of a bad situation.

As if this were not all bad enough to cripple our business! But just around the corner was our very own home grown *'Annus Horribilis'*.

It was mid May, all the rooms were full, the weather was about to turn warmer despite the constant downpours, when suddenly at six one morning there was a hefty knock on the front door. It was one of the ladies staying in the Colonial Cottage. Glum-faced, she declared, "There is *no* hot water!" And she just stood there glaring at me, accusingly.

Oh no! This is all we need. I immediately sought to investigate the problem and discovered that the boiler, which was located in a tiny annexe room off the Claret Cottage, had stopped functioning.

Naturally I apologised to her, and to all the guests that morning for the inconvenience. And offered them the option of using the bathrooms in the main house. Meanwhile I tried to rectify the problem.

These occurrences as any hotelier knows can be very embarrassing, and our literature clearly states:

'That all appliances are maintained on a regular basis, and the management cannot be held responsible – though of course will endeavour to rectify problems with failed equipment as soon as possible.'

Stressful was an understatement! I could not get the darn boiler working, and called in the emergency plumbers. Pronto.

The master plumber checked everything out, and the boiler seemed fine in itself. But there was just no heating coming through the system. Why...?

The man spent ages tinkering around, and then ascertained to my horror that the pipes running the entire length of the cottages encased under the concrete floors must have burst somewhere, consequently cutting off the flow of the system. It was the only explanation for the failure, as nothing else seemed untoward. A nightmare scenario...

This was a disastrous blow! It was as if the gods were conspiring against us to fail in our new venture. Events were spiralling out of our control... He suggested we get the insurance assessors in to advise on our Policy Cover.

Now that was a blast...

This could mean closing for weeks on end, possibly having to dig up all the floors with the outcome of each suite having to be completely redecorated – costing thousands!

The chap from a well-known established insurance company, which shall remain nameless, arrived the next morning to appraise our dire situation...

"There may be a problem..." he sighed nodding his head.

"Uh-oh!" My alarm bells were ringing louder than the belfry at Westminster Abbey.

"It's a classic, sorry guys..." And he closed his briefcase. Mike scowled in disbelief.

"What...?" I cried, perplexed by his sudden ruse.

My premise was... '*That the boiler had crashed as an obvious consequence to the burst pipes encased in the concrete floor*'. (A dubious paragraph did state in the Policy that this should be covered.) However in his expediency he declared that as there was no physical sign of water damage (soiling the interiors), therefore *The Company* would not be at liberty to cover any costs. And that would be that.

What a scam... and we were thoroughly disillusioned...!

In hindsight I should have contacted BBC *Watchdog* that might have got their arses into gear.

Nevertheless I fought tooth and nail over the following weeks to get quoted costs reimbursed, but unfortunately to no avail.

So we were faced with two choices. Either arrange for the floors to be dug up causing untold damage, and expense with months of lost income in high season. Or a simpler quicker option of rerouting the conduits from the roof tanks through the ceilings down into the corners of the rooms, to connect to the radiators, which would be the less costly option. Resulting in minimal disruption, expense, and closure time. Ultimately we had to choose the latter, being dictated to us by the circumstances.

It was an all-time low... And that became an exceedingly trying week. However, there was the saving grace of the hearty breed staying in the Claret and Country Cottages – both couples were sympathetic to our plight, and conducted themselves with stoic British reserve. In fact they did not seem too bothered by cold showers at all, even though they had the option of using a bathroom in the main house as a substitute.

Meanwhile the two ladies in the Colonial were bloody awful about it... holding us personally responsible for their inconvenience, as if it were some cataclysmic event like a tsunami tragedy of untold suffering. Naturally in order to gain free passage for their entire stay, I might add...! They would march into the house sour-faced, sullen, moans and groans, take their showers in the master bathroom, and then march out slamming the front door behind them.

Of course everybody was offered a fair discount, ingratiated with boxes of chocolates, fine wines, and flowers to assuage their inconvenience. But on departure: 'The Sisters of Perpetual Indulgence' as I dubbed them, insisted ungraciously on free bed and board for their entire seven-night stay. Despite the fact they were moved to the Oak Room in the house, where the poor darlings were supplied with constant hot water for the duration of their stay.

Consequently, theirs were the second names to go on my '**BLACKLIST**' this time adjunct with the term 'Spiritually Bankrupt!' I couldn't help myself it was my private sweet revenge of putting a mark of *persona non grata* to nasty individuals who tried to capitalise on our misfortune.

Paradoxically, the couple, keen cyclists, who were in the Claret rejected our discount outright, and preceded happily to provide us with a rewarding tip. In fact they commended us on our professional handling of the situation.

I came to the conclusion that when dealing with the general public on a day-to-day basis... It was a minefield!

Shortly after that bleak episode, a ray of hope came in the form of some very good news...

Matt's mother had agreed to bring the dog over to Holly Lodge to meet us. With all our troubles it would have been very easy to have informed them to forget the puppy, but I instinctively felt compelled to go ahead, which proved beyond a shadow of a doubt, that we might have passed up the opportunity of owning a *diamond* of a dog...

Holly Lodge closed for the next three weeks. The necessary works were carried out. And all due reservations for that period – though threadbare – were relocated to neighbouring guesthouses and hotels. Disappointing... but beyond our control.

The builders were back. Hey-ho. And we just had to get on with it... Fortunately, the day came when we were about to meet our beloved little whippet puppy.

He jumped straight out of their 4x4 bounding in with a hop, skip and a jump like a ray of sunshine through the front door. A kiss for me, a kiss for Mike, straight through into the lounge plonking his backside into the comfy wicker dog-basket in front of the Inglenook, which we had presumptuously bought. And thereupon made himself at home. Bless!

It was love at first sight... Matt's mother, Teresa, and her husband Keith sat on the Chesterfield to vet us as prospective new owners...

Suddenly the little dog, a bright eyed bundle of joy, jumped up onto the *Knole* sofa. He shuffled, and squeezed himself betwixt Mike and me, where he preceded to pass the smelliest of farts! It was risible... Consequently Teresa declared, "Well, he's sure made himself at home now...!" And smiled with grand approval.

Barney as he was originally called, snuck down and with his wet nose, tapped Mike on the knee, shook his blessed head, stared at him, and then side-glanced towards the garden.

Teresa interjected to point out that... "He is telling you that he wants to go out to do his business." We were dead impressed.

And Mike rushed to the French doors. The little fella scurried across the terrace, and sloped off behind a shrub to discreetly do his stuff – without being seen. And that's when we discovered not only did we have the handsomest of creatures resembling the *horse-piece* on a chessboard, but an intelligent *gentleman* to boot! There and then we renamed the little mite Barnaby although his sweet tender nickname at times would become Boo.

He came trotting out from the shrubbery wagging his tail buoyantly cajoling us to play with him, and we frolicked around with him as if he'd been with us for years. Teresa and Keith nodded. We'd been approved...

Arrangements were made for our new ownership and we were to pick Barnaby up from their home in Newmarket in a fortnight – much to our relief!

Barnaby has the most expressive chocolate brown luminous eyes, a lustrous velvety-smooth fawn coat, white socks, neck blaze, and unusual geometric double-diamond white markings on his upper neck merging into his fawn and white head. Not forgetting a little white dash on his rear rump as if someone had accidentally spilt some bleach on his fawn coat, *or* I like to think it's a signature of his creator: a statuesque, sleek, elegant, pedigree, masterpiece! "Don't I make you sick?" And at the risk of sounding completely cloy, this dog would become the perfect pet in every way, with the most loving, affectionate, and smart nature imaginable. We were truly blessed with his arrival, and in our time of crisis too... (heaven must be missing an angel!).

Apparently he'd been the runt of the litter, and was hand-reared by Teresa for the first few weeks of his precious life forming a strong bond between them. However after the disappointing homing experience with the couple that had separated, she was very reluctant to re-home him and had to be persuaded by her son Matt to give us a shot.

We discovered that this remarkable woman was indeed like a dog *whisperer;* very skilled in handling her successful show hounds, and most revered amongst the whippet fraternity. She has skilfully bred many award-winning dogs from this fascinating breed. Her lounge is full of rosettes and trophies. And in actual fact, we later discovered, that Barnaby is from an amazing lineage of many champions most notably his great, great grandfather 'Pencloe Dutch Gold', who was the first whippet to win *Best in Show* at *Crufts* in 1992. No wonder he was so darn handsome, resembling a thoroughbred racehorse... There I go again...

We have been so fortunate never to have to consider kennels, as Teresa would always be more than happy to look after him, should we go away. She became appropriately known as 'Mother Teresa'. And I know I'm gushing... But she is our *saint*...

The next two weeks flew by, with work nearly completed in the cottages, and fortunately as it panned out the re-routing of the pipe-work caused minimal damage to the décor.

It was the beginning of June... we had counted down the days to collect Barnaby-Boo from Newmarket. He came bounding over to us as we entered Teresa's house, recognising our voices instantly. In fact he jumped up so high Mike caught him in his arms, and it looked like he would never let him go *ever* again. Whippets are totally *moreish*, and happen to smell like buttered toast... We were introduced to rest of Barnaby's clan too. One by one they came cantering out of the annexe to meet us. We were mesmerised...

Sophie, Barnaby's mum, lovingly greeted her pup, Gina, a striking grey and white brindle (his sis), and Flash his larger more boisterous bro made a blubbery fuss of us. Then a stunning pair of very blond fawns (showstoppers) elegantly sashayed in, named Jade and Jasmine, winners of numerous rosettes. It was like a bevy of beauties vying for attention! However, our eyes were transfixed on our... Lucky Mascot! Because, believe you me, our luck really changed thereafter.

Teresa's insurmountable knowledge regarding sound advice in caring for our new *surrogate* baby meant we were in good hands... A surprising fallacy is that whippets and greyhounds need hours and hours of running out exercise each day. When in actual fact an hour of two half-hour bursts will suffice. Another anomaly is that we discovered that these dogs are very much like cats, when it comes to cleanliness – preening themselves more than you'd expect a dog to do. And for fear of sounding horribly mawkish... Oops! Barnaby is the only canine I have ever known to dodge dirty muddy puddles. No kidding!

'Now; that's what I call a perfect pooch for a couple of fussy gay guys...'

It was a revelation to discover that Teresa even refused to take payment for him, her main criteria was the dog's welfare at heart, and that he had a good home. And she even presented us with a starter kit. Of course we insisted on some form of payment, but she just would not have it. And there began a wonderful relationship with a sincerely special lady.

I'll never forget when we left that day. Tears streamed down her face as we said our goodbyes, and Mike swept the little fella up into his arms, to sit in the front of our vehicle. Barnaby lent out of the open window, whimpered, and licked her face as if to say goodbye – it tugged at my heartstrings, and we were all in buckets!

That night he whimpered long into the early hours. I came downstairs gone two and placed a ticking clock into his bed next to his cuddly bear to simulate the heartbeat of perhaps a sibling. However his first night trauma in strange new surroundings was just too much for him to bear as his whimpering continued gone three.

Finally, Mike could stand it no longer, and dashed down to the boot-room, and brought him up to bed, where we snuggled up with him, allaying his fears as he lulled into a deep sleep.

First thing, I awoke startled to cold moist licks splashing across my face, heavy panting, and then a snuffling in my ears. **THE PUPPY SILLY... NOT**

MICHAEL! His large soulful eyes bore into me. Bless, our new arrival was prompting me urgently to get him to the garden for his routine business – already housebroken, and gentlemanly enough – to patiently make sure he did not have an accident in our room. *'What a good boy!'*

We still had a few days grace before we'd be open for business as usual, so that morning we jumped in the campervan and headed to Holkham Beach with a very chirpy excitable puppy.

At first we were reluctant to let him off the lead being insecure that he might run-off into the pine forests never to be heard of again, but he dragged the lead so much in a bid to run free, Mike just suddenly let him off!

He was a sight to behold as he ran out across the dunes towards the sea (whippets are the fastest animals alive for their body weight), leaping over inlet streams like a wild Springbok. He reached the shore-shallows, stuck his paw into the water cautiously, and then trotted through the surf seemingly un-fussed by the cool droplets splashing onto his body (this is uncharacteristic of whippets as they are inherently not fond of water).

I know both Mike and I are probably guilty of being wholly anthropomorphic, but Barnaby displays many human qualities by his suggestive behaviour patterns, subtle nuances of his decision making for example, especially when dealing with capricious human emotions or dilemmas... *'I can almost hear him thinking it through...'* His expressive mannerisms that we have grown to know so well, as well as his clever telepathic abilities go to show he has a conscience, and more importantly a *soul*! Our own **'Can...Einstein'**.

The game was back on. The talks with the unions resolved the petrol issues for the time being and the cottages were now ready for occupation. June rolled away... People came and went in a flash, and with the arrival of Barnaby-Boo, a brand new optimism now distracted our thoughts; allaying the unutterably harrowing events that beset our lives that spring.

Thank God, everything was looking rosy in the garden once again, and those dark oppressive storm clouds cast over our first full debut year did indeed reveal: a very *shiny* silver lining after all.

Handsome Barnaby on the sand dunes at Holkham Bay.

CHAPTER 10

GOING FOR GOLD

The severe financial repercussions of our loss of income for the month of June, and the costs of repairing the central heating system in the cottages were no doubt a major setback. And despite the horrors of the Foot and Mouth crisis still ravaging the country causing havoc to rural economies, we ploughed on into the summer months as best we could, forgiven the dire circumstances. Fortunately, with Barnaby added into the equation, our spirits were lifted out of the mire as we focused much of our precious spare time into nurturing our little puppy.

One sultry afternoon under a ponderous sky in August, the house shook with the vibration of two (classic) *Harley-Davidsons'* racing up the drive in a whirl of dust as they made their way onto the gravelled forecourt. The black and chrome motorbikes gleamed in the afternoon sun – blinding my vision for a fleeting moment, and then two leather-clad bikers suddenly appeared at the entrance. No, this is not another fantasy!

The woman lifted off her helmet and shook a wild mane of jet-black hair, which cascaded onto her padded shoulders. Her companion lifted his visor to reveal a broad engaging smile, albeit gaping with a shiny gold front tooth. He handed me his booking confirmation letter, and it was the Wolfe-Jacobsons down for the annual motorbike rally in Norfolk.

Oscar was a university professor who spoke with the resonance of an upper crust Lord belying his biker-dude appearance. He sported clipped facial topiary highlighted by a silver goatee on tanned weathered complexion, which he would stroke continuously. While his wife Donna reminded me of Morticia from the *Addams Family*, albeit, a more suburban version with luminescent green eyes – emphasised by heavy Goth make-up – hamming up her ghostly pallor.

She sexily slid off her jacket to reveal a bright fuchsia singlet stretched tightly over a pair of remarkable XXL faux boobs. And I took a double take, especially because every square inch of exposed flesh was covered in Celtic and Tribal tattoos…

Oscar did not disappoint in the tattoo department either. Extensive designs of organic dragons, reptiles and Japanese imagery were crawling all over his upper body. Between the pair of them they had an elaborate tapestry of more ink-work than a Punk fest parading down King's Road on a Saturday afternoon – circa 1980. The couple must have been sixty if a day: 'Ageing Punk-Rock Chick meets Nutty Mad Professor on Prozac…' Bless!

I advised them to park their bikes in the garage as the sky had become increasingly leaden. And of course they were offered the customary *Pimm's*. The heavens opened, and the rain relentlessly battered the Lodge for an intense twenty minutes, and then in a typically English fashion, capricious sunny blue skies ensued…

The phone rang about ten minutes later. And as expected by the highlighted entry in my diary… my Irish friend was at the end of the drive announcing his imminent arrival.

Naturally I was supposed to have no idea who it was; "Yeah right!" It was a little shy of a full year since the last inspection from the Tourist Board, and my heart was now racing in anticipation of the dreaded outcome to our all-important next star rating. I was almost tempted to text him: "WE R READY…"

The suited and booted individual arrived on spec as if he just left a boardroom meeting. He must have been sweltering in the humidity that day, and we went through the usual registration routine – verbatim! Perfunctory pleasantries were exchanged; the summer cocktail followed, and then I escorted him to his room.

However en route, I was taken by surprise to find Donna (Morticia), now de-clad of her leathers, modelling the skimpiest black shiny PVC bikini, with leopard faux-fur trim, and precariously stretched over her impossibly thin, albeit very busty – frame. She wiggled her snake-like hips. Animated billboards in Times Square had nothing on her – as she contorted her body-art every which way... She happened to be hanging out her Union Jack undies over a garden chair, just concurrently as the inspector and I passed by.

"Oops..." I uttered under my breath, I thought there goes a star from our rating. Clang!

"Howdy," she cried out with a coquettish smile, as she clawed at us with her black painted talons.

"Catching some rays," I said nonchalantly.

"You bet," and she giggled raucously like a schoolgirl from St Trinian's...!

The inspector recoiled, but nodded politely and hastily went through into his cottage.

"Hey ho!" My day of terror has just begun. I could feel my anxiety levels heightening by the minute. I mulled over the arresting scene consciously thinking... that my Hell's Angelina Jolie – Rock-Chick had no idea that our lives hung on the outcome of the judgement by our visiting Tourism Inspector. To her he was just another guest – to me the harbinger of my future.

Mike warned me to keep calm at breakfast the next morning... Unfortunately the initial calm turned into a raging storm behind closed doors with an unforeseen calamity about to beset our routine that morning.

Oscar and Donna emerged a la Morticia and Uncle Fester from their dark crypt bang on time for the start of breakfast. The gruesome twosome, were decked-o t to the hilt in full studded leather regalia replete with hardware accessories – clinking and clanking to announce their arrival. They seemed to fit right in with the Baronial setting of the dining hall. Moments later they were joined by a couple that paled into sheer insignificance within their flamboyant presence. They all sat down to breakfast...

Mike now engrossed in his serving rounds, recounted that they were animatedly regaling the joys of motor-biking on the sparse Norfolk country roads, and seemingly boring the socks off the pair of straight-laced churchy types, who were down for their annual pilgrimage to Walsingham.

The Inspector then arrived, and sat incongruously at the end of the refectory table watching everything like a hawk. And that particular morning we had an extra couple in from Lancashire – a doctor and his wife down visiting '*Pensthorpe*' (a stunning Nature Reserve nearby). Apropos new arrivals could often arrange for breakfast the same morning, while their bags were left for collection in the holding area – for check in later.

Hence we had a total of seven in for breakfast. The breakfast routine had now become like driving a car on cruise control, foot down on the accelerator and automatically away you jolly well go!

That morning, everything went swimmingly until that is the most darnedest unbidden storm swept in. Suddenly the power was disengaged as I prepared the main course. (Perhaps the macabre combo of our devilish riders and our own in-house spirit were conspiring to weave a web of destruction in their wake...): The kettles, percolators, hostess food warmer (tabletop), and my electric range all ceased up, the music went silent, and the lights went out. And I became like a maniacal screaming queen with the stress of it all! The foods that were sizzling under the grill in the range simply stopped cooking. It was panic stations...

Mike ran out the back door to the garage to grab our three portable gas-stoves, which we had used to cook with, whilst living in the cottages; luckily the canisters were relatively full. We emptied all the drawers to utilise all cookware for the semi-cooked foods to be shifted too. Saucepans, frying pans, and griddle pans everything I could lay my hands on was requisitioned. Profanities, speedily rolling off our tongues...

Remember, I just said everything is usually on automatic pilot. Well, believe you me that fateful morning everything went bloody *manual*! Pans of water were now boiling away to facilitate coffees, and teas; toast was wrapped in foil, and inserted into the range, which fortunately still radiated some heat. Everything else had to be cooked on the makeshift stoves, and to be synchronised accordingly. We had our reputation at stake with our special breakfasts at the Lodge. And I did not want to let the side down, under any circumstances – especially that critical morning... Sod's blinking Law!

Mike came back into the kitchen with the used plates from the first course buffet. The guests were chattering away to candlelight oblivious to our plight. I could tell he was very tense, so much so, he was humming *Libiamo ne'lieti calici* (Drinking Song) *Brindisi* from Act 1 of Giuseppe Verdi's *La Traviata* , which was the last track playing when the power went down. This was very uncharacteristic of Mike – singing in public – not him at all!

I became surly and very snappy, as I was racing around trying to assemble the breakfast dishes, which were a very complicated assortment of orders: four Full English breakfasts, two with scrambled eggs, one without mushrooms, and the other without sausage, but an extra rasher on the side, and no hash browns. One with poached eggs, no tomatoes, only one rasher of bacon, and no fried bread wafer; and one with fried egg over-easy, two rashers, and an extra tomato, but no sausage. Two House Specials (egg filled croissants), one with cheese, and no Parma ham – one with basil, and no cheese, but with Parma ham. Smoke salmon and scrambled eggs on bagel, but with low fat butter spread. And one plate of kippers with extra tomatoes with a four-minute boiled egg shelled on the side... Blimey!

I tell you it was a nightmare to say the least, concocting the vast array of menu combinations that particular morning. My role of *Master Chef* was tested to the hilt that muggy morning... And I was wired to the point I thought I would combust at any moment. Help!

Finally all the dishes were prepared and ready to despatch. I quickly changed my sodden shirt and loaded them onto the serving trays.

Then in a fit of impromptu madness... Here goes... we swung open the kitchen door singing a very shaky (*Italiano* style) rendition of *Let's Face the Music and Dance*.

The respective platefuls were served to our bemused guests with a messianic flourish: now not knowing what to expect on that morning with no power? Suddenly, a huge round of applause ensued with gleeful smiles of satisfaction all round. And even the Inspector disarmingly called out with a pleasing "Bravo!" as he tucked into his nothing less than a perfect Holly Lodge breakfast.

Phew... how we pulled-it off – I'll never know...

The guests buoyantly departed the dining hall. And by now the biker couple had exchanged phone numbers with the doctor, and the doctor was already preparing prescriptions, which sounded ominous...!

The room fell silent for a moment, and then the lights flicked on, as the music started playing. Routinely, the inspector presented us with his business card, and we played out the obligatory game.

"Oh... I would never have guessed it..." I declared. Mike looked at me as if the Lord above might strike me down at any moment...

We went through to the lounge to discuss our assessment... He began by congratulating us on such a well-run establishment, and not only had we maintained our five star rating, but we had earned a much-sought-after "Gold Award" – to our utter amazement... He even suggested he would recommend other B&B proprietors to come and stay here to see how it was really done at this level.

Wow... Naturally, Mike and I were overwhelmed with the achievement, and seriously delighted by his generous candour. *And* with all those dramas earlier, it felt like such a coup!

He added we were now of the calibre with these qualifications to be entered into *'The Regional Excellence*

Awards in England', if we so wished? "You bet... we so wished!"

So there we were on our way into an elite club at the luxury end of the market, the recognition played into my psyche, as a major step towards burgeoning my vision of becoming the *best* establishment in the county. The prestigious assessment had infused us with a newfound *enthusiasm* especially after such hard times.

Did you ever see the film the *Money Pit* with Tom Hanks? Well, Holly Lodge was eerily similar – very high maintenance! And kind of reminded me of that house, which drank money at an alarming rate. The Lodge simply slurped the stuff like a desperate alcoholic falling off the wagon. Old houses just do, no matter what we did something would always rear its ugly head, crying for attention! It was so frustrating just when we thought we'd made some extra cash, bang it be gone in an instant putting something or other right. The other thing of course, which most good proprietors will recognise, is the immense amount of stuff one needs to cater for the top end. Consequently we were always shopping. OK it is my one *big* weakness, what *gay* guy doesn't love to shop, but it becomes laboured when it's for dreary necessities.

We'd often joke... our neighbours must have thought we were secret Lottery winners; gathered by the amount of shopping bags we'd be seen laden with on our forays Oh I can but dream...!

Although that may have meant, I would never have written our story of life at the Lodge, which you are now reading.

So it was timely that Mike's flat in Kensal Green came into question. Still inhabited by an ex, dating way back when, refusing to compromise, and to buy Mike out of his lion's share of the property, whilst still cheekily demanding regular funds for maintenance on the flat too. Even though Mike had not lived there for around ten years.

Faced with no other alternative the matter went to court, where the Judge ordered in favour of Mike, and declared that the property be sold immediately, with the predominant portion of the proceeds from the sale being reimbursed to Mike after the mortgage had been settled. It was a very painful episode for Mike. And a chapter finally closed after many years of angst over the issue.

Mike chose to invest the proceeds into the Lodge, and combined with the sale of my investment bonds, this provided us with enough funds to develop the back garden plot, and at the same time to create a new living area – to be a separate private guest lounge annexe in the form of an Orangery. Hurrah! I drew up plans for both ventures, which would be the making of the Lodge. And thus bring my vision to fruition the following year for phase two of the *Dream Sanctuary*.

A brand new plaque displaying our recent Gold Award was proudly fixed to the front gatepost, and one afternoon while avidly polishing it, a slick black *Daimler* limousine swept past me up the drive – almost pinning me against the sign.

It was a party of six down for a wedding at '*Voewood*', a beautiful Arts & Crafts country manor house in High Kelling. A unique architectural gem based on a butterfly-plan, and an extreme example of Norfolk neo-vernacular design – combining a melange of flint, stone, tile, and concrete into rich decorative patterning giving the façade an extraordinary majesty. And oh, it is set overlooking a magnificent formal terraced garden. The owner is the very charismatic Simon Finch an antiquarian bookseller aficionado, who has cleverly restored this fine building for posterity. And which he also offers for hire for functions like weddings and parties making it a truly special venue. Which in actual fact became the scene one glorious Sunday in June, many years later for our very own "Civil Partnership" luncheon celebrations after our ceremony at Cley Mill, exactly a year prior to me writing this book.

At this juncture, I have to come clean about my perceptions of *our* wedding guests. Please don't think me a party pooper... And without tarring them all with the same brush, it's just that these episodes were a fact of my experiences with *them* back at the Lodge – disrespectfully abusing the accommodation – their crash pad for the night.

The *Daimler* dropped off the party at the front entrance delivering onto my doorstep an assortment of three generations: septuagenarian grandparents, fifty-something parents of the groom, and two frightful sprogs: a girl thirteen, and a boy fourteen, bridesmaid and pageboy respectively. Naturally they were all stressed out, extremely hyper, and then they had good reason to be. OK... I have given them enough excuses; so let's get down to the nitty-gritty of what really happened that morning after they left for their wedding. We entered the cottages for the usual turn-round. And it was pitiful...

It transpired that the young lad had dyed his hair blue depositing copious portions of dye streaking through a conglomeration of towels, cushions, bedspreads and throws, and the young miss had smothered gallons of glitter makeup onto an antique wall hanging from Rajasthan, a beautiful Kilim rug, and the pair of deco armchairs, consequently spoiling the coverings. A CD had been jammed in the *Bose* player making it irretrievable. And it was total carnage in the Colonial...

Meanwhile in the Country Cottage, darling Mother had not only self-tanned her own body, but managed to have smeared her *St Tropez* tan all over our Egyptian cotton white sheets too, the TV remote had by the looks of it been stamped on, and there was a rip in the padding of my beloved retro tailor's dummy: a model for many a fashion creation – remaining unscathed for the last two decades – until this very day...!

However last but not least dear old Gramps, and sweet *dear* little Granny in the Claret, had ever so thoughtfully soiled our beloved *Bokhara* rug with the foulest smelling scent, and puddles of black coffee, blocked the toilet with reams of tissue paper, and the odd *Carmen* hair-roller, cracked an expensive vase, left burnt cup-rings on the fine Georgian side tables, and somehow managed to have tested her lipsticks on our marble bust in the alcove. What chutzpah!

They were hooligans of the highest degree. Our Barnaby had more manners than all of them put together... We were appalled by the morning after scenes.

At breakfast the next morning Mike and I were absolutely seething to boiling point. However without saying a word we waited for an expected apology, which I am afraid to say was not forthcoming. I kept buttoned. And then on departure I presented the father (of the groom) with the most *astronomical* bill covering all the damage they had instigated to our property.

He was heavily hung-over, and for a tardy moment moaned under his breath as he scanned down the *very* long inventory list of items to be replaced and repaired. And then he snapped to his wife, "Darling – cheque book – now!" Rubbing his head, he simply wrote me a cheque for a hefty four-figure sum, without any apology whatsoever – would you believe it...?

Everything was conducted in complete cordial efficiency and a rather embarrassing silence ensued...

As they were leaving his beauty-queen daughter turned on her heel. The precocious little *minx* screwed up her pixieish face, and stuck her liquorice-dyed tongue out at me apparently when nobody was looking, and cattily remarked..."Whatever!"

I must confess I did the same back to her, but with bells on. And she ran shrieking to their car. Good riddance!

Their names were naturally added to my special 'BLACKLIST'. And little horrors were barred from here on then. Mind you with those folks as disastrous role models it's no wonder: perhaps a typical case in point of a Blair-Brown Britain in the nasty Naughties.

Each time as with many of *our* (inconsiderate) wedding guests, we would have some dreadful occurrences, but that disrespectful bunch took the cake – excuse the pun!

One time though, we had to come and rescue some rowdy types from the splendid Gunthorpe Hall nearby designed by Sir John Soane, who was appointed to architecturally design the Bank of England in 1778. They'd collapsed blind drunk in the middle of the floor of a great

175

marquee in the grounds. The slobs were retching in our car all the way back to the Lodge – it was horrendous. Yuk! And then they proceeded to keep all the other residents up the entire night by revelling in the garden at all hours. I daren't mention what we found in their room, it will put you off your supper.

We did not relish most wedding revellers; "Heaven forefend!" staying with us. They were just simply more trouble than they were worth... end of.

In complete contrast, we would have the most wonderful people staying at the Lodge over the years, and I have to emphasise that most were pretty fab. One such lovely person was Maggie Beaumont, whom with her brother Ted, were both evacuated to the relative safety of Norfolk, from the heavy blitzkrieg of London during the World War II; when they were both around the tender age of sixteen.

She brought some sepia photographs of how Holly Lodge looked back then, with nostalgic pictures of the village, which were fascinating. And of course she would have met our resident ghost, when she was very much alive, and well.

Maggie had not been back since the 1940s. But on her nostalgic return to the Lodge, she could not wait to drag us to the old flint wall of the tumbledown in the rear garden. Apparently some old copper coins were discreetly embedded in a nook – nestling between two flint cobbles. Amazingly, as she foretold the little stash was still there; after all these years unbeknown to us, and previous owners.

However more remarkably, this is the tale of how she had met her future husband in the orchard during an apple scrumping fest one afternoon. Their eyes simply locked under the bunting-bedecked trees, and it was love at first sight. They spent a memorable day at the Lodge, and even threw a copper coin between them in the old well for good luck! Maggie had made such an impression on her new beau, Sam, that he hid another two coppers at the time (King George V: 1912 & 1915) in the wall of the ruin. A sentimental gesture just after she departed to take her train back to London.

Sam worked the land as a jobber for local farmers, but spent his precious spare time studying the complex world of banking. He lived in a nearby village, and they wrote to each other over the next two years. Finally though, he did go to London, and initially got a job as a bank clerk, they married, and he eventually became a city high-flyer. Sadly he died last year. However he mentioned prior to his death, details of the whereabouts of the two coppers he'd secretly left embedded in the wall in a superstitious hope it would one day symbolise their union. Of course it worked, and the rest was history.

Naturally I offered the coins to Maggie as a keepsake, but she insisted on them being left be, as a kind of memorial to him. Mike and I were in buckets as she recounted her story; I'd never heard of anything more romantic... And it happened at the Lodge, which was so very enchanting.

Maggie is a darn special lady, one of the best, and we were besotted by her warm yet vulnerable persona. Fifty-seven years of married bliss to the love of your life must be extremely hard to forfeit... I just wanted to hug her forever; she had that effect on me!

The following Christmas a plain brown paper parcel tied with coarse twine arrived. But... oh inside was the most beautiful crimson cushion, with which she had embroidered with fine gold thread – letters scripting: '*Holly Lodge*'. A treasured thoughtful gift, and often much commented upon... Dear old Maggie!

Christmas was teaming at the Lodge; our second Yuletide in Norfolk had arrived, after a roller-coaster year of disastrous lows, and astounding highs. We decided to shut our doors on Christmas Eve, and nest quietly at home.

I could smell the delicious aroma of Mike's most wicked roast lunch wafting through to the lounge, the comforting fire crackled in the Inglenook as the BBC morning service of Christmas carols filled the room.

Barnaby curiously prodded his goodie-filled stocking beneath the Christmas tree. He tore away to open the mesh with his paws as he inquisitively made his selection, choosing the nice chewy hide bone. He picked the prize up in his mouth, and proudly cantered over to his basket by the fire, enthused with his find, and wagging his tail profusely. I climbed off the sofa, and sat by him, his shiny intense eyes looked lovingly at me as I stroked his dear head.

I look around at our festive warm home and thought if only it could always be as peaceful as today.

Mike cried out, "Lunch is ready," Barnaby's ears pricked up in eagerness of his bowl of titbits...

And we were finally home alone at Holly Lodge that perfect Christmas Day...

The Claret Cottage Suite

An ensuite bathroom at Holly Lodge.
photo Courtesy of Tonyhalleyepix.com

The kitchen where we produced those award winning breakfasts.

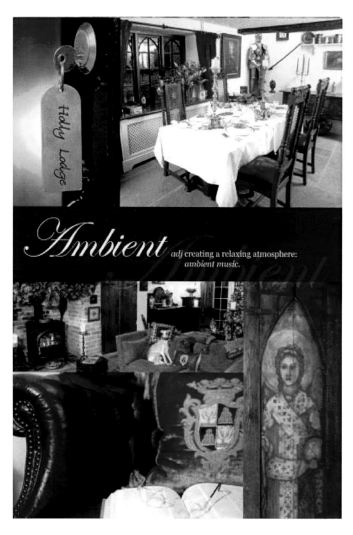

From our brochure: living room and
dining room

The Oak Room as featured In *Country Homes and Interiors*
Magazine
Picture courtesy of *Tony Hall,* <u>tonyhalleyepix.com</u>

A feature in *Now* Magazine: Spying Seals in Norfolk.

Pictures from left to right: Standing by my VW campervan - Sheringham Station (The Poppyline); First Christmas with Barnaby-Boo, Mike, me and Barnaby by the sunken terrace; Stunning Stepmother, Violet In her mid-70s.

CHAPTER 11

THE LADDER OF SUCCESS

Insomnia has always been the bane of my life, especially with a major project on the go. Mind you, it didn't do ole Maggie Thatcher much harm – they say she existed on four hours a night. No wonder she was known as the Iron Lady. Poor dear… I tell you, I can go round the houses for hours in my mind's eye working a virtual tour of a creative vision.

More often than not Mike would be in one of his deep slumbers (comas), that guy could sleep through a nuclear warhead exploding! For example on one of our first trips away together we found ourselves a peaceful spot on the Red Sea in Israel. Or so we thought…

One morning I awoke suddenly to the horrific vibration of the entire hotel shaking, the bed swaying back and forth, the French doors rattling violently, and a terrifying rumbling sensation like an underground train coming through and followed by a tremendous jolt. Initially I thought we were under missile attack. But no, it was a frigging earthquake!! (Nearly six on the Richter scale.) Mike slept through the entire ordeal completely oblivious to the scary episode. And only believed me the next morning around eight, because as we were leaving the room there was a tremendous rumble rendering us both weak-kneed with terror. He is the deepest, soundest sleeper ever – the lucky chap! Thankfully we survived to tell the tale.

It's no use; I jumped out of bed with my mind buzzing into the early hours on that freezing January night. The house nestled in white winter solitude evocative of a Canadian wilderness lit by a bright full moon. No howling wolves though, just my little Barnaby curled up at the foot of my desk.

Full of inspiration I broached my design draft for the guest lounge extension. My Orangery would be based upon the colonialism of *Raffles* hotel in Singapore, as my mind harked back to my travels there, whilst working in Hong Kong: tea on the atmospheric veranda (a most civilised affair) an echo of the grand hotel's imperial past. That's it!

Although my concept would be more of an eclectic mix: an exotic combo of empiric eastern and western nostalgia meets vintage travel vibe meshed harmoniously inside the shell of a neo-Gothic inspired structure.

Viewed from the southerly aspect, the main gabled pediment would be topped with a proud glinting finial at its apex, and mounted on four classical Doric-style pilasters. A deep wide lounge bay would be created in harmony as viewed on the perpendicular. The hardwood structure should blend effortlessly – sympathetically painted in my lichen colour to match all the exterior woodwork of the house. Tall slim Gothic framed windows serried in pairs throughout would enhance the generic character. I sketched feverishly...

Reclaimed Norfolk pamments are as good as old and would be used as flooring surfaces throughout – extending onto the surrounding terrace too. A hand-made ceramic tile with an ancient patina made from regional clays ranging from terracotta, reds, through to pinks, buffs and white shades: very apt of the Norfolk vernacular.

Mike and I chanced across a warehouse full of interesting artefacts outside Holt run by local entrepreneur, who sourced many of his wares from the Far East. Here we found a fantastic suite of original 1920s' teak and wicker furniture that looked exactly like it had been teleported from the very veranda of Raffles Hotel. The set became the mainstay for the interior scheme.

Four bronze pavilion lights with glass-moulded flame-shades accented the look perfectly; these wall sconces were fitted to the interior pilasters. An old iron and glass table languishing in our barn was brought back to life as a walk-around centrepiece (housing a huge glass urn to be filled with candles or flowers as suits). Our prized Georgian lithographs (eight in all) featuring historic country houses including Althorp, were hung on the lichen painted tongue and groove panelling that now clad the back wall of the new garden room. Finally to complete the Orangery effect an abundance of exotic plants were placed in situ creating a dramatic lush ambiance. And think gnarled vine-creepers clamouring up the inside frames for a Georgian-plantation-house feel.

I found a local specialist company to carry out my plan, and the owners were very *simpatico* to my design.

The new Orangery became a triumph! It was completed in October, and without doubt became the icing on the cake at Holly Lodge. Well a triumph eventually... Sadly you will see what transpires later...

Now my attention turned to the rear garden. So, armed with my inspiration from that amazing coastal garden we had visited at the Old Vicarage in East Ruston, and a wonderfully inspiring book, *Designing with Plants* by Piet Oudolf: an innovative Dutch garden designer specialising in prairie grasses *de rigueur*. I set about to landscape design our acre back plot with immense fervour. This refreshing naturalistic planting, that I had in mind, would blend effortlessly with the wild surroundings of a Norfolk landscape.

Fortunately I have a well-versed self-taught knowledge of plants through a keen interest over the years, and nurtured by many exciting projects. Hence I was able to put my plans here to maximum effect.

Without getting too horticultural, basically we created a walkabout circuit, starting at a new Mediterranean sunken terrace surrounding the Orangery replete with clipped topiaries, olive trees, and hot coloured potted plants en masse. The guests could access the garden through a (charming) Gothic-arched studded oak door incorporated into a lofty privet hedge. The hedge was then clipped into a dramatic *wave* design echoing the back of the Loch Ness monster – it looked eerily majestic (think *Eddie*

Scissorhands). And it acted as a natural curtilage between the main house and guest cottages.

The objective being that once through the ancient door, a vista would be created – opening onto a secret magical garden, taking our visitors on a meandering journey through a rousing élan of merging themed-garden zones.

Their journey began... proudly flanked by two huge fantastical gargoyle dogs, aged by years of weathered patina. Meandering paths would wind via vast kidney shaped beds filled with all manner of feathery and plumed billowy grasses, some with long golden awns. These were interspersed with swathes of the tallest flowering perennials creating ebullient textural drifts (mesmeric in sunlight). One path would lead along a verdant shrubbery to a tranquil enclave overlooking a field, where Hayley and Pea lived (two statuesque horses), while the other continued on out of the prairie garden...

And past the tumbledown overgrown with red poppies: very emblematic of Clement Scott's *Poppyland* (Norfolk). Here the visitor would pass along a desert garden reminiscent of a dry riverbed filled with mega-huge boulders – that strained our backs for days manoeuvring into place. Drought loving plants including spiky Agaves (Aloe-Vera) punctuated these gravel paths.

Here the route forked: either straight on, or sidetracking left onto a merging path into a lush tropical zone filled with dramatic architectural plants: hardy Fan Palms, Cabbage Palms, Tree Ferns, magnificent Phormiums (New Zealand flax) – a respite to while-away lazy afternoons in a sleepy hammock.

Alternately, not straying from the main path to ultimately arrive at the pièce de resistance – a stunning wildlife pond, surrounded by a sweeping decked area, and a jetty that appeared to float stretching way out onto the water.

These expansive water-gardens were planted with many native species: Norfolk Reeds, Bulrushes, Water Irises, Marsh Marigolds, Bog Beans, and my favourite Pickerel Weed (*Pontederia cordate*), with its shiny translucent foliage, and rampant purple flowers. Prolific Water Lilies suffused the surface echoing a Monet. A wayward stream cascaded into a gentle waterfall sending ripples through the glimmering surface that reflected the great Norfolk skies. And a bubbling boulder set in the marginal shallows at the opposite shore end would gently soothe the senses with its rhythmic flow.

Retro steamer-chairs serried on the deck beckoned the visitor to rest amidst this glorious profusion of waterside nature.

Barnaby, the sun-worshipper (like his perma-tanned Dads), often lounged here his favourite spot – that is in between shelling the zillions of hazelnuts abound on the deck. He would amuse our guests with his party trick, and his discerning palette, by spitting out the discarded shell of the nut before chewing his trophy.

The pond quickly morphed into a very naturalistic wildlife water-garden with a boggy lagoon created along the water's edge aside the jetty. And where a Gunnera grew to humongous stately proportions, under which Barnaby once satiated with the afternoon sun would shelter – appearing Lilliputian.

The guests would delight with how it became a magnet for wildlife… sprightly black and white pied wagtails would swoop in skimming the water, and wag their long fluttering tails as they do, the odd enigmatic kingfisher would take a star turn caught in a fleeting glimpse; ducks and moorhens would make their way to our oasis, and become part of our wetland habitat, and extended family too… Daphne, Brittany, Imelda, Zachary, Osborne, and a matronly moorhen with a flame coloured beak that we called Winnie – were just some of the regulars at our waterside bar.

Then there was Maximillion, the awesome white barn owl swooping in at dusk to finally land on an old post to gauge dining possibilities…

Sometimes the dreaded heron would stalk our precious fish through the long reeds in the shallows. Great crested newts, very rare, and sadly now in decline inhabited the pond – some could be a whopping six and a half inches long, and looked very exotic. And there were masses of frogs too – very effective in protecting my collection of Hostas – averting lace-curtain syndrome from the marauding snails. But most of all, my indelible memory is of a typical late summer's afternoon when the metallic turquoise dragonflies and damselflies would entrance with their impossible aerial displays; balletically dancing over the water lilies like ethereal fluttering fairies shimmering in a myriad of rainbow reflections... *Fantasia* had come to the Lodge.

Our gardens became a great hit – no doubt adding to the pulling-power of the total package, and really only took very few years to flourish. And oh, how they flourished...

Our guests really thought we fed our plants on a diet of anabolic steroids. Everything just grew and grew to gargantuan proportions in no time. Most were dismayed how recent it really was, as the ambiance created felt centuries old.

Eventually we were cajoled to have open-garden days, which were very satisfying for all the right reasons.

With a little bit of wisdom, trickery, the blessing of fertile soil, and tons of hard labour vigorously contouring, digging, raking and turning the soil, we managed to get it all planted in one fell swoop that spring.

However, as with all labours of love, there are growing pains (no pun intended). Initially, the entire plot resembled a garden nursery with row-upon-row of baby plants. It did look pitiful in its infancy... And then there was the problem of the dreaded moles... Yikes! They would run rings around my plants digging them up continuously; leaving them high and dry. It was soul destroying! I'd constantly be firming the little plants back into their respective holes to stop them dying. Eventually I became so fed up with the pesky little varmints, that one afternoon picture this absurd scene... Barnaby ready to pounce and me lying in wait in premeditation armed with a shovel – poised ready to clobber the bugger... What a complete and utter dork!

When I recounted my deployment tactics to Richard, a local gamekeeper who helped us with the garden, he howled with laughter at my naïve city-boy antics!

The summer season was upon us... bookings were up compared to the previous summer season with all its calamities. And we were raring to go with the flow that year...

Outside on the forecourt, there was a tremendous commotion – a blue car was having trouble parking. The car jarred back and forth in jerking motions, and then it catapulted across the lawn hitting an apple tree... Blimey! The horn blared and I rushed over to see if anybody was hurt.

I clocked the disabled sticker on the windscreen, and out popped a head on a dwarf-like figure, it was the 'Darlings' arriving for their summer break.

"Don't worry! Erm... we are fine, sorry about the dent in the tree." His cute button-face beamed at me from under a cap. He apologised profusely, that parking was not one of his finer points.

"Hi there, I'm Martha..." said the squeaky little lady seated next to Walter Darling.

They both had the most infectious voices as if they just inhaled helium from one of those party balloons; I was tickled and wanted to crack up initially, but bottled-it thank goodness! Otherwise I might have been reported to the *Politically correct Police.*

I helped the couple disembark. They were no more than four and half feet tall... if that! And then their disabilities became even more apparent.

I did feel guilty though, what with first impressions... Although before me, barely able to stand were two of the most engaging fifty-something characters. Identically dressed in bright red *Adidas* tracksuits, matching *Ray-Bans*, Yankee baseball caps, brilliant white trainers that had never seen a muddy track ever, and enough jangly bling, that would out-sparkle the Crown Jewels. They looked like a pair of overgrown teenagers from the hood in Miami. A complete conundrum!

Of course due to their impaired movement, everything became a laborious affair, and after faffing-on for around an hour or so, they were finally installed in the Colonial Cottage.

We were debating whether to join the Tourist Board's 'National Accessibility Scheme', as we would occasionally get all sorts of disabled visitors. Fortunately the cottages were all single storeys, with wider than usual entrances allowing for wheelchair access, one even had a ramp in place. We had tried very discreetly to incorporate aids for such guests, and we were even considering Braille menus and Braille information literature for the visually impaired.

Of course there would be a tipping-point with all the necessary signage and appropriate paraphernalia needed that care should be taken, so Holly Lodge did not appear like a Nursing Home. By the by the twee name suited though, and was *one* thing that always bugged me. Why hadn't I changed the name of our establishment to something more palatably in-vogue as a marketing tool? But I guess we ran with it initially for some continuity of business, and then it just stuck... But hey, it didn't put off the trendy punters or hamper us being featured in the stylish glossies.

Nevertheless, we'd do everything within our power to make these guests have as comfortable and enjoyable stay with us as possible.

The Darlings booked breakfast for 9.00am the next morning. We offered them the alternative of room service, and any assistance if required, however they were fiercely proud, and totally independent, and chose to come into the dining hall without any help. Normally it would take a minute or so from the cottages to the main building...

But the next morning gone half past nine, I noticed them through the dining room window making their way at a snail's pace to the entrance. It took another thirty minutes before they finally got to the front hall; by the time we got them seated and propped up with about five cushions each at the table, it was gone ten thirty. Phew...

The Lodge was full and the atmosphere that morning was very convivial, what with the Darlings being pretty jovial characters full of witty repartee...

"Why do birds fly south in the winter?" Walter asked me.

"I don't know why do birds...?" I replied.

"Because it's too far to walk..." he declared with his cheeky grin.

"What on earth does one do at our age when one's rear drops south?" Martha asked Mike.

"I don't know, what on...?"

"Simple... you sell up, and move north!" she quipped with a chuckle.

And this is how it went throughout breakfast that morning, and every morning of their stay. They were natural born comics... Perhaps I should have become their agent and vied a spot for them on *Britain's Got Talent*.

The tour bus was hooting. Walter handed me his menu for their breakfast, ticked for their serving at nine the next morning. Um...?

I must confess, Mike and I hatched a devious little plan. And while doing their room turnaround, we sneakily put all the clocks forward by forty-five minutes in the hope they would make it on time for their next serving... I felt thoroughly ashamed after the event!

Consequently the next morning they were as punctual as the nightly News at Ten. The topical banter was well underway and we prepared breakfast.

However, the foxy Darlings full of derring-do had us rumbled as they sussed out our little game. Somehow with the help of perhaps another guest, Walter had changed the time on our dependable grandfather clock (our precious time barometer with its baritone chimes announcing to all and sundry 'Breakfast Is Now Served'). He'd cannily moved the hands forward by forty-odd minutes, throwing us into a state of confusion...

"Good grief... Sorry for the glitch this morning," I exclaimed to everybody.

In cahoots with the conspiracy they all responded with curt, wry smiles. Oops... And I have to admit we fell for it. True to form the atmosphere that memorable morning became more than side-splitting as Mike and I were deservedly stumped.

On departure Walter cocked his head around the door and declared, "By the way... that was a *Death R*ow breakfast to die for!"

Walter and Martha were truly adorable little darlings! An inspiration to us all...

One blazing afternoon that summer, while we were knee-deep in chores, I suddenly became aware that perhaps Barnaby might have gone missing. We'd always get sporadic glimpses of him around, but he was nowhere to be seen that day.

We searched high and low, over every nook and cranny. Five hours or more had passed, and still there was no sign of him! Mike trawled the village, while I scanned around the orchard and grounds. Horrible thoughts crept into my mind, as there had been a spate of kidnapped pets in the area recently, and reports had filtered through of large ransom bids.

"Don't even go there..." Mike suggested to me with an alarmed telling look.

Because in the unlikely event of this happening they may have known that we'd given anything to get him back...

Early evening was drawing in, by now we were beside ourselves... We'd been over our grounds and the village with a fine toothcomb; it was baffling... where he could be...?

I sat in my office with my head sunk low in my hands. I glanced over at the line of pencil marks on the doorframe; each notch lovingly made to gauge his growth month-by-month from a tiny puppy to adulthood. He was even my main screensaver image on my desktop computer.

By now my despair was turning to frustration. The light was fading fast, and I was on the brink of printing posters out – to nail up during a night search.

I peered out over the orchard; it was well after dusk. And suddenly I took a double take as I rubbed my eyes in disbelief. There, coming up the drive was the Museum caretaker, Peter with Barnaby in tow. Mike ran out to greet them and I could not get down the stairs quick enough.

Barnaby had been found in the kitchens of the Thursford Museum... Bless. No doubt on the hunt for some divine delicacy. Phew... what a relief! And we thanked Peter no end for bringing our hound safely home. Apparently he'd slipped out of the side-gate that might have been left ajar by one of our more *careless* guests.

This only ever happened on one other occasion. But believe you me – it was one more than I could bear... I must confess I'd become an overbearing, madly diligent, almost totally paranoid dog owner when it comes to my dog's safety.

In fact so much so that my friends got a T-shirt produced – printed for me with the slogan: '*Where's Barnaby-Boo*?' So if you ever see a shaven-headed, muscular swarthy chap wearing that T-shirt? You know it's me!

The highlight of that autumn was the arrival of a letter from the East of England Tourist Board to inform us that Holly Lodge had been selected as a finalist in the B&B/Guesthouse category in this year's 'Regional Awards for Excellence in England'. Yippee! Subsequently World Video came to film the Lodge for the footage to be screened at the ceremony, that year to be held at the Imperial War Museum in Duxford on the 9th October 2002.

Naturally, Mike and I were jubilant. I counted down the days to the ceremony. Finally the much-anticipated event arrived and we were buzzing with excitement. Barnaby had to be dropped off at Mother Teresa's. He was in an almighty huff all the way down to Newmarket. But in the excitement of it all, and with the combination of road diversions due to major works within the area we ended up horribly lost, and *unfashionably* late for the big day.

The ceremony itself was held in the main hall of the 'Officers' Mess' building at the Air Museum.

Eventually, we screeched to a halt in the car park, which was full to the brim. I raced around frantically looking for a space, and just managed to squeeze into a forgotten corner tucked down the side of the building.

The adrenalin kicked-in, and we made a sprint to the entrance in our Sunday best – storming the building like marauding paratroopers. The attendants hastily pressed our special pass badges onto our lapels, and we dashed down the long hall crashing through the doors of the auditorium – where the glossy parquet floor had been polished to within an inch of its life. Our heels noisily echoed: squeaking-clicking-clacking as we trod. Oops...

A sea of faces confronted us with disapproving glances of our late arrival no doubt. And to make matters worse a great kerfuffle ensued, as typically we were seated bang spanking right in the middle of a row – way down the front of the hall.

"Excuse me! Sorry! Thank you!" we muttered, as people were up and down yo-yo like to allow us through. I was totally embarrassed. I hate being late for anything!

And finally just as we got seated, I was astounded to see Holly Lodge flash up on the large screen. It was surreal! I heard some chaps behind gasp, and say, "They must be the winner..." That filled me with delusions of grandeur!

The camera panned over our establishment, and we were chuffed at how impressive it all looked. Subsequently the next contender came up on screen, and to be quite honest it just appeared dreary and old hat in comparison. My mind raced with a presumption that we'd conceitedly clinch the award if that were the only competition in our category.

Everything happened in a flash, because no sooner had we sat down – than suddenly we were summoned to the stage. They had announced the winner. But confusion reigned. And I think even the guest presenter Sandi Toksvig was not quite sure who'd won either.

Mike and I enthusiastically went to greet her at the podium, confidently thinking we'd won. But, hey what...? Another couple suddenly joined us up on the stage and swept past us. Sandi handed them the trophy. And we were handed the framed (*runner-up*) certificate, as Holly Lodge was *'Highly Commended Guesthouse of the Year'*. Oh dear. And I was utterly devastated!

Later at the awards dinner in the magnitude of this historic museum of aviation, the winners graciously came over to tell us how lovely Holly Lodge looked. Naturally we congratulated them on their great success, but I ashamedly deep down thought we'd been *robbed* of the title.

Please don't think me ungrateful B... It really was a tremendous achievement at the time in only our second year of trading, but truth be told... *'I WANTED TO FUCKING WIN...'* I whined like a spoilt Jewish princess at home after the awards. I can be incorrigible you know... a notion perhaps of allegedly being descended from a European countess on my father's side, but the less said about that the better!

Mind you... I'd never won anything before to speak of. But, as Mike so eloquently reminded me in my darkest hour of disappointment, that once I was voted the winner of 'Most Favourite Customer' by the till-ladies of a well-known supermarket in Muswell Hill winning a bouquet of flowers. And on offer I surmise, ensuing with a hugely embarrassing round of applause by hundreds of Saturday shoppers...

How camp is that...! So at least now... *"You should thank your lucky stars,"* he said comforting me with derision. And I hung my head in shame...

But nevertheless, I swore to myself we'd be back to win it next time for East Anglia and for our adopted new home of Norfolk...

Pictures from left to right: Mike with his brother Darren, and his fiancé Nicola on the terrace at Voewood; Afterwards at Voewood for our Civil Partnership luncheon party; At Cley Windmill for our Civil Partnership ceremony with close family and friends; Big bro Tony giving his epic speech (Adele his wife, left and stepmother Violet, right).

CHAPTER 12

SUCH SORROW

Avon calling, perhaps... The vivacious smile redolent of an official representative of some kind, just marched straight in out of the blue. Who was she?

It transpired, that our Lodge had been recommended to her most prestigious organisation by one of our guests. This time *totally* unbeknown to us we'd been inspected by one of their assessors... She cheerily informed us that our B&B had been approved for entry in no less than the much-coveted *Michelin Guide* (Red Book). We were completely bowled over by the amazing news. And another fine feather was added to our cap.

Ah, the sweet smell of success... The *AA* had just awarded Holly Lodge with 'Five Red Stars' elevating our establishment into the top ten percent in the country at this level. And *VisitBritain* had confirmed our gold, and five star status at their last rating. We were on an incredible roll...

The newly well-appointed (orangery) annexe guest lounge opened that Christmas season as the icing on the cake. And the guests seemed to relish the splendid new facility! Usually around teatime they had the option of complimentary drinks in the Orangery to meet the other in-house residents in what often turned out to be a social whirl of daily activity. We'd layout a sumptuous spread of festive fare for their bubbly welcome.

Uh-oh, of course it was all just too good to be true... Because unbeknown to us, the landscaping team had created a serious fundamental *flaw* within the engineering of the drainage system from the new sunken terrace surrounding the annexe. Unfortunately this played out with a vengeance one dreadful morning in December during a horrendous spell of torrential downpours...

The old proven tried and tested drainage conduit normally would extract all the excess water that accumulated onto the sunken terrace from the farm fields beyond. Subsequently, the water would drain away into the gulley drains onto the front boundary by the road. Sadly, this pipe had now been blocked off, to be replaced by two soakaways, recently excavated as the replacement new overflow system – to alleviate any excess water. However, their inadequacy became alarmingly apparent due to adverse weather conditions – much to our horror that fateful morning...

Our brand new Orangery suddenly morphed into the ill-fated liner, the RMS *Titanic* on her maiden voyage. The entire terrace was flooding at an alarming rate; pots and debris floated around chaotically, and we were just about to serve breakfast. Mayday! Mayday!

There was so little time to think. Instinctively we removed all the furniture, and anything that was in contact with the pamment floor, and stored it all in the barn.

The guests were ushered through the front entrance into the dining hall; we locked off the side entrance, by bolting the Gothic door in the hedge, which would have been the alternative back-access route through the guest lounge. Breakfast got underway. Our guests were completely oblivious to our plight. And we both *prayed* for dear mercy...

In the meantime I called out the boss of the landscaping team in an emergency 999 call!

Mike and I were really concerned that this potential disaster could destroy our lucrative all-important Christmas season, which had only just kicked off. The repercussions did not bear thinking about.

Breakfast was now in full swing. The skies were as black as night with the heavy pounding rain relentless that morning. And torrents of water were gushing from the roof gutters too – hammering onto the flooding terrace – just to make matters worse. I kept monitoring the situation by the minute, and then I noticed to my absolute terror, water leak through the base frame of the French doors into the Orangery.

Uh-oh. *Groundhog Day* is here again. Panic stations…!

How does one pretend everything is fine when one's house is about to be flooded?

Well, stoicism… We just got on with it that morning. Our guests were none the wiser. Mine hosts were mine hosts as per usual.

That is until… I spotted several inches of water now accumulating in the Orangery and precariously lapping onto the doorstep to the lounge of the main house. F…!

I dashed into the lounge with piles of towels and old cushions, to curtail the water. I vigorously swept puddles back into the garden room, and then I raced back to the entrance of the dining room. And just managed to get a grip in time to compose myself, take a deep breath, and then entered…

The dulcet tones of Chopin emanated serenely as our bons vivants were tucking in to their gastronomical delights – as if all was normal. But, of course in the utter urgency, we were quaking in our boots… with the ship about to go down at any moment if help did not arrive soon!

We kept checking the time, and monitored the level of the water rising by the minute. Now it was getting really desperate…

"How much longer?" Mike said anxiously.

"It's got to be anytime now, an hour or more has passed, and the engineer promised they'd be here within forty-five minutes."

By now water was seeping through my makeshift sandbags, edging its way perilously nearer the lounge floor. The heavens were relentless. A feeling of totally helplessness engulfed us…

Sadly just then, faced with no alternative, we felt it best to terminate breakfast. I came out of the kitchen to announce…

"Ladies and Gentlemen, I am very s…"

Suddenly at the corner of my eye, I glimpsed two vans and a car roll up the drive. It was like the US Cavalry had arrived... I held my announcement mid-sentence. Mike ran out at breakneck speed to meet them, as the guests looked on inquisitively, obviously wondering what the hell was going-on... But I just shrugged it off with a brave face front of house, immediately changed tact with a reassuring smile.

"How about a spot of Sinatra?" I suggested to their quizzical faces. '*Bewitched, Bothered and Bewildered*' – words to that effect as Frank sang most aptly – while all hell broke loose outside...

Mike directed the crew around to the back. They hurriedly set their water-pumps to action on the terrace. Just in the nick of time... the moment the water started to flow rampantly over the floor of the main lounge.

Holy Smoses! Thank the dear Lord, the pumps did their job and moments later the floodwaters gradually subsided, with another disaster narrowly averted with only seconds to go... and we high-fived with great relief. Phew!

The company boss deigned with an obliging apology and naturally agreed to bear the brunt of any costs due to their *amazing* technical blunder.

Basically we were left with two possible solutions: (haven't we been there before?). Either a noisy pump could be fitted near the terrace to control the excess water in future, or the entire drive of around 200 yards or so, would have to be dug up to increase the gradient of an overflow out-pipe from the new deeper terrace... Shock horror!

However, I really did not want the expense, and inconvenience of a permanent *noisy* water pump, so I chose the latter option, because, in the long run it was more practical – although we'd be faced with a major upheaval yet again. Thus we decided to broach the works at the top of January 2003 (during low season).

The Christmas season had been saved, albeit without our beloved Orangery – rendered out of action, while it dried out. And our doors were finally shut to the public on Christmas Eve for a well-earned rest. The year had been long and hard, and quite frankly we were both utterly exhausted, and needed some downtime. So we battened down the hatches to nest quietly from the world. And even excused ourselves from spending Christmas with Mike's mum up north that year.

It's all very poignant now. But I had a cheery chat with Norma on Christmas Day during the festive celebrations over at her sister's, Helena. I clearly remember us berating ourselves for not being up in Yorkshire with the family. Then on Boxing Day, we had a very disturbing call from Mike's brother, Darren, to tell us that his mother had collapsed, been rushed to hospital, and was now in a deep coma. Mike immediately caught the next train home, while I held fort for the next couple of weeks until the drainage issues were sorted. I then joined him in Yorkshire. Fortunately by now Norma had come round, although still in intensive care, and wired up to all sorts of ominous machines.

Mike look shattered, he had kept vigil at all hours, and I discovered that the prognosis was not good. Apparently the doctors had advised the family to switch off the life-support equipment. Both brothers declined in the hope their brave mother would pull through. And there were days when she certainly seemed to be making good progress. So the vigil continued and I returned to the Lodge to continue my duties.

Sad, lonely weeks followed during that bleak winter. The house became a silent vacuum, save the reassuring company of Barnaby, cuddling into me at every opportunity, and seemingly to intuit that we were having the worst crisis possible, I laid low during that harrowing period. The only person I ever wanted to talk to was Mike. And I prayed long and hard for his mother's recovery, because she too had now become such an integral part of my life, a confidant and dear friend. After all, I could converse with Norma like no other person; especially on family matters.

I would lie awake in the still of the night – thinking endlessly, listening to the house settle and groan. The owls hooted, the wind rustled through the trees, and the birds tiptoed over the pantiles, whilst I was lost wistfully in my thoughts.

This highly emotional situation was evocative of my own trauma of losing my mother; questions still unanswered: Why had she deserted me when I was still so young? What really happened? Was it suicide? Why had I been left at the mercy of an abusive stepmother? For whom after all this time I still harboured hostile feelings somewhere deep in my psyche.

And what of my father...? If only he had rescued me from her sinister clutches and not been blinded by her guile; resulting in years of a deep malaise festering through the veins of my family. Morbid thoughts plagued my conscience night after night during this emotive time and started to bring me down. However I had to be strong for Mike – he was going through the mill. And I could not afford to become a manic-depressive again with these negative messages, so I pressed the *delete* button and *refresh* mode for Mike's sake.

Then on Valentine's Day as I was slavishly doing my chores around the Lodge, there was a sudden knock on the door as Barnaby galloped excitedly down the stairs. I opened up, and Mike stood there before me, with his radiant smile albeit shining through hollowed sleepless eyes. At that moment it felt like the best present ever! I was so astonished to see him – it seemed ages, because it was just not expected forgiven the dire circumstances. Apparently his mum had stabilised, and he needed a break, and what with the spring opening nearly upon us, the chores would be a welcome distraction for him. I did feel selfish for wanting him home with me. But the impact of his decision to leave his mother's bedside would sadly haunt him for years to come.

Some more weeks passed and we were in constant touch with the family up north. But it all came to a head one desperate evening...

We had decided to hold an overdue dinner party to reciprocate the tremendous generosity of our supportive neighbours. Everything went swimmingly – although we both felt uncomfortable entertaining, as our thoughts were obviously with Mike's mum.

And then, it's as clear as yesterday... I was about to serve desserts, when the phone rang. It was Mike's brother, Darren.

"Come now... it's close, mum is..." his voice faltered in utter desperation.

I looked at over at Mike and my heart sank.

The dinner party was immediately terminated. We packed our bags at breakneck speed, practically threw Barnaby in the back of the VW, and drove through the night up to Yorkshire.

It's always a hell of a drive, and in a very foggy Lincolnshire the motorway police stopped us. Uh-Oh... I thought I was going to get done for speeding. But he reprimanded me for failing to have my fog lamps on. And allowed us to move swiftly on.

Finally, we anxiously arrived at the hospital in the early hours. Family members were gathered, and a priest had just visited, I think to read last rites! It was very traumatic, and extremely distressing that night...

Mike stayed until dawn, I brought Darren home to have some kip, and got Barnaby settled. Darren had been with his mum constantly, day after day. Totally devoted. And then cruelly just in the way it had happened to me, when my father passed, and on the rare occasion that I was not at his bedside: Norma passed away that very afternoon – just as her much-beloved Salvation Army were playing past the hospital. Perhaps the Higher Power has particular reasons?

Shock does weird things to people... No doubt and through the devastation of their loss the grief stricken brothers needed me more than ever. Somehow I went into overdrive and took charge to do the best I could to make sure their mother would have the type of funeral the family wanted. A very intense week ensued. In fact a week like no other: making all the necessary arrangements, trips to the funeral parlour – working through all the necessary documentation – and the flowers of course.

The funeral was to be the following Friday. The turnout was tremendous with hundreds in attendance from far and wide, going to show what a *special* lady Norma really was.

She had always been an ardent fan of Elvis, so the boys chose one of her favourites *Love Me Tender*, the rawness of the version played – touched everybody. It was a very fitting send off at the Crematorium, and there was not a dry eye in the church.

We arrived back in Norfolk with heavy hearts. Mike was inconsolable, and just sobbed, and sobbed for months on end. It was heartbreaking. I knew that once Mike had joined this exclusive club bereft of a significant parent, he would never be the same ever-ever-*ever* again...

A timely poignant reminder was ever-present back at the Lodge though. Mother's Day was just around the corner and the daffodils we had planted in our first year were now amassing in abundance. Yellow heads nodded vibrantly in swathes throughout the orchard. You see the *daffodil* was Norma's favourite flower... No matter wherever we are, whenever we see a daffodil, she will always be in our thoughts.

That sad spring, we threw open our doors and lost ourselves in the daily grind. Busyness, a much-needed tonic became a very welcome distraction. Mike was understandably fragile, but I was always there for him.

One such distraction shortly after we opened manifested itself one bright afternoon – a seriously snazzy red *Ferrari* zoomed into the car park at the Lodge. Out-stepped a glamorous sun-kissed couple. A new age sporty perfectly tanned Metro-sexual male with his bottle-blonde hottie in tow, your typical Essex gal, and I should know because I am an Essex boy. And, "No, I am not wearing the trademark white stilettos – if that's what you are thinking..."

Let's call her Tiffany, a name that suited her to a tee. She had made the reservation, with a particular request for the Claret Cottage. And for its fridge to be copiously filled with bottles of vintage *Laurent-Perrier* champagne for their arrival and more to be chilled on tap as required.

She had also expressly asked for large fresh strawberries, smoked salmon sandwiches, and oh... a huge bowl of the chap's favourite sweets – Smarties! We will call him Cole to protect his identity too, which suits his slick, vacuous, handsome hunky persona...

Cole and Tiffany were obviously used to the finest. And dinner was booked at the upmarket Morston Hall's acclaimed restaurant bursting with Red Rosette awards, and sporting a *Michelin* Star.

Cole was very familiar, although I could not place him. And the weird thing was, that throughout breakfast each day, he never removed his *Prada* shades once, as if he was shying away from something. While, on the other hand... Tiffany was the belle of the ball, brash, with that look-at-me constant hair flicking. Though only twenty-eight, she was botoxed to within an inch of sanity, flirting outrageously – fluttering her spidery lashes over her baby-blues, and pouting her enhanced plumped-up lips. Everything about her was carefully considered in her role as the adorning totty: her perfect pearly-white nails (perhaps, courtesy of Beverly Hills beauty salon of Chigwell?) her plunging V-neck sweater bursting with a *Jordan*-esque cleavage, and hipster-skinny jeans practically sprayed on to that svelte figure. And naturally her wrist was bedecked with a prerequisite blingy (eye-popping) designer watch as part of her dedicated uniform – to prove she was most successful in her field as the *Immaculate Deception* of the perfect WAG...

These epicureans knew how to have a good time, and drunk our cellars dry, so to speak. I don't think in my entire time at the Lodge had anybody requested so much room service after all it was supposed to be a Bed & Breakfast. They just reeked of heady musky sex to be quite honest! And who am I to complain about libido – as long as they paid the bill?

On departure, Cole flashed his laser white teeth, and insisted on cash... he brought out a wad of fifties to settle up, and requested for Tiffany's credit card to be refunded for the deposit. Mwah-mwah. They breezed out. And I was left with the lingering scent of an intoxicating perfume in the front hall.

Suddenly, Mike called me over to their room to take a look. This gets better. Imagine what we found after they boarded his fiery-red-*Learjet* on Thunderbird wheels...

I opened the door. And just stood dumfounded...

A trove of expensive clothing and accessories had been left casually lying about. Naturally, we thought that they must have forgotten to pack the stuff, but how...? Astonishingly there were: four *Turnbull & Asser* gorgeous bespoke shirts from H.R.H. Prince of Wales shirt-makers in Jermyn Street, London, three *Dolce & Gabbana* silk ties, an exquisite *Missoni* scarf, four unopened boxes of sexy *Calvin Klein* underwear, a brand new bottle of *Paul Smith* eau de cologne, *Giorgio Armani* perfume, some gift-wrapped *Marc Jacobs* beauty potions, two *Yves St Laurent* belts, *Fendi* sunglasses. Inhale... and a hardly-used luxury-bumper *Harrods* food hamper of every gastronomic indulgence imaginable: Including *Beluga* caviar!

How could anybody overlook such valuable items? Ridiculous! I called Tiffany on her mobile, and this was her surprising response...

"Babe, h'iya! Your 'otel is rockin' innit? Listen hun, sorry 'bout the mess." She drew a deep breath... "Don't worry, keep 'em all on us! Nah problemo! Luvya. Luvya, Ciao. Ciao..." rang her diminuendo in my ears! Huh...? I was gobsmacked!

Mind you, such eye-popping guilty retail pleasures on offer could be construed as an unexpected perk. And oh, they left the most excessively crumpled sheets I'd ever seen. Hmmmm!

These happy punters not only knew how to have a good time, but also had more money than sense. We figured there must have been at least two-three grand's worth of belongings left behind.

However, I am not finished there... A couple of weeks later, I walked into the lounge, and just caught a feature on the late news – immediately recognising the good-looking sporty chap on the screen. He was being interviewed with his wife and kiddies. But, and a very big BUT... The woman, his wife on the TV was most certainly not the *gal* he romantically liaised with at the Lodge. What...? Of course I have to keep *schtum* as to his identity? And my lips are sealed...

Although I decided to pull this thought from the cutting-room floor as a final footnote: *In hindsight, maybe all the luxury items left behind were indeed an indirect bribery after all...?* I beg the question to this day...

That brings me to another downside of the business. What guests get up to in the privacy of their rooms is one thing, but sometimes what they leave behind as unequivocal evidence is another...

I tell you some items found were bewildering, and others damn right naughty: all manner of sex toys, handcuffs and once, we even found a rubber gas mask, whip and spiky gauntlets under the bed, I wonder what that was all about... Um? Then there were the more mundane items: the odd shoe, socks, books, scarves, mobile phone chargers, and electric toothbrushes etc, which we would have to wrap up, and forward on, making an extra trip to the post office. One time we even found some false teeth... Yuk! How on earth could someone forget them? We always thought if all else fails, we'd open a curiosity Gift Shop for (Lost and Found) items from hotel rooms!

One of the funniest and most bizarre situations we ever experienced at the Lodge, happened that year, and most certainly put a much needed smile back on our *mourning* faces.

A couple had booked into the Colonial Cottage. On arrival they requested... "No housekeeping would be required for the duration of their stay," which was very unusual, because it was standard practice. Anyway they'd gone out for the day, and a bulb blew in the neighbouring Country Cottage, which had tripped a switch to the communal circuit board located in a hidden cupboard in the Colonial. An issue we did need to address that sometimes affected all three cottages.

Mike naturally knocked before entering, and surprisingly a trill voice replied...

"Gooo...d morning. Gooo...d morning!!"

Mike asked if he could enter and explained why he needed access. Again came the reply...

"Gooo...d morning. Gooo...d morning!!"

Almost as if it were a tape recording...

So, he knocked again, and gently turned the key in the door. And this time cautiously poked his head round.

Suddenly as he leant around the side of the door, a voice shouted...

"Fuck off! Fuck off!"

And he was astounded. Shutting the door immediately.

He came to fetch me, as obviously something was untoward.

We knocked again, and again, and heard a repetitive trill response of...

"Gooo...d morning. Gooo...d morning!!"

So we entered gingerly, and then to our surprise heard more offensive expletives. "Fuck off! Fuck off!"

We were peeved with the abrasive reply, but went straight in, regardless. We glanced about the dark room, as the shutters were still closed. Strangely it appeared nobody was there. And I flicked the light on.

"Hey, what this?" I exclaimed. I could not believe my eyes.

"Arrgh! It's a blinking parrot..." Mike looked completely bewildered by the discovery.

I pulled the cage out from the corner beside the wardrobe, and was utterly amazed to see the exotic bird eyeing me suspiciously from its perch.

"Anyone for fucking tennis!" it squeaked and shrilled, ruffling its feathers. And then guffawed.

Initially, we cried with laughter at the surprising find, and fawned hopelessly over the sight of the colourful bird of paradise.

"Perhaps they booked the Colonial to make it feel more at home..." I cried.

However they had broken our house policy rules as pets were only permitted at our discretion. Of course they would have to be reprimanded.

I went to see the couple on their return later that morning. They explained that they had been let down at the last minute by a neighbour, whom usually cared for 'Giles', as he was called, when they went away. So they thought on this occasion faced with no choice they'd smuggle him in.

"What's with the profanities?" Pray tell us.

"Well, he gets crotchety with strangers... and yes, he has picked up some rather nasty habits – probably from an unruly half-boarded-up council estate – that he was rescued from. Sorry!"

Anyway the deed was done with no harm caused. Giles the pretty-boy parrot seemed happy enough, and was such an adorable little fella to have around the Lodge that week! And oh, he really swore like 'Nan' from the *Catherine Tate show* and then some...

We would have many strange encounters with the most unusual visitors, but for me one of the strangest encounters was one of the Third-Kind that summer...!

If my memory serves, it was sometime around ten, after Mike had crashed out. And I was shutting down the Lodge for the night. I had been calling out for Barnaby – he had been let out to do his business. Usually, he would come cantering back after a few minutes, but I guessed he might be off investigating some creature or other out in the Prairie garden. It was a particularly dark Norfolk night with only a soft crescent moon obscured by a hazy cloud. I traced the beam of my torch in search of him... and moments later, found myself up by the water gardens.

Intuitively I looked up over the farm fields beyond. I gasped. There and behold in the sky was a translucent sphere hanging statically motionless perhaps between fifty to hundred feet over the neighbouring field. There was no sound, but a corona radiating from its outer edge with maybe thirty beamed lights emanating into the night sky.

I stood there mesmerised for several minutes, trying to reason what was in my line of view. I ruled out lasers, holograms, low flying aircraft, or hot-air balloons, and even some kind of weather phenomenon. There was just simply no logical explanation.

Unsuspectingly, I heard a rustling nearby. I won't mention to you what I thought for a beam-me-up-Scotty moment, but you can well imagine what was going through my fertile mind... I shivered.

Suddenly, out bolted Barnaby from the shrubs tearing towards me at lightning speed. And I nearly jumped out of my frigging skin...

The UFO was there for a quite a while. I pondered, lingering a few more minutes trying to figure out what this silent rarefied apparition was in the night sky practically above Holly Lodge. Until I decided to go and wake Mike, but by the time I got back to the bedroom, he was in such a deep peaceful sleep I let him be, and that was that.

The next morning, I recounted the experience, and he laughed incredulously, until at breakfast when some guests commented they had seen the UFO too, which backed up my sighting. East Anglia is notorious for frequent sightings of many inexplicable objects in the skies, and it just so happened around that time there were news reports of UFOs in the region.

Another page turns on life at the Lodge, bringing with it a new passage of daily activities for me to record in my diaries. Marked that autumn with the symbolic planting of a special tree in memory of Mike's mum. The *Robinia pseudoacacia Frisia* with its ebullient lime-green foliage like the one in the middle of our 'Courtyard' in Muswell Hill, which she so loved... It was planted within view from the Orangery. We would watch this tree grow and flourish each and every year, and were always comforted by the knowledge of her spirit watching over us.

CHAPTER 13

REUNION

Enjoying rare mornings off, almost became a special occasion at the Lodge, whereby I mean if we were closed, we were well and truly closed for some much needed rest. However on that particular morning events took a surprising turn that hey, I just would never have expected...

Mike was having a comatose lie in. I'd been up since seven, taken pooch out for his constitutional, and was ready for some precious me-time...

Uh-oh! There was a loud knock at the front door. It was around eight o'clock. Damn!

The knocking persisted accompanied by ominous yells. And then I heard footsteps sneak around to the back of the house. Cheekily, some persistent visitors had opened the side-gate to let themselves in.

Crikey... This must be a matter of life and death for these accommodation seekers, or perhaps they might be opportunists casing the joint...?

I crept downstairs and scuttled past the windows hoping no one would clock me. Pathetic...

And then as I crept out of my recess, and leant around into the open doorway of the kitchen. I flinched.

Well, well... Who do have we here...? Suddenly our eyes locked in bewilderment.

A slovenly elderly couple were gazing intensely at me through the kitchen window. Of course they'd sussed that we were in. I'd even heard them discussing the escaping water down the rear pipe from my bath. How invasive is that!

Then they peered closer – pressing their noses onto the windowpane.

I lip-synced, "WE-ARE-CLOSED..." But the shifty couple just leered at me. So I gestured – pointing to the front door. I had a disconcerted feeling about our pushy visitors.

They must have been in their early seventies at least: He was unkempt, dressed in a tatty grey-marl hooded sweatshirt, with a florid pitted complexion and straggly grey hair, and his wife, I guess was purporting to be Gypsy Rose Lee, but a rather shabbier portrayal with a grimy yellow hooded top over a folksy dirndl skirt.

"We're closed, it's our holiday break," I announced.

"Well, 'ow the 'ell are we supposed to know..." he retorted in a laconic Irish brogue (there was no closed sign displayed). And he stood there disgruntled, scratching his top feverishly, as if he had nits.

I apologised, and at the same time rebuked myself for forgetting to change over the sign. However, I politely directed them to another guesthouse in the village that might have rooms available.

The bedraggled fellow stood there tugging at his gold hoop earring nervously, and seemed agitated. And his wife glared at me with menacing eyes. I felt very uncomfortable, and just wanted to get rid of them.

Then, just as I was about to shut the front door, he obstructed it by jamming his foot in the gap, which really unnerved me...

"Excuse me... Look we are closed, I am sorry," I said. His bloodshot eyes widened with fury, and his wife began flailing her arms about. Especially redolent were the jangly gaudy bracelets and the sovereign bedecked fingers.

"We 'aav been bleedin' misled," she yelled, and pointed at me accusingly.

"OK! OK! What can I say... my error, but we are still C-L-O-S-E-D..."

"Stick your guesthouse... I bet tiz not as gran' as they say tiz anyway," he replied churlishly, and they both swaggered back to their car and drove off.

I rushed to the phone to call the owners of 'Blueberry Cottage', to warn them about the implausible duo, and not to let them in under any circumstances, as they seemed bogus and incredibly truculent. (I felt guilty for the recommendation I'd just made before the *contretemps* at the front door.)

I ran upstairs threw off my dressing gown, hastily got dressed. Mike asked me what the bother was...

"Don't worry, go back to sleep," I hushed as I gently closed the bedroom door.

I got down to the front gate and hastily hung the closed sign on its hooks – standing with my back to the road – a car slowly chugged behind me. And then something hit the back of my head...

"Ouch!" I cried and an empty milk carton hit the ground. I looked round, there was that dastardly couple who had been at my door minutes earlier, sitting sniggering in their car, with their music blaring.

He leant out of the window and shouted... "Blueberry fucking Cottage is full. Arsehole!"

His wife cackled, and made an offensive V-sign at me, and to top it all, they tipped a bag of rubbish out of their open window, spilling it all over the entrance to our drive.

It usually takes a lot for me to lose it, but they were really pushing it now! And despite their age, it was just completely unacceptable behaviour, verging on an assault really...

I must admit that I became so incensed and caught up in the moment, that uncharacteristically I actually picked the rubbish up, and threw it back at them in the car, tipping a quarter of a bottle of fizzy pop over his lap in the process. Furthermore, and really riled, I stuck my head inside their vehicle almost abutting up to his face, and fired off, "I have had enough of you two obnoxious old farts – now just sod off...!"

His wife howled with laughter and I smelt alcohol on her breath; in fact they reeked of it...

"Hah... we'll report yer ter the Tourist Board," she hollered, and actually spat at me, although she just missed my face, and her ghastly saliva dribbled down their dashboard.

"Yeah, yer'll be shut down, when they git wind of this," he sneered uncouthly and flicked his fag end, hitting me on my arm as I pulled my head out from inside the car.

This could have really escalated at this juncture into a brawl. I took a deep breath, and composed myself. I realised it was inane, dealing with such ignoramuses, so I backed off, and locked the field gate on them.

There seemed to be an impasse for a minute or two as we stared each other out. Then I turned on my heel and ambled up the drive. Instinctively, at the top I glanced back. And then took a double take... The old man was now standing with his trousers unzipped taking a leak on our gatepost. What...?

"Oi!" I shouted. I went ballistic... and sprinted down the drive towards him. I furiously fumbled with the gate lock, he sniggered... cowardly jumped into his car, and they drove off at lightning speed, cursing me, and blowing their horn like a pair of rowdy delinquents.

Blast! There I was in the middle of road panting with anger, and just too late to record their number plate.

Hmmm, the little shit... God knows what I would have done if I'd have caught him...?

They really were a pair of unruly hoodie wearing *septuagenarians*. The hood-wearing connotation associated with the 'Yo' culture of teenage Chavs, who usually get all the bad press, should now be applied to certain individuals in that age bracket too: especially after what I experienced that day. They truly were worthy of an ASBO...

In hindsight I should have contacted the police, as during that year, they had posted warnings up in the area – for proprietors to beware of bogus callers. And in some cases these unscrupulous characters had scarpered from guesthouses before settling their bills, and even on occasion absconded with valuables. The odious couple did reek of that possibility too...

I would say ninety-eight percent of our business was booked via e-mail or by phone. Naturally though, we would have visitors drop by unannounced on the off chance for a room.

Sometimes, we solicit great new custom this way. One such dear couple were a delightful pair from Wandsworth, who became ardent regulars year after year. Of course it's a question of better judgement whether unexpected visitors can gain entry for accommodation...

So, having an idyllic home in the country – down time for relaxation should become par for the course... I'm afraid not!

Far from it at the Lodge as we painfully discovered... our time became consumed at every turn, endless chores would fill our spare time, which was albeit brief, and then there were the guests to constantly pander to, when open.

Although, during those early days I was hopelessly enamoured with the place, and nobody or nothing could rain on my parade!

So, the tantalising prospect of a holiday filled our thoughts with a longing. Mike had been very rundown, what with all his personal grief, and the arduous tasks of the business to deal with on a daily basis. And besides it had now been years of hard graft since we both had a real break.

Ironically, my older brother Tony would come up with a timely solution. We'd grown ever closer over recent years; the gap was bridging our generation divide now we were of an age. And he had somewhat stepped into my father's mantle on certain subconscious levels – his sagely advice was always welcomed. He and his dear wife, Adele, would be due to visit shortly as it had been quite some time since we'd last seen each other.

Hah, the things we remember... especially when I was a cheeky little devil of around six – back in the day when these childhood sweethearts were courting. I used to sneak up on them when they were canoodling on the swing-seat by the rose garden. One time though, my I-spy cover was blown as I fell arse over tit to avoid some stinging nettles. And big bro wanted to kill me...

Naturally, I was keen to show off our achievements at the Lodge, because his little bro had come a long way. None of the family would have expected the course I'd taken over recent years insofar as the *twist* amazed everyone.

A slap-up meal was booked at the very atmospheric, 'Lord Nelson' in Burnham Thorpe, where Nelson's father had been the village Rector.

By the by, this renowned pub, and eatery really is the original of its *eponymous* name, built in 1637, and formerly called The Plough. It became the 'Lord Nelson' after his victory in 1798 over the French at the Battle of the Nile; and thus named in his honour.

However after Trafalgar, his corpse was sent home in a barrel of rum, which ran dry of the spirit because apparently sailors had taken a *nip* of the so-called 'Nelson's Blood' for good luck!

The barrel was then topped up with brandy and other spirits before being transferred to a coffin for a posthumous state funeral at St Paul's Cathedral.

The secret recipe of the brew dubbed 'Nelson's Blood' available either by the bottle or just as a *tot* is blended here. It is a very unique concoction of one hundred percent proof rum, with mixed herbs, and spices making a great tipple especially on a cold winter's night... You can even sit in his very chair, a high-backed settle, and soak up the history of the place, which has changed very little since the time of Norfolk's greatest son.

Tony, forever on a tight schedule must be the most well travelled person I know... That guy has been round the world too many times to mention, there is not a country he hasn't visited. He is possibly responsible for the entire *Global Warming Crisis*. Joking aside it's the nature of his trade and he has to fly here, there, and everywhere to attend to all the demanding facets of his business. A business that in fact keeps armies of fashion savvy teenagers attired in the latest state of the art footwear from London to Los Angeles – from St Petersburg to Barcelona – and then some!

By 10am, big bro (the Simon Cowell of the shoe-world), who has always been an extremely early riser even before God on most days, had become fully acquainted geographically, and historically with the entire coastline here. And was ready to be quizzed on *Mastermind* replete with his newfound specialist subject on 'North Norfolk'.

I think it must be a family trait. He really is a tremendous polymath of the highest order.

This is leading me on to our forthcoming holiday. Tony had been on no fewer than twenty-five cruise-ship holidays, I would go so far as to say, 'he was an *authority* on the subject': Which cruise line? Which ship? Which destination? Which itinerary? Which restaurant to book? And where? And even which excursion to book at each destination, etc.

His *mantra* for the best way to travel is: 'Book a Cruise' – no doubt as a welcome alternative to his constant jet-setting lifestyle. But we had always been put off, thinking perhaps it was packed full of the *Saga* generation exclusively. Eventually though, he managed to sell us the idea. We were just gasping to be pampered in some far-flung destination. And besides I might pick up some more ideas for the Lodge, which was constantly evolving with the passage of time. Sold... and we booked up our first Caribbean cruise holiday.

Unfortunately about six weeks before we were due to set sail, Mike had contracted a severe bout of shingles, and was bedridden for weeks on end. He had been so worn down I suspect mourning the loss of his mum, and coupled with the gruelling demands at the Lodge: that I guess this horrible illness just manifested itself as a result of his weakened immune system...

Fortunately after a touch and go month, he managed to recover somewhat, and insisted he'd be well enough to make it, which was just in the nick of time by the departure date.

Naturally this meant a lot to me, he'd been through so much and I felt he deserved a darn good rest. We both did!

We flew to Barbados to set sail on the P&O liner, the *Oceana,* in February 2004, cruising around seven of the most beautiful Caribbean islands. I must admit I felt like Bette Davis in the romantic film noir classic '*Now, Voyager'*, only for a minute – mind you...

Picture this, we were on a jungle adventure, in deepest St Kitts, we couldn't have be further away from Norfolk. Right in the middle of an exotic thicket: parakeets and pendulous primates shrieked and leapt overhead. The great canopy was teaming with wildlife. Then, suddenly out of the blue our *wild life* took an unsuspecting turn on this safari. A middle-aged couple came bounding over calling our names with familiar eagerness.

We were flabbergasted... I had to pinch myself – it was Brenda and Ron, regulars at Holly Lodge every year since we'd opened.

So we had come to the far reaches of Planet Earth to escape from the business. And lo and behold, our very own 'Holly Lodgers' appeared right in the middle of the flipping jungle. It was astounding!

Oh... there was no escaping them and even on that vast ocean liner... Blimey, man-overboard!

The *Oceana* was an awesome ship we could not fault it. The service, the food, and the accommodation were all truly superb. I have to take my hat off to *P&O*! How they manage to maintain such a high level of quality throughout, beggars belief! Our cabin had the added luxury of a balcony, which made all the difference, somewhere private to chill out, and enjoy the spectacular views to and fro all ports of call.

Apropos, we were to discover that the *Captain* of the *Oceana* just happened to live a few doors along from us in our own little hamlet. We had heard there was a cruise-ship captain in the village, but we would never have imagined in a million years, that he would be the *very* Commander of our ship. It really is a very small world! (Recently he was made Commodore of the entire *P&O* Fleet.) What a champ!

All the islands were of course stunning, and so abundant in their exotica (High-Definition) colour. But my favourite had to be St Lucia for its breathtaking scenery. We'd spent a memorable day at Marigot Bay, where *Doctor Dolittle* with Rex Harrison was filmed in 1967, and I half expected that giant pink snail from the said movie to come sailing into the picturesque bay, as we were wading through the clear turquoise surf, and sipping fruit cocktails...

Interestingly, the far north of St Lucia was a complete anomaly compared to the rest of this lush tropical paradise, and not what would be expected... Its barren rugged shores are weirdly reminiscent of Cornwall. Contrarily though, this landscape was punctuated with indigenous towering cactuses clinging to its jagged coves. And wild horses roam the terrain, redolent of the Camargue in France. A rugged beauty pervades here! And loving it...

My beloved brother was a life *guru* after all... Bless. As this turned out to be the most relaxing, re-energising experience, a much-needed tonic at the time to put us in fine fettle for the adventures of 2004.

That spring I was to get a most wonderful surprise. On the guest list of arrivals one day was the name 'Hope' which meant nothing to me except that it's a pleasant sounding name. I did the usual correspondence confirming their booking, nothing out of the unusual.

However, when I opened the door to greet them, I was immediately struck, and riveted to the chic vision that stood before me – the epitome of stylish elegance, with her captivating vivacious smile. And I recognised her instantly. It was my old friend Margaret from 'The London College of Fashion' days. I had not seen her for twenty-five years or more; she looked remarkably the same, unblemished by time.

This African beauty from Sierra Leone had been in the senior year above. She always seemed to hold her own whilst all about her were losing their heads in this heady world of madcap fashion, including *moi* on occasions, I must admit!

Ah, in actual fact a sweet time so evocative of that carefree blazing-hot summer of 1976: boyfriends, girlfriends, young loves of the fickle variety, a ditzy affair with a famous radio DJ, who shall remain nameless. And then my first intense gay love affair that lasted quite some time beyond my college years.

Margaret was accompanied by her daughter Jamilla, herself a stunning young woman with the most alluring, charismatic charm. Mike and I fell for her, hook, line and sinker!

A thank you letter was discovered on the roll-top bureau in her room. A deep profound essay with the most touching words, and written with such poetic eloquence by a lady with tremendous talent who has gone on to become a very successful radio personality in her own right.

Margaret and I have rekindled our friendship, but stronger than ever, and remarkably, her and her husband Ron, fell in love with North Norfolk too, and have since moved to a charming old Rectory not too far from us. Apropos it was my dear friend Pat from those *good old college days,* who arranged this reunion so I must mention her as a tribute to her fine deed.

That summer, we had a near fatal encounter for our beloved Barnaby-Boo. One afternoon after leaving an upstairs window open, he literally sprang through the opening from the first floor, and landed acrobatically – thank goodness like a gymnast, but on all fours – unscathed onto the lavender path below.

It was death defying. And miraculously he had a very lucky escape! Our little mite ran about dazed profusely wagging his tail with the shock of it all. Baby-Boo kept kissing us both – almost as if to tell us he really was OK! We knew he'd never attempt that stunt again.

Whippets are extremely agile creatures, and we have seen him high jump many an object to land perfectly smart, although this breed are prone to neck disc problems; so we don't encourage him to perform aeronautics.

Without the risk of sounding cloy Mike and I have come to the conclusion that our dog really is a reincarnated sixties' *hippie*! That is why we sometimes call him Boo, which is not before considering: Brook, River, Skye, Summer, or even Dude. Please let me indulge in why this is so...

Barnaby needs complete *harmony* in the household. If ever we are involved in a domestic, you know one of those tête-à-tête fracas that might become somewhat invective... his ears prick up on cue, then he jumps between us, and literally taps us both in-turn on the nose in a kind of reprimanding stance as if to say... 'Now, now gentlemen, please... we'll have none of that!'

He'll stare intensely into each of our eyes as if he really means it. Then he'll plonk a kiss on both our noses in turn. He has diffused many a heated row with his 'Peace-man!' hippie-dog way.

But even more remarkably, he has another clever tack too. He will literally stick his paw on the TV remote control to either switch the telly on-or-off as a distraction to diffuse any tension. I kid you not! He is a highly sensitive creature, perhaps a *woof-dah* at times, but that's our Barnaby-Boo...

Two years had nearly passed since that *runner-up* Highly Commended Award. The rule is you cannot enter the process over two consecutive years. So in June, after receiving an intriguing reminder from The East of England Tourist Board, I re-entered by filling out the obligatory registration forms, especially outlining all the developments and improvements we had made to the Lodge since. As well as highlighting our approach to the ecological aspect reflecting the current *Zeitgeist*: How we were trying to address (Green) issues such as waste, and energy.

Naturally, we tried to recycle as much as we could. All applicable food wastages would be reconstituted into garden compost. And all foods, products, materials and extra labour required for the business would be sourced locally. Outside lighting was operated by solar-power; however low-energy light bulbs were a tricky one – as aesthetically they were so ugly back in the day – incongruous with most light fittings. They were only used where they could be concealed, although vast improvements have since been made to bulb designs now currently available.

Solar panels and ground source heat pumps, were a consideration for the Lodge; unfortunately our budgets at the time would not have stretched to accommodate these costly changes. Although financial assistance in the form of grants can now be applied for with certain eco-energy installations – yet cost effectiveness will still only be *beneficial* in the very, very long term.

On the other hand we had planted hundreds of shrubs, copious trees, and created those wildlife attracting water gardens, so that itself must be considered eco-productive too. Also we prided ourselves on being organic with our homegrown produce.

Holy Moly! All this endless recycling lark... disingenuous, and ambiguous rhetoric in thrall to this holier-than-thou new religion called 'Climate Change', *hallowed be its name*! Dumped on us by global warming alarmists. And god-forbid you are a doubting Thomas: Huh... You'll be crucified as a 'Flat-earther'.

FYI... This could be the biggest con of all time... Doom mongering has become big business on the political eco-gravy-train to curry favour to Brussels to propagate punitive stealth taxes, and hector a chased-change to all our lifestyles.

Paradoxically, aside from recent reports of statistics being allegedly massaged, the reams of ostensible meteorological theories, and data purporting to *Climate Change* could well-be-part of the earth's *natural* cycles anyway! There has to be room for debate too...

OK, we all know Planet Earth is under a tremendous strain with our insatiable consumer demands... But if it's that, *that*, utterly desperate – uh, hello! Logical! "POPULATION CONTROL!" Oops... I'll stop jumping up and down now for fear of letting rip further and causing a gross indecency to those pious incumbent dilettantes of the status quo... End of.

Once again the inspectors from both Tourist Boards had visited, and we had successfully maintained our status: five star rating, with our Gold Award happily still intact.

A seminal letter arrived from the East of England Tourist board in September, I anxiously opened the missive, and it announced that we had been selected by the judging panel to go through to the final of the *'Regional Awards for Excellence in England'* in our category, this year to be held in October at Ipswich Town Football club. Wow wee!

I rushed out into the garden to tell Mike the great news. Naturally he was delighted... But warned me not to be disappointed if we did not win again; unbeknown to him I was already preparing my acceptance speech in those first few minutes of the notice. Yep... you know now how incorrigible I can be. But hey that's me...

Please don't think me cocky! But how could we be runners-up this time around? That would be purgatory... because, if they'd gone all-out to the trouble of placing us in the final yet again, they must be planning on giving us the title this time. Surely...?

And the winner is...

CHAPTER 14

AND THE WINNER IS...

"Holly Lodge..." The name echoed in my ears. *I simply don't believe it...* That unforgettable whinge of the irascible *'Victor Meldrew'* from the classic Brit sitcom resonated in my head as I tried to grasp the reality of the moment.

"Yes, Yes," we rejoiced and collided palms with the most jubilant high-five imaginable...

The cheers rumbled as though a game were in progress at the club's stadium. I glanced out over the vast green baize visible through the viewing windows from the Sir Bobby Robson suite (The Galleria) and for once I was speechless.

David Sheepshanks, Chairman of Ipswich Town Football Club and Jonathan Bowman, Chairman of the East of England Tourist Board, both welcomed us as this year's recipients.

It was a fine moment no doubt being named 'B&B/Guesthouse of the Year 2004', out of six regional counties (East Anglia). No mean feat... Imagine how many establishments there are in the East of England alone, and how many that would vie for the title. We both felt truly honoured to receive this much-coveted award.

As regional winners, we were now automatically eligible for entry into *VisitBritain's*, (National) *Award for Excellence'*, earmarked for next year, and considered the ultimate accolade known as the 'Gold Oscars' of the Tourism Industry.

Isn't it strange that after such an event in retrospective acuity – I may have foretold the outcome by the seating arrangements alone at the pre-awards luncheon. The mere fact that I was inserted next to a VIP: the much-revered Tess Wright, the incumbent managing director of the East of England Tourist Board should have been a hint in itself, the privilege kind of felt like being seated at the top table. Nerve-racking...

Mike though bless, can find these events rather awkward. Heaven forefend... he's thrust forward centre-stage. He just did not relish these ceremonies at all. However this world became very much part of our lives back then. And of course there was me dragging him through them by the scruff. Poor chap!

A film interview took place in our new Orangery. And the footage was played back at the ceremony...

"I can't believe that's our place up there on the big screen," he beamed with pride.

"We've well and truly earned our stripes now." And I meant that from the heart, because we'd come such a long way to this day.

We returned home elevated to a new level of provenance with this auspicious achievement. Suddenly Holly Lodge was now fast gaining the reputation as a hot *boutiquey destination* on the increasingly hip North Norfolk coast. Reporters were pitching for interviews, press-features followed, and the phone rang incessantly. Basically it took-off!

2004 turned out to be an incredibly busy year... At this juncture I have to come clean about Mike's acquiescence towards the business. He was showing signs of tiring from the constant demands: there was no doubt that the severe bout of shingles had worn him down physically too.

But now the cogs were spinning faster than ever, and the machine needed more and more *energy* to keep up with the gathering momentum. We were unequivocally a great team then, and still are today. However, Mike being the great guy that he is simply rode along with it. That's commitment...

Although deep down, I knew the die was already cast. And me at the time... Well, I was hopelessly in denial being carried along in the strong torrent of a tide of success that would become even greater before the year was out.

Nearly five years at Holly Lodge, and we still did A-Z of everything ourselves. It was a *very* hard slog! The fast exhausting pace was taking its toll, so I insisted that we bring in staff. Cleaners would be hired to take some of the pressures off, especially for Mike, who is *very* meticulous about such things to the point of guarding the housekeeping fiercely as his personal domain.

Ever since I'd known him, I'd always suspected he was in denial of his (OCD) cleaning mania, even making light of his rituals. Guests would often comment, '*One could eat off the floor at Holly Lodge*'. No bad thing for our reputation of course.

Ultimately we hired Wendy who lived in the village, and then Sue, who were both terrific. Absolute gems...

Mike seemed appeased with the new help, although now he was beginning to question the constant intrusion into our home life.

We discussed options like converting the Nissen barn into separate private accommodation as new living quarters, which would enable us to then let the five bedrooms in the house – full-time to expand the business – to capitalise on recent events.

I drew up plans and applied for the requisite planning permissions. This new space would adapt well to a contemporary open-plan barn style home, and would be set in a quiet recess in the very back of the garden. Consequently the third phase was on the drawing board, no doubt an expensive prospect! But perhaps a necessity if we were to continue happily here in the very long-term.

The Lodge was teeming that summer. A chap called, making a reservation expressly for the Claret Cottage. He requested the room to be filled to the rafters with dozens of fragrant long-stemmed red roses, as it was to be a very special occasion.

He arrived promptly at 4pm on Friday 13th August, which seemed prophetically significant as the plot thickened to this particular tale.

It panned out that the reservation was made for one of our favourite regulars at the Lodge, however a regular like no other! She was the incomparable, and very cinematic Mrs Vandergeld. True to form she would swan-in making an entrance, as if she were arriving on set. However this time, accompanied by a suave and debonair gentlemen in tow, whom I shall name Mr Black due to the nature of his fate.

Elena Vandergeld was our very own 'Black Widow – *Femme Fatale*'. Each husband had either died tragically, or had left her in very dubious circumstances, she would often relay to us all the ambiguous gory details.

The thing is, she was so personable, with a really vivacious countenance in her fabulous Ascot-esque hats, floral summery frocks, just revealing enough décolletage to be stylishly appealing for a woman of her years. But then again she was very well preserved... Especially redolent was her chosen scent, *Christian Dior 'Poison'*, which seemed most apt. And reminded me of a certain lady I used to date way back when.

This glamorous beguiling creature would cannily entice her victims into her web of intrigue. Once bitten forever smitten...

All the necessary arrangements had been made for the next morning at breakfast. The dining room was bedecked in dozens and dozens of red roses. And it became a very riveting affair.

Standby: Lights. Camera. Action!

On cue, I played *The Look of Love*, sung by Dionne Warwick, for the romantic interlude. And the scene was set...

"Elena, my dear, will you do me the great honour of giving me your hand in marriage?" Mr Black presented her with a sumptuous black velvet box from a certain Bond Street jewellers – exposing the most magnificent opulent gem.

She sighed and gently patted the back of her shock of titian hair, and cast her ravishing green eyes deliciously over the sparkling four carat *Marquise* diamond set in a gleaming platinum band. The room fell silent for a nail-biting impasse...

All eyes were drawn to the alluring spell of her enigmatic presence with a god-given *X-Factor*. Her ruby lips quivered for another spellbinding moment... She knew full-well how to hold an audience in her palms. The suspense was tantalising as we all held our breath. And then she arched an eyebrow...

"Kind sir, I would be honoured to become your Leading Lady, of course my darling..." She smiled graciously at her distinguished beau – bowing her head in acceptance, as he slid the prerequisite *whopper* of a gem onto her significant finger.

Again on cue as prearranged, I cracked open a bottle of best *Bollinger* – bubbling into our finest *Baccarat* flutes for all to toast the happy couple. And given her scene-stealing powers, applause ensued with each and every guest utterly driven to tears.

Her suitor was captured, pre-nuptial contracts would shortly be signed in accordance, glasses chinked, and they amorously embraced – politely controlling their passion under the prying eyes of all in the room that morning.

A stellar performance by this seasoned starry actress played out before us as a repeated production. We'd seen it all before, but of course with a different leading man in the role.

Our setting became the perfect 'Seduction Scenario' for her prospective husbands adding another soapy episode to her string of sequels. Mike and I would shudder in anticipation to the outcome of this one. We really hoped in our heart of hearts, that he'd be an *ideal husband* (no pun intended) for our *Oscar* winning veteran.

Unfortunately spouse number *four* met an untimely end – aptly histrionic as others that went before. As she recounted tearfully to us one rainy afternoon that autumn...

It happened about a month after they had returned from their romantic honeymoon on the Orient Express to Venice. Elena had been imbued with *la dolce vita* from her sojourn, and naturally this time thought her new love was for keeps.

One morning he complained he felt unwell, but nevertheless went to the club to play a round of golf that day. Unfortunately he literally fell off his perch so to speak, dropping dead at the twelfth hole from a fatal heart attack. Naturally she was utterly devastated, and so were we to hear her sad news!

Elena, forever a consummate survivor, and after a respectable period of mourning returned to the Lodge exactly one year on, but this time it was after a dalliance with a Russian oligarch. They had met at an art auction at Sotheby's, whilst they were both embroiled in a bidding war for the same Modernist painting.

And a luncheon date followed at *San Lorenzo's* in Beauchamp Place, that very afternoon.

However, it turned out to be more of a pseudo-proposal that played out under the dappled shade of our rose arbour bedecked in blooms that May. You see the burly Russki of no fixed address except a magnificent Super Yacht, the *Tzarina,* moored in the glitzy waters off Monaco, had a penchant for club hostesses, one in Paris, one in Milan, and who knows where else...?

Subsequently the engagement had to be broken off hitherto Elena's discovery of an unsavoury note found in the inside pocket of a flannel suit that she was despatching to *Jeeves*, (the ritzy drycleaners) in Belgravia. The sleazy scrawl on a sheet of stationery from the fabulous Hotel *Principe Di Savoia*, Milano; sadly said it all. Consequently, 'Sergei' the lusty lothario from the Siberian Steppes, though he may have been mega-loaded – *marriage* material he most certainly was not.

Naturally, Elena was disappointed with her paramour, and subsequently to make matters even worse, unearthed the fact that he was still married too. The rascal...

It was time to revaluate. And true to her new ethos, she decided any future trysts would be ones of pure unadulterated, dare I say... Sex. Well, for the time being at least. It appeared that our cougar had morphed into an insatiable panther on heat. And oh, now cubs were on the menu...

This manifested itself late one afternoon, literally only a month or so later – when she booked into her usual suite...

Indefatigable Elena sashayed in, linked to a dusky buff Latin dancer, a specialist choreographer in the Argentine Tango at least half her age, and then some. The air around them was charged with electricity, wired for another erotic vignette no doubt. Uh-oh... but thankfully as it transpired no proposal was in the offing. And she was so over that *'From Russia with Love* Thing...' The *Do Not Disturb* sign spoke volumes. And I have to add that I'd never seen dear Elena Vandergeld so beatifically dishevelled at breakfast before. Ever!

And finally, although I can't report a happy ending to Elena's tale, of a life of high drama as intriguing off-camera as on. But it has come to pass at the time of me writing her segment that she is currently dating a recently divorced chap, whom she'd met on a Nile Cruise. Some kind of ex-military bigwig, I believe.

Redolent images of Cleopatra wooing Mark Antony – now Caesar was out of the mainframe sprang to mind. Although we sincerely hoped our leading lady would get her prince (consort) in 'The End'. So watch this space... for any further developments in perhaps a newer edition of my book. Although, more than likely, word will spread across Twitter of Elena's latest conquest... I'm sure!

It seemed with every twist, and turn we'd encounter another surprise at the Lodge, and this transpired next in the form of a curious letter.

An intrepid young couple came to stay with us under the pretext of visiting relatives in the area. However the real reason for their visit was to study our formula for running the Lodge. Apparently, they owned a coastal hotel that they wanted to reinvent.

In fact their letter asked our permission if they could assimilate many of our ideas into their establishment. So seeing as it was not in our area, we had no objections whatsoever.

Actually they invited us down to check out their improvements based on our format. Mike held fort while I paid them a visit the following year.

Their boutique establishment turned out to be very cutting-edge, and they proved to be exceptional hosts, who actually went onto to win much acclaim with their well-appointed hotel.

And by the way... it ironically transpired that they were the *very* couple that had lost out in the race to buy Holly Lodge back in 1999.

Snoopy contemporaries or investigative proprietors in the hotel biz did try to catch us on the hop on a number of occasions, and would rarely let on as to the nature of their visit. But hey, it was a tremendous compliment...

Ahem, please look away now... if you have a strong affinity with the Scots. **(WARNING!)**

Because this was another most memorable encounter that year that I just couldn't resist rescuing from the cutting-room floor.

God help us... Mary and Alistair Loomas had arrived with Paisley, the West Highland terrier in tow. (Dogs were allowed by arrangement only; but on this rare occasion seeing as they travelled from Scotland... I kept schtum.) And this is how it all played out...

The moment the crass couple stepped in they were very derogatory about all things English... I wondered why they ever ventured south of Hadrian's Wall – against the dichotomy of Barnaby and Paisley falling madly in (puppy) love at first sight.

On arrival at breakfast as I offered them the usual morning drinks, the spontaneous response from Mrs Loomas was nothing short of retaliatory...

"Ah could nae possibly be drinkin' the wa-ter in yer hoose it's absolutely houghin'... Ye must import pure Highlan' Scottish wa-ter, an' as for yer music... for heaven's sake jimmy (man), somethin' *Celtic*. An' the weather in Norfolk is awful!" And so it goes... delivered in her thick Glaswegian accent with the most annoying snarl!

It just so happened that that weekend Norfolk was experiencing the worst weather in the country, whilst Scotland, and the rest of England were basking in glorious sunshine. Typical!

"And what would Madam prefer...?"

"Somethin' bonnie Scots. Och aye!" she shrieked.

I raided my music library and unearthed a freebie CD from a Sunday supplement: *The Edinburgh Military Tattoo.*

Our other guests winced in horror. And Mike recoiled to his particular pet hate: The Bagpipes.

In the meantime Barnaby and Paisley were canoodling in the lounge by the fire, while a *Jacobite* uprising broke out in the dining room.

The insolent duo, started whinging on about their bed! They had booked the Claret Cottage, which clearly had a king four-poster bed as indicated in our literature, and now all of a sudden, they wanted to change to twin beds, as apparently they always slept in twins at home, furthermore in separate bedrooms.

Oops! Now that was an uncalled for declaration about the parlous state of marital affairs, publicly aired for everybody's consumption.

The falsetto whining, nit-picking and querulous remarks plagued-us-no-end. Even the table roses were the wrong shade of white. Uh! They almost drove me to bipolar depression... And Mike, who was usually desensitised to such petty-minded comments, was on the cusp of having a word.

"Just sometimes the customer is not *always* right," he muttered as he beat a hasty retreat from the dining room.

It so happened that Mrs Loomas had a phobia for wasps, and *Sod's law* that week, a nest had formed in the roof overhang to their cottage.

She came rushing over to the house mid-morning flailing her arms about her. "Hehlp! Hehlp!" crying hysterically.

"There is a swarm of wasps in mah room..."

Which was grossly exaggerated as there were only about two or three wasps buzzing around outside, and the rest were crawling tightly in the nest; but of course it was the *one* in her room that was naturally the *Queen* Bee, which was going to kill her!

I attempted to calm her down and I inquired if she was prone to anaphylactic shock?

"Och nooooo! But... how about a wee dram?"

I happily obliged her with the intoxication. In fact she was welcome to the blinking barrel, and every last drop, the lot – if it would zip her goddamn awful gob...? Pest control was then called out.

I left her to marinate, and went to see Mr Loomas over at the cottage. He was flapping about with a can of insect repellent spraying all and sundry: including me with the toxic stuff. No doubt he was fretting in fear of his gob of a wife.

'*Mary Loomas was a DRAMA QUEEN of mega-proportions*'.

Meanwhile, Barnaby and Paisley were getting on so famously behind the bike shed near the cottage I now feared, Mary Queen of Scots, might end up an in-law. Blimey!

The next morning as I was collecting the finished plates, she inquired...

"Is yer bacon local...? Och, it's quite naice... An' ah know ah was mouthin' off about Norfolk, but...?" And she prattled on and on... The dialect was almost forgiving, but the pretentiousness was so unbearable I just wanted to slash my wrists there and then. What did she want? Blood!

"Yes it is... just try, you never know you might find something to like about our fair county," I retorted cynically. I just could not help myself anymore; the words tumbled out thick and fast in the face of this nauseating creature. "It's high time you just settled down, and stop behaving like a moaning-Minnie. Or leave!"

Mary, mother of Jesus... There! I have committed a cardinal sin to a paying **Guest** by being blatantly sarky. Now I bet she thought I was a *Sassinak*...

The room fell deathly silent; she looked stunned and just gawped at me... I could imagine she was already preparing her elaborate case, a solicitor's missive would follow, and I would be dragged through the Highland Courts for my degenerate crimes against the '*Bravefarts*' of the glen.

"Guilty, take the defendant down," the Judge's sombre tone would condemn my actions in a hushed courtroom for being a very, **VERY RUDE** Proprietor."

"It's her, the woman in the *Argyle* twin-set and pearls..." I'd yell, as she skittishly danced the Highland fling around my verdict.

Naturally, I'd be made a pariah, and poor ole Holly Lodge would go down the pan, what with *Political Correctness* gone ape-shit these days...

Now in my acuity of recalling a week of horror with one, Mary Morag Loomas – I can see her haughty demeanour and squinty eyes set in that sardonic face – she so deserved to be born with, whilst an inexorable cacophony of repellent statements spewed off her sour tongue for an eternity.

Don't get me wrong some of our nearest and dearest are from bonnie Scotland, but these characters were so blinkered. 'Heaven forbid it we're not dressed in **Tartan**...'

On their penultimate morning, even our faithful regulars from the Yorkshire Dales, Lloyd and Anita, became so fed up with her exhausting snipes, they actually told her to zip-it and pack. Huhhhhh...

An uncomfortable silence ensued. I'd never heard guests slight one another before. Was all hell going to break loose? Actually, Mrs Loomas in a sudden change of unctuous tact started backtracking, perhaps as her way of an apology to be fair...

My god... she was now burbling on about discovering the *wee* delights of Norfolk. Her ranting became hideously mawkish... Everybody just yawned!

Suddenly the door burst open, Barnaby, and Paisley, ran in from the garden yapping, and running rings around the table. Pandemonium broke out, which thankfully quelled the slight...

Constructive criticism was always welcomed, and when a guest mentioned something that could be improved upon, we were the first to instigate the suggested changes for everybody's benefit. However when it was unfounded just for the hell of it, and delivered in a snide insulting manner, then it was hard to cope with.

On departure the wretched little woman with grimace, had the gall to haggle for a massive discount. I knew she'd give that one a go! I point-blank refused. And she practically slammed the front door abruptly in my face.

Poor Barnaby though was heartbroken on Paisley's departure, as the pretty little terrier gave him one last *fond* look before jumping into their car. He took to his bed, bereft for days. Sadly, Mrs Loomas made my '**BLACKLIST**'... End of.

I must digress here to make a very important, and oh so up-beat announcement...

The old Bakelite phone rang in the hall, and a voice delivered the most unbelievable message like a magnificent bolt out of the blue. I had to ask her to repeat the statement: Twice...?

"I am delighted to confirm that Holly Lodge has been chosen as *AA Guest Accommodation of the Year for England 2004-2005.*"

I seriously impugned the message with total bemusement. Stunned into silence... and really thought some friends were messing around, until a missive on letter-headed stationery promptly arrived with the amazing news the next morning.

It was absurd... no-way... It can't be true! Surely there had been a terrible mistake? And it would turn out to be some other establishment called Holly Lodge receiving this jaw-dropping award.

We were utterly euphoric. I wanted to do cartwheels all over the place: fifty-piece orchestras were playing in surround-sound in my head, "Congratulations and Celebrations..." fireworks were exploding as if it was New Year's Eve, claxons sounded off, banners proclaimed the declaration, and the sky filled with smoky jet-streamed script... '**Holly Lodge – The Best in England**'. And the jubilation danced around in my head for days on end... This is how it truly felt.

The brochure for the award ceremony stated, and quotes...

'This particular award represents the inspectors' personal choice of somewhere they would choose to stay themselves or would enthusiastically recommend to friends and family. Introduced in 1994, the award is the pinnacle of achievement for B&Bs in England'.

Peter Birnie, the AA's chief Hotel Inspector said, and quote...

'Holly Lodge provided the closest ideal of what a Guesthouse should be, offering warm hospitality, a beautiful location, and excellent food.

A combination of both traditional, and contemporary style with beautiful furniture, and tasteful personal pieces create a welcoming atmosphere'.

The Award ceremony took place in the Grand Ballroom at The Carlton Tower Hotel, Cadogan Place, just off Sloane Street on 29th September 2004.

It was short notice and rapid arrangements were made for our stint to London. The books were chock-a-block, so at the last minute, Mike's aunts, Helena and Anne were called in to take the helm.

Barnaby sloped off in a huff, while we were ironing, and packing; he'd watch us hawk-like, and then curl up in a ball as whippets do. 'Dog's really are children in fur coats', and we did not relish leaving him ever. He was now so much part of us. Although this time he could stay home at least.

I remember so vividly, the elegant Hospitality Awards luncheon, like it was yesterday, however on this occasion there was no waiting to learn our fate – it was a sure-fired thing! Luckily.

As we wandered in off Sloane Street into the hotel lobby, representatives from the *AA Hotel Association* greeted us warmly: They made us feel very special on that memorable day.

The Luncheon was a gastronomic feast of exceptional fare, which of course was appropriately in keeping with such illustrious company present from the finest chefs, restaurants, hotels, pubs all there to receive their respective accolades as judged by the AA.

Back in 2000, my aims were high, but this epic title swept me off my feet. Who'd have imagined *this* would really happen to us...?

It was mind-blowing, when we went up to the stage in the grand surroundings of the Carlton Tower Ballroom to collect our Award.

A specially commissioned most beautiful watercolour painting of Holly Lodge was presented to us as a symbolic prize of our achievement, and which we'd treasure always. There was a gilt-framed certificate, a full page free-entry into the front of Britain's Best Bed & Breakfast Guide for 2005, and so much spin-off free publicity through trade magazines, and press releases, that we'd never have been able to afford it on our own backs at the time.

However the surprising fulcrum of the proceedings for me, now forever etched on my mind... Was when my most favourite of culinary heroes, whom himself a recipient that day of *AA Chef's Chef of the Year 2004-5* kindly came over to our table, warmly shook our hands, and generously called us 'Geniuses' with his charming Gallic smile. Unmistakably it was the one and only *Raymond Blanc*. Both Mike and I were gobsmacked... Previous iconic winners were *Gordon Ramsay, Jean-Christophe Novelli, Rick Stein* and *Michel Roux*.

Holly Lodge received some wonderful reviews in a slew of leading national newspapers including *The Sunday Times*, and *The Guardian*. And local regional papers headlined our scoop of the AA award too.

Richard Parr came down from the *Eastern Daily Press* to photograph the interiors, and to review our establishment, which he generously featured in a full double page spread.

Here is a snippet quote from an editorial 27.11.2004 – titled:

'JUST PAMPERED IN PARADISE'

'When you turn into the driveway of Holly Lodge, the knowledge that you are arriving at England's top guesthouse 2004, as judged by the AA that you are in for something really special during your stay, and indeed you are!

'Once inside you feel you are in another world of Baronial, and Gothic splendour exuding a quiet relaxing ambiance.

'Having stayed in the Colonial Cottage reflecting nostalgic influences of the Raj, I can understand how guests return again, and again.

'If you think the overnight accommodation is a treat just wait for the wonderful breakfast in the dining hall.'

Tony Hall, renowned freelance photographer, whom has worked with many a top national interior magazine, came to interview us and to photograph Holly Lodge. An impressive six-page spread in *Country Homes & Interiors*, and a fabulous feature in the *Eastern Daily Press* county glossy ensued – much to our delight...

Actually I'd been trying to get in touch with the elusive man for ages and now the accolade brought him to our very door. Ironically we have struck up a fine relationship and Tony has been very supportive in many of my subsequent interior design projects – producing many dynamic spreads since.

An official letter arrived from The House of Commons addressed to us from our Member of Parliament for North Norfolk: Norman Lamb, congratulating us on our Accolade, which was such a boon!

We arrived back at Holly Lodge where our stand-ins had done us proud in our absence, although they described some of our guests as most challenging during that period, and that the phone was ringing off the hook, since word had got out.

Barnaby went ballistic when he saw us, and bounced around from room to room before settling down into a temporary huff, his *Gromit* smart way of scolding his masters for leaving him. And then true to form he soon curled up on the sofa between us sharing his love out in bucket loads.

Now everything really had changed forever! Our business had come of age, going from strength to strength, the results were tangible. Mike, although thrilled with our success, was still ambivalent about the business; nevertheless he still indulged me in the moment.

Just as we were catching our breath... a golden invitation landed on the doorstep, but this time from *VisitBritain* though, announcing that Holly Lodge had actually now qualified onto the shortlist for their (National) 'Excellence Awards' – to be held at the British Museum in the spring of 2005.

My god... it felt like we were now being launched into the stratosphere amongst the really big players of the industry to slug-it-out in the pantheon of ancient relics.

Um... 'This golden chalice (The Tourism Oscar) was up for grabs! And little old us were in with a chance'.

Could this be an unprecedented triple...?

VisitBritain requests the pleasure of

Robert Greenfield

at the **Enjoy England Excellence Awards 2005**

The British Museum
Queen Elizabeth II Great Court, Main Entrance, Great Russell Street, London WC1 3DG

hosted by Sandi Toksvig
Tuesday 19 April 2005

Doors open 7.00pm
Ceremony 7.30pm
followed by 'Champagne' Reception
Dress code: Lounge suit

VisitBritain: promoting Britain to the world and England to the British

Please bring this invitation with you for security reasons

VisitBritain requests the pleasure of

Mike Bell

at the **Enjoy England Excellence Awards 2005**

The British Museum
Queen Elizabeth II Great Court, Main Entrance, Great Russell Street, London WC1 3DG

hosted by Sandi Toksvig
Tuesday 19 April 2005

Doors open 7.00pm
Ceremony 7.30pm
followed by 'Champagne' Reception
Dress code: Lounge suit

VisitBritain: promoting Britain to the world and England to the British

Please bring this invitation with you for security reasons

Our invitations to the *VisitBritain Excellence Awards, 2005*

CHAPTER 15

SURPRISES

A gale-force flurry of enquiries blew with the emblematic nature of our recent awards. Now nationally!

The impressive kudos imbued our expanding reputation with an overwhelming number of enquiries, which implied we'd have to expand the amount of letting rooms in *needs-must* urgency to capitalise on our good fortune...

I'll never forget my first morning back at my office. There were just hundreds of e-mails in my mailbox, and my answering machine was bleeping to the max with messages for bookings and brochures etc.

Finally I turned in bushed gone two in the morning, and was up again at six as a very bleary-eyed proprietor heading into another hectic day. Although this was to be a special one...

Wally Webb from BBC Radio Norfolk arrived to interview us that afternoon, so I had to have my wits about me. Mike, as usual always shy of media attention made himself scarce, and he actually wound up sitting in our VW listening to the interview on the car radio, whilst I gave a running commentary to Wally about life at the Lodge.

"It was surreal listening to your distinct voice echoing over the airwaves." Mike seemed impressed with my narrative, regaling many aspects of the business. I was a nervous wreck though.

Subsequently, I couldn't count the amount of times my mobile ringtone sounded that afternoon as many friends and acquaintances had heard the live broadcast. The exposure through this medium is staggering.

In fact a local farmer, whom we'd never met before, dropped by to congratulate us, and generously stated that: Thursford, forever known for its Museum would now be known for our establishment too. That spoke volumes, and it really hit home the significance of our burgeoning achievements.

So that summer we arranged to personally celebrate with some of our mates, especially the hosts of that Millennium night party all those many moons ago. And who recently followed in the footsteps of our dream. Naturally we sincerely hoped all would work out well for them too; luckily they could collate their information based on our experiences, whereas when we came to Norfolk we did not know a soul, and our experimental journey, was a journey into the unknown. And of course not everybody's dream of escaping to the country is based on the same criteria...

I'd booked tickets for an open-air concert in the height of summer at Blickling Hall to see the *Opera Babes.*

I chose the venue, because it is my favourite National Trust property in Norfolk, and besides the stunning setting by the lake should go down a treat for our sumptuous picnic celebration...

About fifteen minutes before the show was due to start everything was set. Our table was covered with starched white linen, a copious array of mouth-watering treats, and even silver candelabra were placed in situ. What are we like...?

Although we discovered we were not alone in our decadent endeavours that day. Hundreds of portable tables like ours emerged all over the lawns of the great park. Here's the thing... we Brits seem to carry out this kind of stratagem with military-style precision – an away-day campaign to include all the home-from-home creature comforts. One table looked more outstanding than the next. *Keeping-up with the Jones's* must be a quintessentially English trait... Eh?

"Ready, everybody!" Mike lit the candles to our centrepiece, and just at that moment a sinister cloud ominously appeared overhead. The sky went *Doomsday* leaden. And the heavens opened with the most violent torrential downpour, lightning bolts catapulted into the horizon, and thunder roared to biblical proportions. Bloody hell...

In a freeze-framed moment of utter bedlam, we just all sat there dazed as we looked upon the destruction to our poor celebration feast. Then as if being fast-forwarded from a paused movie still, we dashed around manically trying to salvage some semblance from our supper. Chaos ensued all over the vast parkland; brollies and straw-boaters collided in the mayhem.

"Now that's what I call a deluge..." That certainly blew my own petard.

I do have a penchant for that sultry moist, almost tropical atmosphere created after a summer storm has cleared the air. It's very sexy... but not this time I'm afraid.

We all huddled and shivered together in the hammering rain, whilst torrents of muddy water gushed over out sodden feet. And weirdly, we started to sing in a stoic defiance: *Singing in the Rain,* which spread like a contagious chorus throughout our corner of the park. Suddenly I became a bizarre *maestro* of sorts to hundreds of people chanting along with us too. It was a beautiful albeit *cringing* moment!

Fortunately, moments later when the worst of the storm had passed, the orchestra revved-up, the stage lights illuminated, and the *Two Divas* made a grand entrance to a rapturous applause. And thankfully a tone-deaf diminuendo aided by howling dogs (including Barnaby) sank in favour of an epic vocal master-class! Crowds of fans looked on in awe drenched like an army of water rats...

The finale was a spectacular fireworks display shimmering over the still lake. The great house at Blickling was flash-backlit into a shadowy silhouette. Those outstanding turrets, and extravagant gables, flickered eerily in the smoky fall-out evocative of an archaic film inside a Victorian projector.

Nothing could dampen our spirits though; we were on such a high all that summer, with extraordinary events unfolding around every corner.

I know I have rambled on about typically English (volatile) weather per se, but I am convinced after living in this region for some time now, that North Norfolk has some kind of microclimate. Often, while the rest of the country is suffering atrocious storms this coastal enclave is invariably dry, sunny, and warmer. It seems that the storms, and severe weather systems sweeping in from the Atlantic devour Cornwall and Devon, cause havoc through the West Country, and then often veer up north to my Mike's neck of the woods; largely bypassing this county.

Studies by the University of East Anglia have also shown that levels of frost in the counties of Norfolk and Suffolk are similar to those of Cornwall and Devon, although in the winter months when those bracing winds drive off the North Sea, I dive under the duvet, or head for the nearest wood-burning stove. Believe you me…

There was a new breed of *Holly Lodgers* descending upon us, a trendier city crowd of media, film and music industry types. The A-Z list of celebs were probably attracted to new byword labels attributed to us… Such as 'The Boho Beauty' bestowed upon our little Bed & Breakfast by a certain glamorous travel magazine, suggesting:

'Bohos will love the chilled-out vintage décor at this gorgeous award-winning B&B: Indian-inspired Colonial, Shaker vibe Country, and Gothically romantic Claret'…

An unforgettable couple arrived that summer, down from Clerkenwell. They were involved in the media, as I gathered from their initial spiel. They had seen a feature on our abode with the slogan:

'This versus the West End on a Saturday Hmm…'

As they sauntered in to register, they declared this little sojourn to Norfolk might turn out to be something special, and indeed it would be; one that would change their lives in fact!

There is an obligatory uniform for outdoor-pursuits, especially here on the North Norfolk coast that most adhere to…

Firstly, we have the Gore-Tex and Gaiter crowd: ramblers, and hikers, durable windcheaters come all weather-wearers. Secondly, we have the Voyeurs: painters, photographers and twitchers here to record the visual cornucopia of delights in this blessed region; all donned in their eclectic mix of town & country-coastal (practical) apparel.

And finally we have the big players… The tweedy old-moneyed landed-gentry, incumbents in this landscape for aeons (think… classic Norfolk hunting jackets), but now obliged to rub shoulders with an influx of what I call the nouveau riche 'Blakeney Set'. The second homeowners, and the pleasure seekers in-the-know.

These hearty yachting-types down for their weekend breaks, especially the ruddy-faced chaps will usually be sporting apparel by marine clothing specialists *'Henri Lloyd'*. A must! Then of course there's the obligatory mannish brand of their beloved *'Hackett'* (polo/rugby shirt), and no doubt that distinctive Polo Player will be sported most discreetly of course. (Mr *Ralph Lauren* will do nicely for the gents, and the ladies too.) Ah, the 'Yummy Mummies' having escaped the urban school run and gone all country-chic. Those charlatans with chic-chicanery purporting to be country gals: the *Barbour* jacket brigade will be dressed-to-chill down to their sheepskin *Ugg Boots*.

Eat your heart out Paris Hilton! Dinky Chihuahuas were so last season – because the latest must-have accessory is the *'Boden'* bedecked (catalogue) kiddie in tow. *These are the Naughties of North Norfolk.*

Well, the new arrivals seemed to fit right in. Although they added their own uber-appendages: he with a straw Havanna trilby, and she with a tweedy Gatsby cap. Country-Cool…

Our two itinerant guests were keen bird-watchers; so both sported field binoculars, and all the requisite (outdoorsy) accoutrements including that classy *'Dubarry'* footwear completing the ensemble for their muddy hike. So here you have a snapshot of our two dashing protagonists fully attired for their North Norfolk coastal safari.

Ah, one of my flights of fancy had always been to set up a fleet of Safari Jeeps (don't ask...), bedecked in some kind of logo-imagery akin to the region's famous bird watching landscapes, to porter visitors out on expeditions over this expansive terrain by the sea. The key would be to collaborate with the hotels, guesthouses, and eateries in the area to fuel the fleet that I have in mind. Perhaps someone might cotton-on, and beat me to the idea now...

Actually as it turned out, Gerard and Lucy had both met on an assignment to Kenya having been keen conservationists, and each morning after breakfast they would recount exuberant tales of wildlife preservation in Africa and Asia. Mike and I would be enthralled for ages listening to their stories – especially as this is one topic very dear to our own hearts.

In fact their very first encounter during a safari was not for the faint-hearted as their jeep developed a flat in the middle of the Masai Mara. A terrifying ordeal ensued. Firstly a wayward elephant charged them, and then as if that were not bad enough... Secondly they were then subjected to hours of interest by a pride of lions in the rolling savannah. Only to be rescued long after nightfall by a search party.

Finally late that night back at base-camp, unbeknown to Gerard just as he was about to hit the sack, a snake had ensconced itself in his sleeping bag. And sure death would have ensued had it not been for the fact that his electric shaver had somehow fallen into the bag and perhaps assisted by the movement of the slimy predator – had actually switched itself on. Subsequently Gerard was alerted to the danger within.

"Now that's what I call a close shave!" Sorry, I couldn't resist...

Each day they would rigorously explore the area, but on their third morning during one of our after breakfast chats, they unexpectedly announced that they had fallen in love with the North Norfolk coast. In fact so much so that they even made us a seriously tempting offer to buy Holly Lodge *on the spot,* much to our surprise... I think Mike wanted to bite their hands off! But after some persuasive deliberation my end: we *both* declined. Although the seed might have now been sown as to the marketability of our residence!

A couple of mornings later, I think the day of their departure, they enthusiastically disclosed that they had actually had their offer accepted on a coastal house near Burnham Market, North Norfolk's (glitterati) epicentre aka 'Chelsea-on-Sea'. And if I were interested they would like to commission me to interior design their new home as soon as they completed the purchase.

A strange anomaly was that so many of our guests aired their views of wanting to move here. So much so, I feared that all our customers would end up living in the locale, and subsequently our business would all but dry up... What a schmuck!

Well, despite my obligations about six months later, I somehow managed to prepare my designs for their new house, which I computer generated into 3D virtual visuals sending them direct via e-mail (PDF) to their loft warehouse in Clerkenwell. They seemed impressed, and I was hired.

My concept was based on an eclectic mix of more current retro-inspired schemes with an ultra-contemporary edge for their glass and cedar-clad beach house. The fun-inspired project became a success, and ultimately we forged a tremendous lasting friendship. Thereafter I ached for more like-minded projects here on the coast...

OK, are you ready for another little gem about to be disclosed from my dog-eared diary...? Well, the one time we decided to let the place for a chic fashion shoot it almost backfired into a major debacle, especially as the Lodge was approaching its high profile apex at the time.

A hipper-than-thou entourage disembarked from a deluxe tinted-glassed minibus: six drop dead gorgeous models, a crew of West End stylists, one ultra-camp set director, and a hip photographer – all swished in from the hubbub of Covent Garden on a sultry summer's morning.

Key areas of the Lodge were commandeered: boudoir shots in the Claret, club cocktails in the orangery, country gingham in the orchard, and *risqué* swimwear by the wildlife pond... Hmmm?

It was sweltering that afternoon, when I wandered up to the water gardens with a tray of *Pimm's* to refresh our fashionistas. Talk about risqué swimwear, the tiniest bikinis ever created in the sheerest of vibrant techno-coloured fabrics. (The wearer might as well have been butt-naked in a birthday suit...) I just prayed no other guests were around for the show-stopping spectacle.

When I signed the contract to allow the filming of the fashion range at the Lodge, I had no idea it would be so provocative. More fool me...

Malcolm, the set designer sporting some serious guyliner came mincing-over in his flouncy floral shirt, practically open to his navel. Slut! Exuding his *Gaydar*, proud and *very* loud. He spoke with a potent lisp, and relayed to me all the relevant data...

"Isn't it fabulousss...? Next spwing's new Weady-to-Wear collection called 'Wural Waunch' (Rural Raunch) for the Twance-Clubber-ss." (Trance-clubbers)

The design samples were just hot-off-the-press, created by the latest up and coming protégé being backed by his super-duper mega corporation. Naturally it brought memories flooding back to my own fashion career, when I was somebody's latest protégé, so I thought I was used to the hype of a cutting-edge collection.

Malcolm pranced about, while the hairless bronzed muscled gods save a hint of stubble, and lithe goddesses sashayed sexily back and forth; Ike, the cameraman vied for the best shots, and the stylists preened, and prodded the models to perfection. This was the finale to the shoot, which surprised even me with its blatant lasciviousness, which in today's culture is becoming the norm... Just then I heard the bell ringing on a pushbike, and a croaky voice hollering, "Cooee... it's only me collecting for the Red Cross..."

Blimey! That voice was unmistakeable.

Marjorie, Miss Goody Two-Shoes from a local Christian group had let herself in through the double side gates.

Suddenly she stopped dead in her tracks, and shuddered...

"Oh dear..." she exclaimed, and lowered her eyes to the ground – not knowing where to look...

This was our Lady from Walsingham doing her saintly rounds, and it just so happened she caught the entire decadent pastiche at its most climactic sequence, that could have been evocative of a great Caravaggio.

She turned and looked disapprovingly at me nodding her head in disgust, pausing for a moment possibly to assess the situation.

"Eh...?"

Uh-oh. I could literally hear her mind thinking all sorts... All this scantily clad eye-candy cavorting around being filmed in the privacy of our back garden. What on earth do they get up to at the Lodge...? She must have thought. And I was mortified...

Malcolm intervened as he caught onto my embarrassment in front of our *holier-than-thou* visitor.

In fairness his overt camp persona was not his fault. He tried his best to put her right with what was going on, anxiously sweeping his over-highlighted Rockabilly quiff off his botoxed forehead, with his heavily bejewelled hands. He lowered his diamante-studded shades, and spluttered his words in a screeching lisp; but the more he tried to explain the deeper, and blacker the hole became. And she just did not get it at all...

I guess being privy to this type of diaphanous outré apparel revealing more than a just a hint of nether regional Boyzilians, and that's just the guys for starters, huhhhhh... was just completely unacceptable to her religious order.

She sighed tardily... But nevertheless rattled her collecting-tin all the more vigorously, whilst trying her darnedest to look away from the near-nudity abounding on the sundeck that afternoon. And much to my chagrin I might add as I implored everybody for a most generous whip-round for her benevolent cause…

Copious crisp notes were slotted into the tin in a frenzied flourish, and then I shoved in another twenty-pound note for good measure too.

Ah hah… the bribe might stop her from blabbing now! And curtail Chinese whispers, which I tell you could spread like wildfire around this neighbourhood!

Marjorie though did seem content with her day's takings at the Lodge, probably much more than expected, forgiven the circumstances.

"Mum's the word… toodle-oo!" she shrilled as she mounted her bike, straightening her school-ma'am bonnet, and clipping her moss-green loden skirt safely away from her sensible Oxfords. She hastily made her exit from the lewd scene, but not before leaving a Miss Marple-esque wry smile to linger heavily on my conscience.

"Marjorie, see you next month, with an extra bonus for the cause…" I hollered, schmoozing and gesticulating like a sycophantic moron as she cycled off down the garden.

I gulped. And was having one of my anxiety attacks…

All the models and crew fell about giggling, but Malcolm knew I felt piqued with embarrassment, and apologised profusely, obviously realising I had been ill informed as to the incongruous nature of the outlandish costumes.

Thankfully as it panned-out, the *dear old biddy* kept schtum! Obviously what was an innocent, but visually explicit scenario could have been construed into something covertly unsavoury, damaging our reputation locally. And then of course it might have really got out of hand with the sleazier tabloids at the time having a field day…

'Holly does porn in the back yard', crossed my mind.

Naturally, we'd be ruined by the scandal, and stripped of all our awards, and that would be it. Game Over.

Phew! That was the last time I allowed anything like that to take place on the premises *ever* again.

Another day, another dollar, another page turns on life at the Lodge.

There is a bona fide official nudist beach up on Holkham, that's abuzz in the summer months; the boundaries to this area are clearly marked for the visitor on the western side of Holkham Bay. The nude zone extends for about four miles, and up to half-a-mile wide, it takes about twenty-odd minutes from the car park to access this Naturist Reserve. Naturally ball games are permitted. Um...?

In complete contrast, on a more romantic note, more indelible memories were etched on my mind from that unforgettable year...

A hip trio of Bright Young Things up from Brighton arrived that autumn. The nature of their break was a secretly planned marriage proposal to take place on the windswept reaches of Holkham sands.

Luke, a successful club DJ, had arranged with his brother Harry to come down the day before, prior to his own arrival with his fiancée Hannah.

The plan in effect was that modish-skinhead-bro, Harry, had been instructed to bury a bottle on the beach with a message, to protrude from its neck, and to appear just proud of the surface of the sand. Harry would have to lie-in-wait in the woods to capture the proposal scene on camcorder.

The next day a tousled-headed wiry Luke, and his svelte aubergine-mopped partner, Hannah, arrived on a very blustery afternoon. However, tired after the long drive, she appeared frazzled and just wanted to crash out in their room. But after some wily persuasion, he finally managed to persuade his edgy disco-diva to go for their stroll on the beach that chilly day.

All went according to plan, and after about twenty minutes or so into their walk, he pointed to the mysteriously odd bottle sticking out from the sand. Hannah knelt down with curiosity, and plucked the message, which simply said...

'Will you marry me?'

"Yeah! Oh Yeah!" came a tearful reply from a rosy-cheeked-face peeking-out from under a woolly (Peruvian) bobble hat. Whereby Luke slid off his striped beanie, beamed with a cute dimpled smile, and kissed her like no tomorrow. He then produced a half bottle of champers, along with two flutes that he had discreetly hidden in his puffer jacket.

And right on cue as a prearranged a very magical surprise then ensued in the form of a magnificent white stallion, draped in a beautiful scarlet coat, embroidered with the words...

'*You and Me forever*'... Their names, date, and location scripted below the message as a memorable souvenir.

A smart liveried footman in Georgian dress then emerged from the cover of the trees and led the horse to them. He handed Luke the reins, and they both, being keen riders, mounted the great creature. From trot to canter, they entered into the shallows of the surf and rode along through the lapping waves for several love-struck miles.

Eventually they rode back to Harry sheltering behind a great pine from the bracing winds in his hooded duffle coat, and our mate, Ben, a top bloke, who had kindly donned the livery costume, and who was actually the lucky owner of super-gorgeous Jeremiah too.

Call it cheesy... perhaps? But I tell you when they played back the film to us the next morning, it was wildly seductive, and if *ever* there was a romantic proposal, then that came out pretty near tops... Totally pukka!

About ten months later they sent us a huge THANK YOU card announcing the birth of a beautiful baby girl, most probably conceived in the Claret, and named Holly, in our honour.

'Pleased to have been of service'. And why not...?

Running Holly Lodge would pan-out to provide a base for all sorts of scenarios having major repercussions at pivotal moments in any number of our guests' lives.

Of course this all added to the rich tapestry that was being woven into my diaries as I jotted down these amazing episodes, and highlighting them for fond recall, as today...

Although, some requests went way beyond our original remit; however, *Mine Hosts* were only too happy to oblige – in most cases that is... until I'd be greeted by the next shocker – just waiting around the corner...

CHAPTER 16

SPA TREATMENT

During that frenetic autumn, we grabbed a week in Budapest to recharge us in preparation for the onslaught of the impending Christmas season. However this trip was also to involve research into the spas of the region, as we were contemplating incorporating this voguish medium into our business.

We reluctantly dropped off Barnaby at Mother Teresa's *Dogotel* in Newmarket, and as usual our little *Can-Einstein* knew something was up by all the telltale signs of an imminent departure. Especially when he saw his personal vintage shabby-chic tan suitcase being packed.

I had pulled the dusty old find off a shelf in a charity shop in Sheringham, only to discover it had been monogrammed with the letters 'B.B' (Barnaby-Boo) by sheer serendipity. So our *hound* would always travel in style... And of course in which we could pack his extensive wardrobe of winter doggy coats, and sweaters. Last count eleven ranging from: *Burberry*-style mackintosh to a sporty hooded fleece number. Sad but true...

It's fascinating to see him revert from dog mode to human mode in an instant. His Lordship doth protest... naturally he can't articulate those feelings verbally, but his actions, always spoke louder than words.

Even as we drove down the long road by the racecourse into Newmarket within sight of the silky patchwork of the colourful jockeys trotting in perfect unison, Barnaby knew immediately what we were up to, and where he was going.

He would whimper, then proceed to deliver that classic whippet shake, accompanied by a loud dry-mouth panting...

On arrival at Teresa's house, although Barnaby felt comforted by the destination that he now knew only too well, he would still cling to our side suspiciously. He had it sussed...

The usual scenario would play out over the coming years. Whereby, he'd snuck down off the sofa, and jump up onto the other sofa by Teresa, then with a bullish wiggle manoeuvre onto her lap. Subsequently looking up longingly at her, before planting a smacker on her nose, and then bathing her in affectionate licks; of course, she'd respond by making an incredible fuss too.

It was almost as if he'd cannily play her off against us with a glare of contempt... There! Letting us stew for a lingering moment. Then spin his head around – this time giving us a look of approval as if to say... 'OK boys now sod-off, and have your hols – I'll be happy here with mum; but don't you be long...'

The dog-dorm annexe next door where Barnaby's biological canine family lived would be abuzz with cries and howls as we were leaving. Barnaby would sashay into the adjoining corridor to be warmly greeted by his mother, Sofie, and they'd rub noses in an Eskimo-esque greeting ritual. And both sis Gina, and bro Flash would howl with doggy-delight at the sight of their sibling reunion. We'd tearfully sneak away with the comforting knowledge that our Barnaby was in safe, good hands.

The culturally rich and vibrant capital of Hungary (UNESCO world heritage site) is bisected by the river Danube dividing the (original) towns of Buda, and Pest – now unified as one city. Our hotel was on Margaret Island, which is predominantly made up of parkland set in the middle of this awesome river. We had the luxury of staying in a Spa complex fed by the natural thermal waters from the many springs, prevalent in the area; and mainly sourced from a place called Gellért Hill.

In fact there are well over a hundred natural springs giving this place the title 'The City of Spas'.

These pungent mineral waters are proven to have healing medicinal qualities, as testified too by the millions of visitors each year.

Every aspect of beauty and pampering treatment, even cosmetic surgery, and affordable veneers or crowns for super perfect white teeth were catered for in the locale, and indeed in many health clinics around the city. These Eastern European clinics were now beginning to give Harley Street a run for their money on their beautifying youth enhancing procedures, but at more competitive prices.

Every morning after a pounding workout in the gym alongside some eye-catching (buff) Olympian Russian gymnasts... we would plunge into these therapeutic waters, first a hot-pool, then an ice-cold pool, followed by a Turkish steam bath, and then a relaxing massage before lounging around. Ah, that's the life... we began to feel invigorated in no time.

We returned to Holly Lodge refreshed, full of zeal, and inspired to incorporate this salubrious edge to be programmed as part of a new diverse service, that we were planning to road test. Treatment cards were slipped into the Information Folders in the rooms, offering various types of massages ranging from head, and neck to full-body using a wide range of essential, and base oils for therapeutic, deep tissue, relaxing, and sports massage. Also planned on the agenda were Reiki and Reflexology.

We would commission the services of experienced freelance masseurs/masseuses sourced locally that could provide portable tables in situ to carry out this service in the privacy of the guest cottages to begin with.

The idea being – should this take – we would then apply for further planning permission for our garage block to be converted into some kind of contemporary health spa facility incorporating: Turkish steam rooms, saunas, massage rooms, and *Jacuzzis*. More outlay, but what an edge!

Initially the general consensus was positive, so we knew the potential was there to build on for the future.

Well... our salubrious new offerings went tickety-boo – for a while, until that is...

Early November, when the Kendals arrived from Nottingham, they had booked eight massages between them – each to take place at 5pm daily, a nice commission for our new husband and wife team, who lived nearby in Holt.

Arthur and Hilary Kendal were very keen ramblers, and they had been negotiating Peddars Way for the last three days. The very scenic coastal path originates back to the Romans, and stretches from the brash Hunstanton (Sunny Hunny) in the west to irrepressible candyfloss Cromer in the east providing finite bookends to the vast gentrified North Norfolk paradise nestling in between.

On their fourth day they arrived back quite late; apparently Hilary had become short of breath, while out on the day's expedition, and consequently did not feel well at all.

Adam and Nicola were hanging about for their clients, when at around sixish, the Kendal's Land Rover came speeding, and honking up the drive grinding to an abrupt halt.

Arthur Kendal rushed to the house panicking and yelping that he thought his wife was having a heart attack. She was breathlessly panting in discomfort, complaining about tightness in her chest, and of arm pains. She bravely told everybody not to worry, and that she just needed a rest.

Suddenly she collapsed gasping... The colour drained from her face, she became a deathly white, and there was a clammy coldness about her body. I feared the worst – it was horrible... Mike called for an ambulance.

Arthur looked at me in sheer desperate horror and I will never forget the devastating panic in his scared eyes.

Oh God. Why didn't I go on that *First Aid* course I had been meaning to do for years? The thought crossed my mind as I scolded myself...

"I hope she makes it." I looked over at the dread in Mike's expression. This was the first full-blown health scare emergency we'd experienced at the Lodge.

The tension was mounting in the room, luckily Adam, a bright spark, whom had trained as a medic knew exactly what to do, as did Nicola. She grabbed some cushions from the bed, raised Mrs Kendal's legs, so as to increase blood flow towards the heart, and checked for any throat obstructions before performing mouth-to-mouth resuscitation. Meanwhile, Adam immediately applied CPR.

Adam tried and tried, again and again, compressing the chest region, while Nicola desperately breathed air into Mrs Kendal's lungs. Time stood still, and the lapse seemed to last forever. Nothing was happening, and she was just lying there motionless.

Mr Kendal was by now beside himself, howling in floods of tears.

"When is the ambulance coming?" he cried over and over.

I became fraught, as we stood helpless on the periphery of a dire A&E scene, whilst trying to calm a hysterical husband.

A guest's death in the *Dream Sanctuary* would be unbearable: I mulled over my most morbid fear becoming a reality.

They continued vigorously with the CPR resuscitation - relentlessly refusing to give up. And eventually, these miracle-workers managed to get a pulse; she choked, whilst her chest heaved with life, and thank-dear-God she started breathing again...

By now, Arthur Kendal was sobbing with relief kissing and hugging his beloved wife, who looked about in a daze of confusion mumbling something like...

"I'm OK, it just a little turn, I'll be fine, don't worry, what a fuss..."

Of course the shock of it all had thrown her, and shortly after that episode, she ended up in the local hospital for the obligatory tests.

Blimey... that really was close to *curtains* for the poor lady... And from time to time we would get guests coming down with all sorts of ailments, but nothing ever that serious... Thank Goodness! However, I hear she has made a full recovery.

All I can say is a very big 'THANK YOU' to Adam and Nicola the real hero, and heroine, who both came to the rescue, and did a fine job in saving this woman's life, through their quick thinking, and skilful deployment of their medical training.

Isn't it strange the things that stand out in a time of crisis? I'll never forget the anxious murmurs of our guests milling around outside, and the familiar clicking sound from the neighbouring cottages. Kettles hurriedly being switched on; whilst china cups clinked and clanked in readiness...

What is it about us British, when faced with a crisis? Thinking a cuppa will *solve* everything, "Aaaargh... so comforting: the quintessential English fix..." Which it is said, certainly semi-fuelled the British Empire, most probably because of its caffeine properties. But it has to be said also, that it must be the 'Theanine', an amino acid relaxant, which apparently gives it that calming effect on our systems, and so reduces stress. No wonder I am thoroughly addicted to the stuff. Perhaps my next novel will be titled: *Tea in Time for a Crisis*.

Another thing I found out about tea is that it originated in Edinburgh by a tea-master named '*Drysdale*', who created the idea, which later seeped across the border to be popularised in English Tea Houses. (God forbid Mrs Loomas, our proud Scottish nationalist ever gets wind of this; she'll have field day with the good news...)

This business with all that it entails is a curious one, especially as we felt responsible for caretaking people's lives, whilst staying on our premises. So I guess, when I spent one afternoon delving into its origins to satisfy my curiosity, I discovered some interesting factoids.

Without digressing too much from the main thrust of the narrative, as to explain in detail the history of the Hospitality Industry would evoke a lengthy thesis on the subject, worthy of its own hardback tome, but here is my sketchy take, and where I think it might lead to...

When Mary and Joseph were refused accommodation at the Inn somewhere in downtown Bethlehem, and kicked off the whole idea of this Bed and Breakfast thing, it was the savvy Romans, who then capitalised on the concept in their adopted realms. Although typical of their trademark decadence – these hostelries became rampant pleasure motels too – which must have really wooed their visiting dignitaries.

However, when they departed these shores, tastes changed, and those hooded Monks, who knew a thing or two about *minimalism,* and pudding-basin haircuts became *de rigueur* with their de-cluttered residences or hospices especially with the itinerant pilgrims. *The Less is More* concept suited their be-gowned-pockets.

But, I bet it was those thrill-seeking European settlers, you know the hordes that followed on from the *Mayflower* to the New World, that struck upon the idea of the sassy Saloon to include overnight accommodation aping European Inns.

This evolved, into those more salubrious Bed and Breakfasts catering for well-heeled guests, and ubiquitous travelling salesmen. Still in use today, and preserved for posterity. Pretty New England clapboard springs to mind, historic Victoriana, or y'all deep southern plantation shutter-number; of course with the obligatory rocking chair on the veranda – to pull in the punters.

Meanwhile back in old Blighty. It was those masked Dick Turpins of their day, who really spotted a gap in the market, lying-in-wait on the desolate cross-country roads in between the Coaching Inns. So as they cried out... 'Stand and Deliver' to highway coaches laden with tourists, they surely did lighten their load of heavy baggage twofold: first to line their pockets, and secondly to assuage storage issues in these establishments. Storage space, now here's the thing... that was amply provided to allay this complaint from our customers at the Lodge: with plentiful hanging and shelving space etc. **And no wire hangers, ever!**

I guess that the French refugees with their *savoir-faire* – outcasts from the Napoleonic wars, who managed our early hotels – set up to accommodate officers on leave – were probably the forerunners to the *sprauncy* hotels of the new Industrialised Age.

Then it all went really haywire, when the former valet of pervy Lord Byron, one James Brown, set a new benchmark synonymous with the epitome of stylish elegance, when he created *'Browns' of Mayfair*; and even received the royal patronage of Victoria and Albert.

The Ritz, The Savoy, The Langham, and the fabulous *Claridges* all followed suit, raising the stakes in top-class hospitality.

Of course today new ground is being broken all the time in the world of fine accommodation with six star, and even seven being banded-about as a new rating terminology. Perhaps the relevant Tourist Authorities will introduce a new star rating level at some point to facilitate the new hybrid breed of guesthouse-deluxe in the post-noughties years and beyond. Online customer reviews will be key, and play a pivotal role in the rating process, I'm sure... Scary!

I like to think Holly Lodge was at the vanguard of this new wave of *Deli-Boutiqueries*, as I call them, especially as there has *now* been a renaissance in interest in staying in more *individual* Bed and Breakfasts: *Pensions*, *Gasthaus*, *Paradors*, *Pousados*, *Minshukus* and *Shukurus* to name some of the foreign terms, as opposed to the soulless bland budget lodges flooding the market: The overnight *Tescos* of the hotel world...

Can you imagine the first hotel in space...? Or even on the Moon? With a never before state-of-the-art technology. There would have to be a slew of in-house entertainments, perhaps on the 3D holographic principle a la *Bang & Olufsen*, rooms with sensational views of the galaxy, with optional premiums placed on glass viewing-suites of blue-planet Earth. Cosmic, compact, capsule living will set the trend, space saving, and gravity-free of course... My money would be on stardust lunar bar-lounges, and revolving solar-powered restaurants, interstellar sightseeing travel excursions in high-spec *'Virgin* Spaceways' pods, and family orientated aqua-aeronautic pools. I can but dream...

I dread to think what a rating inspection will be like then. And we will possibly see the first 'Chelsea Lunarscape Show'.

After over six years in the trade, I had found that we would have so many types of discerning clients – guests from all walks: sometimes snooty, sometimes reserved and enigmatic, sometimes rowdy, obnoxious and darn-right rude, sometimes considerate and full of praise, sometimes picky and querulous, sometimes completely lovely, and charming like most of our Holly Lodgers, and sometimes very curious like the four we had in from Chicago that winter...

On arrival, they requested a card table. Fortunately we had our little Georgian satinwood treasure, which probably was the catalyst for many a tortured soul in its day. Can you imagine – they spent their entire five-day stay at the Lodge, riveted to their poker game, stacking greenbacks over the marquetry inlays, day and night in the Orangery. They never left the residence once.

We actually have a seriously good, if somewhat unusual Thai food restaurant in Thursford (don't ask...) – bizarrely it doubled as our village pub too, and every night take-away food would be despatched straight to the Lodge. Their obsessive game playing might as well have been played, back in their hometown of Chicago. It was very odd!

Another unusual request came from a chap from Hong Kong...

"Please Mister Lobert could I have a bowl of *gold* fish for my loom?" he enquired.

Well, it just so happened we beat him to the idea first as the Colonial Cottage did come with our requisite two trophy goldfish we had won at a Country Fair: Donald and Ivana, I kid you not... This spurned us on with the rather Bohemian idea at the time, of installing (stylish) goldfish bowls in each of the cottages: a novelty that seemed to be a great hit with many of our guests, who could not extol the virtues enough of their soporific effects.

The Chius were very grateful, as I know what this means to the Chinese, and perhaps it gave us *good fortune* too?

Mind you talk about slippery customers (no pun intended) but most apt to the next bunch due in, as we discovered shortly... This time another request was made for our beloved little table, but for very different dubious reasons...

A party of four arrived, checked in with nothing untoward, but hey that's what always happens... I brought the table this time to the Claret Cottage on a Saturday evening, where they were all gathered. And that was that, so I thought; thinking perhaps a nice innocent game of scrabble or the like would ensue.

Anyway around eight o'clock, I decided I would offer them a tipple on the house, and for some strange reason I grabbed a bottle of 'Nelson's Blood' (aforementioned in my story), and knocked on their door...

Well, blow me over! They were preparing for a séance with an ominous looking Ouija board laid out. Which really unsettled me... Especially as we had our own resident spirit now firmly locked away in her own Pandora's box.

"And we did not want her re-awakened for crying out loud..."

Mr Hoskins seemed delighted to see me, as I put the tray down of Nelson's brew and he enthusiastically inquired...

"How on earth did I know?"

"Come again... Huh?" was my riposte.

"Nelson dear boy, NELSON!" he said, practically ramming the naval hero's name down my throat.

You see the reason for their séance was to contact an ancestor of theirs, who had fought alongside Nelson, and naturally where better to make contact, than to be in Norfolk of course! Although I asked them the obvious of why they didn't try to book the 'Lord Nelson' itself, in Burnham Thorpe? But apparently they did, and it was full; so they booked into the Lodge instead... "Drat!"

Mike is always calling me a bit of a 'White Witch' as I am often weirdly intuitive; many a time that dumfounds him. Apparently, both my father and my mother had been very gifted in bucket loads in that department and sometimes it got them into all sorts of trouble.

So the mere fact that I grabbed that particular tipple instead of the mulled wine simmering on the stove, which we gave all our guests during the Christmas season, does remain a mystery.

They raised their glasses and toasted dear Horatio, and beckoned me to sit with them...

The curtains were pulled too; the beeswax candles were flickering from the sconces of the Empire mirror hanging over the fireplace, and a shadowy glow was cast over the Venetian red walls. An apt scene was set for their little foray into the spiritual world to beckon their ancestor forth.

Mrs Hoskins grabbed a chair for me to be seated next to her husband, for now what seemed a no-nonsense perverse game of fey pleasure. But I was not a happy bunny... Not at all!

The heebie-jeebies swept over me like a spine-chilling Stephen King classic and I suddenly declined their invitation, and bid them a... good night!

As I shut the door to the Claret, I dwelled for a lingering moment and was on the cusp of careering back in to implore them to stop the proceedings. And I should have followed my instincts, because... our poor *flagship* cottage, (metaphorically speaking) now the scene of their cosy little ritual, might dredge up who knows what from the beyond? And now I was really bothered...

The next morning at breakfast was a very sombre affair. When I inquired if all went well with the séance, I was greeted with subdued murmurs and that they would rather not talk about it. At all! Which sounded very ominous.

It was as if a dark cloud had dulled them, they were all very sullen and the atmosphere became quite morose.

I was extremely concerned by their reticence, which was very disturbing to say the least. But I just could not prise out any information regarding what happened. And now I rued the day I'd become an effete proprietor – action should have been taken to curtail their wretched pastime.

After they left Mike just shrugged it off as just silly childish stuff, whereas my alarm bells were ringing so loudly, I inevitably stuck my head inside the *Yellow Pages*... speedily thumbing through: Priests, Rabbis and even Mullahs to call in to *exorcise* the cottage of any bad karma that might have been caused.

Ah! Dial-an-Exorcist... *Buy one get one free*. So not one to pass up on a special offer, I made the appointment. Mike thought I had lost the plot and berated me no end.

I was never sure what happened there that night. Although suspicions were pungently aroused in sensitive ole me. The exorcism gave me peace of mind through its ritual. It was my tenet!

Things certainly felt better after that albeit with a possible *placebo* effect. In saying that though, hitherto the place being blessed, I found Barnaby one evening jumping up into thin air as if trying to touch something; his eyes were riveted almost as if he were being cajoled by who knows what? It was very unsettling, and completely out of character for him. Even Mike was bewildered...

Our dedication was boundless during that golden period at the Lodge. The guests always came first. And then another request that Christmas, which should not have been part of our *remit* at all, was fulfilled with alarming alacrity to make their Chrimbo stay extra special with us.

"Here guys these are for you!" chanted Allegra the ringleader of a party of six *'Loose Women'* down from Alderley Edge.

They stood around us like a witches' coven of excessively botoxed ancient beauties – about to stir up a wicked brew...

"Santas costumes, huh?" I queried.

"Because you're worth it!" They cajoled.

"Oh my God." We looked at each other in disbelief. Skimpy Santa costumes were handed out to us to show off our well-honed pecs... And the rest!

So, this is what my years at the gym had been all about: servility to some sex-starved cougars at our B&B in Norfolk... Blimey, *we* were now pre-lunch appetisers...

In hindsight, I think the joke was definitely on us... Well, we played along for the *very* last time that Christmas Day bedecked in the most naffest clingy costumes for their festive parlour show.

I choked incessantly on the white fuzz from my irritating stick-on-beard, and to top it all my lousy bobble hat (annoyingly) slid off at every opportunity from my zero-cropped baldpate – making me look like a half-demented, half-naked, Hare Krishna. 'Ho, Ho, Ho'.

Mike was such a flirt too... and looked like *Spiderman* gone-all-Christmassy! And poor Barnaby did not escape either: he was adorned with felt antlers and sparkly trinkets. However, he seemed to inhabit his role with great aplomb as 'Bambi, the Acid-House-Lounge-Lizard-Rapper'. So much so, that they just wanted to take him home with them. No chance!

Well, it could not have got any wackier at the Lodge that year; more surprising twist and turn spins down the vast corridor of new arrivals: doors opening onto the idiosyncrasies of some of our more murkier visitors. And pigs were flying...

CHAPTER 17

THE PINNACLE

The quest for greater excellence was never far from my thoughts imbuing Holly Lodge with progressively more creative ideas. And never one to rest on my laurels I'd step up a gear each season. There just seemed to be no-room to stagnate in this highly competitive game.

Maintaining the quality of our establishment was always paramount, however the key was to keeping it fresh year after year – that would give us the edge. Luckily I have been fortunate to be peripatetic enough in my life to experience a vast array of hotel services, and diverse levels of quality of accommodation worldwide crossing the cultural divide.

Our regulars would really appreciate the keen attention to inspired details incorporated into either the service, accommodation, or refreshing new changes to update the décor.

Plans were afoot to introduce a 'Pillow Menu', and full 'Bedding Menu' offering a wider variety of tog weights and fillings. A range of hollow-fibre (anti-allergenic) to voluptuous goose-down and duck feather fillings would be provided to anatomically appease all body-types. In fact a delicious menu of unadulterated luxury... And oh, fresh (white) Egyptian cotton linen is always preferable as an unbeatable standard classic.

There is no doubt that our acres of high quality bedding including the later addition of Memory Foam mattresses played an integral part in often generating much repeat business.

It's these *core* essential nuances of luxury that define a special staycation, and I'm sure determine if you would want to return to such and such an establishment.

There are so many discreet touches of *luxe par excellence* that can be applied, such as producing our own fragrance pouches: Here goes... my *Martha Stewart* moment; I'm afraid... Using for example: dried lavender, rosemary, Cleveland sage, rose petals, lemon verbena, apple mint and chamomile or tansy seeds said to ward off moths – all grown in copious amounts in our back-door herb garden. These would be gathered, dried and attractively bound into linen sachets made from old pieces of scrap fabrics to be hung inside the wardrobes or placed in the back of lined drawers. *Make Do and Mend / Waste Not Want Not* – that's so topical! But, of course a much cheaper option to being shop bought...

There is nothing worse than a dusty old bowl of potpourri lingering on a window ledge... Yuck!

Alternately, here's a smart trick... Simply sprinkle a few drops of essential oils onto a cloth and dab onto a warm radiator to instantly fragrance a room.

Another useful tip I picked up from an eccentric maiden aunt, was to fill a spray container with one part pure vodka or gin mixed with eight-ten parts water, and add some droplets of essential oils, blends of your choice to make fantastic room sprays. A much more cost-effective, longer lasting and less toxic room atomiser than if purchased over the counter. Although we always suspected my dear old spinster aunt may have been a secret lush, and therefore reversed the composition of her recipe. Yikes! So it's quite possible she may have had the odd swig or two, or three, and so on... God rest her soul...

Naturally being avant-garde with your ideas helps too and it does not have to be that expensive – such a little thing can go a long *long* way... For example I found in a vintage clothes shop in the locale, an inexpensive iridescent crimson wire-mesh high-heel shoe, which might have been evocative of a romantic Baroque Ball. I used some scrap fabric to make a crimson velvet pad to fit inside the heel of the shoe, so it would become a decadent and witty container of sorts, and filled it with (wrapped) chocolate truffles – to be placed on the ladies dressing table of the Claret Cottage to great effect.

Something so *simple* would become widely commented upon even during the presentation of our Awards, and by *The Sunday Times* to boot. I believe it's these little special (attention-grabbing) *touches* that make you stand out from the crowd. And moreover they resonated with the Tourist Board inspectors for those all-important ratings…

My ethic for the (best) guest experience was to cater to all their senses: sight, sound, smell, touch and taste. So to make those sensuous pleasures work in perfect unison to create a winning formula: *Boutique B&B Porn*!

And naturally it boils down to good ole housekeeping too, relentless dedication and hard work, punctilious lateral thinking outside the customary box for every amenity, a *bonhomie* sincere welcome to our guests, and of course two gorgeous *Domestic Gods* such as our good selves did help!

I swore, the next time a smart Alec of a guest asked me "What I did for a day job?" I would march them into the kitchen and give them an apron, "There Cinders… see you in the morning…" Of course it's an innocuous statement, unassumingly said in jest, but when you have been flat-out for days on end, it can touch a raw nerve sending one into a fit of convulsion. "Nurse-my-medication…"

It's a fallacy about this business being a part-time job unless it's just for extra pocket money – all well and good! For us though it was a *serious* business, a means to an end, and was most definitely 24/7. What we put in, we got out in bucket loads of rewards and satisfaction, although there can be no denying it's honestly a *Love-Hate* affair.

Some mornings we would despair at the hard work, whilst others we'd be happily getting on with the job in-hand. A little praise from a satisfied customer went a long way.

During the economic calamities following the Wall Street Crash in 1929 resulting in the Great Depression, many of the unemployed sought extra income by opening their homes for overnight accommodation to travellers or lodgers, subsequently the term 'Boarding House' was coined, and they thrived across America. And today, we are now faced with probably the worst recession ever since those *Brother can you spare me a dime* infamous days. So, this home-based trade, now almost older than the hills *can* provide a decent income to weather these economic vagaries, whether town or country based.

After winning *The Regional Excellence Awards for the Best B&B/Guesthouse of the Year in the East of England 2004*, meant we'd qualified for the shortlist joining the privileged company of every other regional winner in Britain.

This list in each category would be whittled down with approximately four participants being chosen for each of: Small, and Large Hotel, B&B/Guesthouse, Holiday Park, Self-Catering Accommodation, Tourism Information Centre, and Visitor Attraction, as nationwide entrants to be contenders on the night of the awards ceremony.

The specialist committee of judges and assessors representing *VisitBritain* will have digested, and cogitated rigorously before they'll have agreed on their one winner to be chosen out of each category. These lucky recipients will receive the most coveted of prizes in the awards calendar, which is lauded as The British Tourism '**Oscars**'. Even to have made it thus far must be considered a wonderful achievement!

A golden invitation announced the dates and venue for The Enjoy England Excellence Awards 2005 promoted by *VisitBritain*. The *Red Carpet* event would be held on Tuesday 19th April at the British Museum.

I had been surfing the net stealing a glance at the other contenders in our category, each one looked terrific, but when I Googled *St Ervan Manor*, four miles from Padstow, or should I say Padstein in Cornwall, a former rectory now sporting a *Michelin* Star for its very fine cuisine; my heart sank to the bottom of my dreams... How could Holly Lodge ever compete? I was overwhelmed by a feeling of competitive inadequacy, whilst poring over the photographs of this most classy establishment. Even the name conjures up an air of mystique, and for crying out loud it had been immortalised by the poet Sir John Betjeman in a book *Summoned by Bells*.

There was yet another possible strike against our chances of winning the biggie, an issue that could well handicap us! We had been awarded the *'AA Guest Accommodation of the Year for England 2004-2005'*, and as far as I know for an establishment to win both elusive titles from the two *major* Tourist Boards in the country, especially within a year of each other was unheard of. And I believe this may not have been eclipsed by another B&B/Guesthouse to this day.

Nevertheless I tried to remain positive. We shopped for two new dinner suits complete with all the accessories (any excuse to get to the menswear department at *Selfridges*), and naturally I wanted to look my best holding the much-coveted Gold Tourism Oscar, whilst being photographed by the press. Who am I kidding! This only ever happens in your dreams this kind of thing. OK... We had won the AA award, but maybe that had been a fluke, which would stand-alone as a *pinnacle* for most, giving your establishment tremendous cachet that you could live on for years to come. And one could die a happy man! However this was a new tease, because now we are talking *best* in the 'British Isles'... Now wouldn't that be something?

I guess coming from such a competitive background, being the youngest of three brothers, the oldest always being a rip-roaring achiever and having a very successful, workaholic father: I still had something to prove.

I did lose my ambition for a long time, and it even ended up in the doldrums for a time. Maybe because I'd walked away from a successful career, culminating with too many wasted years in a mired desert of distress; that, when all along I'd been seeking a refreshing oasis in which to rebuild the shattered turmoil of my tired soul. And perhaps this was my new creative outlet...?

My ambition was reignited with a vengeance now... We were suddenly riding the crest of an unstoppable wave, I was feeling inspired and wanted to share this success with my life partner; because none of this would have been possible without Mike. His earnest hard work and supportive loving spirit had no doubt made us into a dynamic winning team, and in many ways completely symbiotic!

"Remember be reticent, if we lose out; and please under no circumstances are you to show your devastation, I'm counting on you..." Mike gave me his sagely advice.

I promised like a good Boy Scout in preparation for the big day...

"Dib, dib, dib... Dob, dob, dob, and all that..."

But of course such a disappointment would kill me, and he knew it only too well. We were in too deep and maybe this title was a once in a lifetime opportunity. And I am saying this honestly, because truth be told, it's what most contenders really think during many an award ceremony – I'm sure...!

"Man we've paid our dues that's why we're in it to win it..."

My years of crystal clear clarity have enabled me to understand finally why I can be so driven; something way back had been ingrained into my psyche from my father's convictions of obtaining commercial perfection. These demands on my energies had played out for an eternity. Business achievements were his only deal with me... Whatever I had achieved in the past never *ever* seemed good enough to extract some kind of praise from him to deliver a satisfying compliment, or even a demonstrative hug. I was forever seeking his ultimate seal of approval, and for god's sake to show me some sign of his paternal love. Alas, forever unobtainable in his lifetime...

The big day finally arrived, perhaps a day like no other... We mounted the steps up to the entrance amid the historic splendour of this iconic museum – a spectacular venue for the Tourism Red Carpet Oscar ceremony.

It was a fine breezy evening with the setting sun pelting its rays against the imposing Ionic colonnades. Evoking the essence of when I last visited here as an awe-inspired young teenager marvelling at the archaeological relics found from the ancient world; that so fired my imagination.

This was a poignant reminder, when in those days I used to escape into my private world of magical childhood adventures. I'd travel through the pages of Homer's, *The Iliad*, to such places as the fabulous, but tragic Troy, and thrill to the sea voyages of *The Odyssey*, or glory alongside Prince Caspian on his swashbuckling exploits through the wondrous tales of the *Arabian Nights*. And of course marvel at the mystique of the Pharaohs and the Valley of the Kings.

These rich colourful journeys left an indelible impression on my adolescent self, and would ameliorate my lonely, and often wretched life as a respite from the austere presence of my tyrannical stepmother.

Two guys, full of hopeful expectations mingled with two hundred and fifty VIP guests in the Queen Elizabeth II Great Court. All gathered together to honour the cream of British Tourism for a champagne reception under an architectural masterpiece. A *splendorific,* if ever there is such a word to describe the magnificence of the lattice glass ceiling covering the entire two acre square court, the largest covered area in Europe, designed by the outrageously brilliant Lord Norman Foster. And completed at the dawn of the new Millennium.

We were thrilled to see all the familiar faces from The East of England Tourist Board – regulars we had met through the years of attendance at such similar ceremonies, but nothing before ever came close to the glamour and prestige of that particularly grand occasion.

As homage to the impending St George's Day, patriotic *English* champagne flowed with canapés inspired by local produce echoing the Best of British. The cameras flashed around at the luminaries from our industry, travel-talk by those cognoscente in-the-know resonated through the vastness of The Great Court. Everybody was there in their finery in anxious anticipation of *who* would be this year's winners.

Last year's event had been hosted by Sue Lawley and the Duke of Kent, interestingly this year it was to be broadcaster, comedienne, and writer Sandi Toksvig, who had hosted that event way-back at Duxford in 2002, where we'd received 'The Highly Commended' runner-up award for our Region.

"Hey, she might remember us," I hinted to Mike.

We anxiously waited to see the outcome…

As the crowd poured into the BP Theatre at the museum, my emotions were wired with heightened excitement. I am a lousy champagne drinker; my tolerance levels are very limited at the best of times; so I had to be careful with my intake.

Maybe it was my extrasensory antenna, but I sensed an air of a buzz eddying around us throughout the reception, everyone seemed to be making such a fuss. Perhaps they were just happy to see us get this far, the vibe was curious, yet quite overwhelming. Was it plausible? Mike ever practical kept me in check reminding me to keep it *real*!

I became even more suspicious though as we were ushered to our seats at the *very* front of the auditorium, while the other contenders in our category were seated many rows further back.

I was on the cusp of: A. Asking the Audience, B. Going fifty-fifty or C. Phone a friend. I could not bear the suspense much longer…

"Oh look it's the nice smart couple, the owners of *St Ervan Manor*," I exclaimed; the ones I feared who might be triumphant.

"I bet they're as nervous as we are." I waived in respect, while Mike nudged me to settle down.

I sat next to a very attractive lady, who represented Holkham Hall, up for 'Visitor Attraction of the Year'. Her name was Laurane Herrieven, and she ran the Marketing division for the Great Hall. We were now kindred spirits from our own home-patch of Norfolk, ready to console one another in our hour of defeat, should it be necessary.

There were many awards to be distributed that night for each category, and the ceremony seemed to last forever. Keeping us on tenterhooks...

Then came Holkham's turn in the proceedings. Laurane became riveted with apprehensive tension as the rival contenders were announced, the envelope was slowly opened... And it was a *Gold* for her beloved Holkham Hall. We looked at each other brimming with euphoria as she excitedly went to claim her well-earned accolade on behalf of the Earl of Leicester. On her return we hugged, and kissed as she smiled in relief. And then she declared...

"It's your turn soon," sending a spine-tingling nervous bolt of anxiety piercing through my chest.

I can't quite recall the order of presentation, but it's possible *ours* was maybe the penultimate category. After that burst of excitement with our very own Norfolk winner now calmly sitting beside me, and Mike anxiously glued on the other side, I momentarily lapsed into nostalgic wistful dreams. And, although I have enjoyed many a big bash in my time, this amazing night was only ever evocative of one other extremely memorable gala occasion back in 1989 that might compare...

I briefly rewound my thoughts, and whisked away, suddenly crossing over a great chasm of memories, trespassing through a portal into a time, and an evening, that was so significant during my lost wilderness years, as I call them now...

There we were, my beloved stepmother, Violet, recently widowed from my father, but looking a film starry knockout!

We had both been invited by my dear friends, the fabulous Ryan twins, and their sister Caroline to join them for an evening with numerous VIP guests to attend one of the last great 'Frank Sinatra Concerts' in the awesome magnificence of The Royal Albert Hall.

On the bill were the incomparable fellow rat-packer, Sammy Davis Junior, and Liza Minelli, who is Caroline's godmother, actually 'The Voice-Sinatra' was her godfather too. 'Showbiz Royalty'... (Caroline is the most unassuming person from that background I had ever met!).

I vaguely recall stopping off at some plush hotel, which one truly escapes me now, but we went up to the suite of Marion Ryan, their renowned songstress mother for pre-concert drinks.

Later we arrived at The Royal Albert Hall, which was crawling outside with paparazzi. As I escorted Violet into the arena, heads turned, and perhaps it looked like I was her young gigolo in tow.

It was first class treatment all the way... Here, unbeknown to us we'd be parted to go to our separate seats.

I escorted Caroline upstairs heading to the most amazing vantage point to be seated in a plush gilt and red private balcony-box practically overlooking the stage. Little did I know, we'd soon be joined by a living legend... Just then the most stunning *glamazon* swept through the lush velvet drapes, she glided effortlessly down the steps to her seat smiling demurely, and exchanging pleasantries. And she sat directly behind me.

I immediately recognised that alluring face, every inch the Hollywood movie star, and thought I would faint in star-struck awe... It was Ava Gardner, no less; although no longer in her prime this iconic goddess of the silver screen was still breathtaking!

I was charged with adrenalin, I seated myself, looking down over the balcony, scanning around the sea of glitterati to the very front row of the central arena, to catch Violet being seated next to the Pop Star forever-blond-mopped brothers, 'Bros'.

The great crooner entranced and captivated all with his rich velvet voice and sang through his repertoire of probably the greatest songs ever written. And poor ole Ava was weeping throughout the entire performance, hanging onto every nostalgic note Frank sang with his inimitable style. No doubt lamenting their well-documented on-off epic romance. At one point, I handed her a tissue, she grabbed my hand firmly with thanks. And I nearly spontaneously combusted in appreciation...

Mogambo, *Showboat*, and *The Barefoot Contessa*, some of her greatest screen roles – still radiated from her dazzling persona in my mind's eye.

It's all quite a haze now, but we were even treated to a back stage pass, where a host of celebrity fans were clamouring to congratulate their deities of Swing.

Serendipitously, I shook Mr Sinatra's hand, and told him it was especially on behalf of my father, who was a lifelong fan, but unfortunately he could not be with us this night.

He was very gracious and gave his best regards to my dad...

A poignant moment played out with such an irony... as I grew up to my father constantly playing Sinatra's records echoing through the house.

The show, the evening, the night of a thousand stars was mesmeric; a one-off special event deemed to the annals of entertainment history; a euphoric recall of a foggy distant dream lodged in the inner-sanctum of my mind.

I really don't remember if I ever thanked Paul, Barry and Caroline enough for their wonderful generosity and support during my difficult times; I sincerely *hope* I did!

Suddenly... It was as if I fast-forwarded from this fleeting trance-like reverie. Interrupted... I jolted on hearing the sparkling wit of Sandi Toksvig, standing at the lectern now speaking about '**Country**, **Colonial**, and **Claret**', and then I really perked up, when she mentioned "Robert and Michael have lovingly created... and so on..."

I nudged Mike, "Huh?"

"Shush!" He discreetly elbowed me.

Her speech then resonated with such audible clarity I thought my heart was going to stop and I gulped as she announced...

"It is with great pleasure that this auspicious Gold Award of Excellence goes to none other than the one, and only... Holly Lodge."

The audience erupted with applause as we took to the stage. It was so surreal and we were jubilant! I wanted to pinch myself, savouring every second of this monumental moment of triumph – *The* **Pinnacle.** And it was mind-blowing.

"Words can't fathom my appreciation of such an honour bestowed upon us that night." A fitting acceptance speech perhaps! Although ineffably, with my brevity caught up with such taut emotions in the moment: words can't express and therefore actions spoke louder...

I remember both of us clutching the award amidst blinding flashes, making us pose this way and that. A broad winning smile from the effervescent Sandi Toksvig, who congratulated us with a, "Well deserved, and at last..." And shaking hands with Lord Marshall chairman of *VisitBritain* was such a boon...

And now... we were the feted darlings of our specialist genre. Well at least for the time being, then in 2005. It's official, Holly Lodge *'The Best B&B/Guesthouse in Britain'.* Perhaps now my father would be smiling down from the heavens enjoying the moment "*Son you did it!*" as he embraces me with ethereal congratulations in respect of my capabilities, and finally approving my accomplishments.

The Samling on Lake Windermere was 'Hotel of the Year', and the guest of honour, and final recipient was the Duchess of Northumberland, who received the Outstanding Contribution to Tourism Award for 2005 for her spectacular garden project at Alnwick. Previous winners were Her Majesty The Queen, perma-tanned television holiday guru Judith Chalmers OBE, and Manchester United football club.

We left the BP Auditorium into a blaze of flash photography and press interviews, even the *VisitBritain* press officer, Maddie, was abuzz with *Hello* magazine being interested in doing some kind of feature. I remember I think it was *Sky Travel* dragging me off to some secluded corner to film my reaction, but in the mayhem, Mike had been pulled in another direction, until we later fought through a myriad of hugs and kisses finally meeting up off-piste in the respite of the magnificent domed Reading Room. Where a hallowed silence pervaded...

"Wow! Have we died and gone to heaven...?" I gasped looking up and around in a spin at this vast sanctity of reams, and reams of vellum bound archives that could almost be tasted in their glorious profusion. And a soaring celestial rotunda so utterly breathtaking it dwarfed us into insignificance below. We gathered our thoughts, took deep breaths, and then noticed...

That a special spread of archaeological artefacts had been laid out for the perusal of the winners; this was an amazing treat... as we wandered from table to table admiring the ancient treasures, and distracting ourselves in the sanctuary of this great cathedral of a library.

Mike cavalierly picked up a priceless Anglo Saxon rare solid gold torque, ironically I believe found somewhere in Norfolk. Simply not thinking he began to stretch-open the adornment – to amusingly try it for size – around his neck. The museum attendant scowled and scolded him most severely, and suddenly museum security swooped, hemming us in, and the next thing... took us by complete surprise.

"Oh my God...!" Mike exclaimed. The great doors to the entrance – back to our real world – were slammed closed. It was another breathtaking moment indelibly etched on my mind from that day. I think we created one almighty security scare...

"Do you know who we are...?" I barked.

I thought I'd try that one. And immediately they released us...

Blimey... What a hullabaloo! I really can't believe they thought we were going to make a run for it absconding with this historic treasure and returning it to its rightful place in Norfolk. So not only did we win our much-heralded prize, but we nearly shut down the British Museum that night probably ensuing with a stint in Dartmoor no doubt... Scandalous!

Back into the moment once again, we cheerily rejoined the celebrations before finally slipping away exhausted with so much emotion spent from a night of exulted triumph we would both remember forever more.

The next morning, an exhausted muggins in propensity of all the excitement, actually got lost – a first, getting out of London – delaying us, hours en route to Norfolk. We had to pick poor dejected Barnaby up at Teresa's in Newmarket, who was now out walking her dogs late that afternoon. When we finally arrived, we looked through the sitting room window to catch him staring forlornly into space. He seemed so lost, and then as if he caught a happy fright at the sight of our peering faces, his expression changed into one of sheer joy as he excitedly scampered around howling with doggy-delight. Teresa arrived with her entourage of regal hounds in tow and unlocked the door onto our beloved companion.

Barnaby slobbered all over us, jumping ecstatically up from the floor to lick our cheeks with kisses, in approval that we were now a *pack* once again, and now he could be at his *most* happiest! (Dogs do smile; well Barnaby does, and that's gospel...)

We bundled into the campervan and tearfully waved Teresa a loving goodbye, hitting the road for Norfolk – arriving at suppertime.

As we drove up the drive to the Lodge, colourful buntings bedecked the trees all the way up to the house, hung in honour of our success by some of our dear thoughtful neighbours. There were dozens of bouquets of flowers and bottles of champagne left on the doorstep too; it was an overwhelming display of affection for our achievement. And as we opened the door there were a pile of congratulation cards on the mat too.

Both Anglia Television and BBC *Look East* came to film the Lodge to feature our win on the news, and numerous press interviews and features followed. We were really thrilled, when Holly Lodge flashed up on the TV screen.

The *Daily Telegraph* headlined their article (23rd April 2005) in coverage of the event in bold print over a photograph of us clutching the award and quote...

'The Best Little Bed & Breakfast in England'.

Walter. F. Stowy the unforgiving hotel inspector for *The Sunday Times, Travel*, wrote (17th April 2005) and part quote...

'Holly Lodge is a sort of showroom for how all B&Bs might be! Does it deserve its nomination? Yes, Yes, Yes!'

I can't begin to tell you what it meant to me reading his gracious article reviewing our hospitality, accommodation and breakfast written in his eloquent words. And there we were headlining in our local *Eastern Daily Press* too (21st April 2005), featured with Holkham Hall under the caption, and quote...

'Norfolk mansion and B&B win Gold Awards'.

We were in fine company on home ground... I wondered what the seventh Earl might have thought when he saw our humble abode pictured next to his magnificent stately home.

And that's when I wrote earlier about Holly Lodge, one day being glorified alongside this grand modern day Camelot.

Mike drooled over the front page with pride and joked, "Which is which?" An auspicious spread to be pasted into our scrapbook for posterity. It was surreal how far we'd really come, and quite scary too...

One of the judges, John Philipson, general manager of 'The Lowry' last year's winner of 'Large Hotel of the Year' said, and quote...

'Holly Lodge demonstrates a good balance between design, comfort, and charm – and the hospitality is great!'

This had been a milestone no doubt. Our humble bricks, and mortar had become 'Googleable', now a rare stamp of excellence had been attained from both major Tourist Authorities. Honours we'd have to live up to, maintaining a reputation at the highest level of perfection: there could be no room for error once the gold dust had settled as the plaudits faded out on that triumphant night. Expectations from our customers would surely be synonymous with our accolades.

Guest house scoops top B&B accolade

By **RICHARD PARR**
richard.parr@archant.co.uk

TWO friends who moved to Norfolk from London and created a bed and breakfast guest house have won a top AA award.

Robert Greenfield and Michael Bell have won the Guest Accommodation of the Year Award 2004/05 for England for Holly Lodge hotel at Thursford — despite only being open for four years.

They provide three guest rooms from converted stables, each with its own individual style, and guests have use of an exotic Mediterranean garden at the rear of the site.

And as if being judged as the top accommodation guest house in England isn't enough, Holly Lodge is also a finalist in a top East of England Tourist Board award for guest houses in the region.

The owners are delighted at their achievement, which was announced at at a lavish lunch in London.

Although they do not offer an evening meal, they serve guests breakfast, and residents have use of their Gothic-style lounge which is decorated with pieces they have collected over the years. Their latest addition is a conservatory full of exotic plants.

ATTENTION TO DETAIL: Robert Greenfield and Michael Bell at their Holly Lodge guest house in Thursford.

Picture: RICHARD PARR

properties and were looking for somewhere outside London they could combine as their home and a guest house.

"When we moved up here and decided to buy Holly Lodge it took us almost a year to renovate it. We opened it in October 2000 and it was a

and then moved into the house while we created the three guest rooms," said Mr Greenfield.

Part of their success comes from the fact that they pay so much attention to detail and do everything themselves.

"We do a lot of repeat business, once people stay here they want to come

The AA judges' said of Holly Lodge: "A warm welcome and genuine hospitality has been apparent on each of our inspections.

"The beautiful location and surroundings of this 18th century property add to the charm of this delightful Norfolk B&B."

● Holly Lodge can be contacted on

Courtesy of the *Fakenham and Dereham Press.*

THE BEST LITTLE BED & BREAKFAST IN ENGLAND

Kind permission of *The Daily Telegraph*

Courtesy of the *Eastern Daily Press* and *The Archant Group*

Eastern Daily Press

Norfolk mansion and B&B win gold awards

Kind permission of *The Guardian Newspaper, Travel*

The Guardian
travel

Guardian writers
review the AA Guest
Accommodation
of the Year winners
Star guests

England

Home
interiors

Sarah Hardy pays a visit
to Holly Lodge in
Thursford Green, Norfolk
by *Graham Cannon*

Gothic renaissance

Courtesy of the *Eastern Daily Press* and *The Archant Group*

THE SUNDAY TIMES

TOP 10 B&Bs IN ENGLAND

Kind permission of *The Sunday Times, Travel* and *Walter F. Stowy.*

Kind permission of *The Sunday Times, Travel* and *Walter F. Stowy.*

(The ten contenders for the Enjoy England Excellence Awards 2005 hosted by *VisitBritain* at the British Museum.)

CHAPTER 18

A TALE OF TWO JUDGES

The main wall in the front hall became jam-packed with certificates, and I just managed to squeeze the gold-framed (Oscar) certificate next to our recent AA biggie. They nestled side by side as glowing proclamations to all who entered.

It was almost as if a significant collection of accolades monitoring our achievements down the years had now been completed. For some odd reason it felt like a... full stop. Hmmm. And now I was in a quandary...

Yes, the diary was booked to the hilt, and as far as the eye could see into next year, but in all honesty our takings were not justifying the recognition the Lodge had now received nationally.

Planning permission had just been approved for the barn conversion to eke out more guest accommodation, so naturally that would have been the obvious route to take to expand the business. However at the same time I felt in my heart of hearts – Mike's acquiescence was coming more into question.

Of course he was seriously impressed by our achievements, but sadly for him, this was only ever a *B&B business*, and never a real home. Whereas I was still passionate about the Lodge, I always was... It was like nurturing a newborn baby who had now come of age and brought forth new-inspired ideas with each step forward. However recent events meant that the infant had now morphed into a gargantuan monster roaring to be fed...

I can clearly recall an Inspector once commenting that he had seen them come and go in the business, time and time again, and the natural life-span usually seemed to be around six-seven years as often one or the other of the partners would eventually tire of the trade. But to sell up at the top of our game would be wholly unthinkable back in the spring of 2005.

I came to the conclusion that you either do this kind of thing on a small part-time basis not infringing your private life: *Be all and end all*! Or one becomes all consumed as we were building a Boutique Hotel style B&B with all that that entails making copious sacrifices for an end product. Of course there's the matter of *my* quest for *absolute* perfection for our product too. It can only ever be black or white with me. Washy-grey just won't do. How exhausting...

In the final analysis... I thanked my lucky stars; I had Mike along for the ride... ever patient, ever supportive, ever unconditional with his love, and a real grafter! I am truly blessed with finding a partner like him, because above all, he is my trusted *best* friend.

The one thing though that truly miffed him was when I received an invitation that August from the Head of Publicity at *VisitBritain*, asking for my services to become a *Judge* for *'The Enjoy England Awards for Excellence 2006'* to be held next April at *Madame Tussauds*, London.

What a coup it was to be invited to become a judging panellist and discover the behind the scenes process of determining next year's national winners for our industry. I felt it was a tremendous honour...

Naturally Mike was disappointed because he wasn't asked. He'd even made a light-hearted suggestion in passing conversation to the incumbent of The East Of England Tourist Board during the reception at the British Museum, proposing his availability, should there be a vacancy. I did feel guilty and even offered him my place, but he wouldn't have it... bless him!

So, here we were at an apex, a crystallisation of definitive merits clocked-up and coinciding with this coastline becoming a hipper and hotter destination than ever before. But, now the *reality* wove its way into our peaceful enclave. Our dear little Lodge was teeming in the thick of it!

Even non-residents dropped by requesting afternoon teas – passer-by-drop-ins became prodigious as our reputation spread with the news nationwide. There was no escaping the public traffic at the Lodge: they winked, waved and watched from every nook and cranny.

Although, back in the day I do remember how frustrating it really was... not being able to accommodate all the extra business – much beyond our capacity. Many were turned away regretfully that summer, and recommended elsewhere.

And then... *The shit really hit the fan...*

One muggy and innocent afternoon several months later just as the last embers of summer were turning to a flame-red autumn, I'd noticed a very large group of around ten strangers milling around outside in the front garden.

However *this* time it felt more invasive than ever... I could tell they were non-residents, and they disappeared around to the side of the house where all the garden tables were set out, opposite the cottages.

I was distracted by a phone call and about ten minutes later I wandered out to check on them.

Flasks of tea and packed lunches were spread out under the parasols and they chattered away blithely.

"Excuse me, I am the proprietor, please can you tell me what you are doing here?" I inquired politely.

"Er... well, we'd seen some publicity on Holly Lodge in the weekend supplements, and we thought we'd use it as a backdrop for our holiday snaps."

"This is private property for residents only, you know..." I suggested.

A lady then grabbed me and shoved her camera into my hand.

"Oh, be a dear, place yourself over there, and remember to get the whole group in – quick while the sun is still on us."

What chutzpah... But I was obliging under the circumstances, and took the blasted picture, and even let them finish their incongruous picnic luncheon. But hey I just happen to live here too... (That was it in a nutshell: A RUDE AWAKENING!) Internally, I was suddenly experiencing a catastrophic meltdown during my *epiphany*.

I was aghast as it dawned on me what our high profile status had really done to the place: A Zoological-Piccadilly Circus effect had taken hold in the depths of our peaceful haven.

Some say... Be careful for what you wish for... Well, my world suddenly imploded that afternoon. It was a monumental tipping-point. I slowly walked back to the house thinking the consequence through... And perhaps that Mike was *right* all along.

Maybe I had been in denial for years lost in an *addictive* fantasy without really considering the repercussions...

"Only a business – never a home," I mumbled over and over the haunting thought to myself.

The balance had to be redressed (urgently)... but how? I lingered on the doorstep and looked around at my beloved '*Dream Sanctuary*'. A toll-bell had gone-off sounding the death knell like a significant passing; I felt sick to my core, as if a love affair had died – soured – finished – over! Even the intoxicating sweet jasmine by the entrance lost its seductive fragrance at that capricious moment.

I walked into the hall; the house felt suddenly strange. I was now standing in a cold, official space, all the passionate allure that had once captivated me had now evaporated in an instant. And I was distraught...! I wandered from room to room lost in a labyrinth of alien volume. For now... *I did not know this place...*

Mike came buoyantly in from the garden, he'd been chatting to some guests up by the pond. He was cheerfully rambling on about how they enjoyed their stay, and how they were full of praise for our imaginative grounds. I stood there faltering with a vacant stare and not really listening...

He broke off his flow of conversation, and asked...

"Why are you so sombre – is there is anything wrong?"

I stuttered slowly... for I was about to break some breathtaking news to him.

"It's, it's over... We must put Holly Lodge on the market for sanity's sake... Mikey! You were right all along this was just only ever a business, a means to an end, and never our dream country idyll at all. And I am really sorry babes..." I welled up utterly devastated with profound disappointment.

He did not say a word, but crept over and hugged me as I began to sob profusely; for he knew what the Lodge had meant to me, and how difficult it would be to leave after so much had happened to us here. Because there is no doubt this had been a *pivotal* chapter that had changed our lives and us forever.

I knew too, how relieved he would be; as if a huge burden had been suddenly lifted from his shoulders; and quite frankly we were both utterly exhausted. How much more could we give to the business? It was now consuming us. Totally...

And the other thing of course above all else was that of our relationship being paramount. In my heart of hearts it was imperative that this must never be compromised, because I knew we had something so special and rare. And many had been in awe of how successful our partnership really became. For me it seemed to have taken a lifetime to find as near to perfect a partner that can be found in this world, and I was not going to let the business come between us now. No way!

There! I could justify the decision, reason it was OK, we had paid our dues, achieved something in this field very few have ever done, and now our work was done, and it was instinctively calling-time!

(I tell you the moribund reverberations meant a tectonic shift had shaken the fundamental foundations of my ethos for life at the Lodge that day.)

A few days later, I had a conversation with my friend, Lawrence, for if it had not been for him we might never have embarked on this amazing journey. He was now living in the Greek Islands, and he talked of a 'Great Depression' coming, nothing like we had ever seen in our lifetime.

I sensed perhaps, he was onto something, and it added credence to the fact that if we did not sell soon we may be stuck here for years to come, this time against our own freewill.

The banks had lent indiscriminately to well beyond their true capacities: a false economy of epic rapaciousness teetered on the brink. Payback time was calling... the bubble of the great economic boom was about to explode sooner rather than later.

And boy... what an explosion it became besetting all our lives with its toxic fall-out, one by one the soaring bastions of financial power fuelling our once lucrative economy have spectacularly crumbled before our very eyes.

Lawrence is a wizard when it comes to this kind of thing, and he had prescient wind of the Sub-Prime sector faltering Stateside. And what with his amazing nous had forecasted this cataclysmic *tsunami* brewing long ago. His warnings played heavily on my mind, and of course the rest is now history...

And history does repeat itself. I began to feel emotive thoughts of the time, when I walked... turning my back on a buoyant career in the fashion biz just before the last great recession, which had now become inextricably woven as bookends, echoing these current issues decades later, but eerily similar in portent...

Ah, the human condition plagued with such complexities and such contradictions. Why do most of us aspire to this great goal in the sky...? A driven quest only to discover... *The grass is not always greener* on the flipside.

I had to follow my resolve. My intuit like my father's had always provided me with impeccable timing with such life changing decisions; and *the* decision would have to be the final mind-set.

Now the unthinkable was *thinkable*!

I felt so contrite and racked with guilt though. Especially with the way both Tourist Board Authorities had bestowed upon us such generous honours, which could now be considered in vain for Holly Lodge. Because in reality these accolades go with the owners, just like a *Michelin* Star belongs to its Chef.

'*Expect the unexpected*!' an aphoristic pearl of wisdom first quoted by the ancient Greek philosopher, Heraclitus (c.535 BC – 475 BC) smacked me hard across the face. And my Inner Child was panicking...

I had to remain resolute insofar that past six-odd years of experience in this industry had provided priceless qualifications for us both. And for me I could develop these in a number of ways for our future. Surely I would be a catch for a budding entrepreneurial hotelier? Or indeed maybe for a hotel chain itching to revamp its flagging hotels. My CV would surely be packed with enough qualifications... eh?

A new *void* would scare the hell out of me and my thoughts were jumping ahead with the possibilities. But of course there could be new territories to explore in other avenues for us both, but next time our *home* would simply be just...

'*Home Sweet Home*'.

And poor Mike. He had been dragged through everything; I should be made culpable for what I had done – the onus was squarely on me. Now reparations had to be prepared...

Primarily, a hush-hush affair would have to ensue to keep our sale a well-guarded secret for the time being. Everything must appear normal, no photographs displayed in estate agents windows, no hoardings, no media advertising.

Our private-pact would be conspired with a specialist estate agent, who would be carefully chosen, and one who would be our only ally in cahoots with a furtive escape-plan.

The next six months were to be the most harrowing of all. Playing out the final sequence with the aplomb of convincing well-versed actors, never showing any inkling to our customers of our future intentions.

When knowledge is abounding of a hotel business about to be sold with change of ownership, we both assumed a shadow would be cast with the associated negatives. So this became our caveat.

Any prospective viewings would have to be arranged for late mornings or early afternoons, a time when most guests would be out for the day. Initially there was a flurry of what were time-wasters, just indulging their curiosity. Sold... Not!

You see in another ironic twist our success would sometimes play against us. And often many prospective buyers seemed daunted by the prospect of stepping into our shoes at the Lodge. It was a somewhat disturbing paradox... when suggestions were raised about our *Michelin* Star style breakfasts. And Gordon (*fucking*) Ramsey sprang to mind because at that point, I'd even started to play down our successes to try, and clinch a quick sale. Doh!

There was one lady though, that came on numerous occasions, declaring that... "Holly Lodge is a Christmas house and I always buy my Christmassy houses..." She was very passionate about the place and wanted to continue the business in a similar vein. I was convinced she'd go for it. However it turned out her husband was not up for the business as much as her. She even wrote me a heartfelt letter airing her sorrowful sentiments of not acquiring the Lodge.

In the meantime we had a business to run and of course I still intended to fulfil my obligations of becoming a Judge for *VisitBritain*, which was something I very much wanted to honour...

It was so ironic in a Yin-Yang sort of way that, that autumn one of the most awful guests we'd ever come to experience was to be a Judge. Perhaps some sort of divine retribution resulted in this interplay with bad karma...

This invidious encounter created the last *Guest from Hell* to be added to my '**BLACKLIST**', and underlined to be passed onto the next generation of owners should they care to continue to run the property as a hotel.

So with the pressure mounting... it all came to a breathtaking showdown with 'Judge-Dread', as I called him, who arrived that fateful day.

On the surface all seemed fine, he was a portly South African fellow, built like a pocket-rocket terrier with a blush thread-veined complexion and a curly shock of the whitest hair. His towering raven-haired wife was so very jolly-hockey-sticks in her tweedy ensemble. Even during breakfast everything went swimmingly. Although Judge Dread was despairingly loud and his bumptious voice bellowed through the dining hall, ricocheting through everybody's conversations.

But in contrast, mild-mannered Mrs Dread was charm personified, and especially noted the Latin names of my mixed seasonal arrangements as if she were a horticulturist...

During this period, we had some of our favourite regulars staying with us: Fran, a very courteous, always impeccably turned-out lady, and Bert her husband, who is very urbane. If ever there were the most truly affable guests, then these genuinely warm-spirited folk fitted the bill to a tee. And they stayed every year about this time.

There was also a very arty young couple down from London; if my memory serves they were jewellery designers, and they had been raving about a day out at the magnificent Houghton Hall. Lord Cholmondeley's, ultra-swanky Georgian pile near Sandringham: once home to Sir Robert Walpole, England's very first Prime Minister.

All was well during breakfast the next morning, then around ten o'clock, the kitchen door burst open, and Judge

Dread just stood there... Fuming like a prize bull. It kicked-off something like this...

"What the hell do you think you are doing? Our belongings have been rearranged: we couldn't find any of our clothes left out over the armchairs..."

He gasped for breath, and then continued as if we'd committed a cardinal crime, with a hefty sentence about to be cast in the offing.

"Now listen here and listen good... I am a paying guest and therefore the cottage is my property. While I am in residence, our possessions are never to be touched in any way...

"DO YOU HEAR ME CHAPS?"

His face was puce with rage; he then grabbed me by my shirt collar and intimidated me by protruding his sweaty face right up to my nose and repeated...

"DO YOU HEAR ME...? **MY PROPERTY**!" shouting vociferously, as his spittle splashed across my cheek.

Mike jumped up from the kitchen table rallying to my side; I pushed the judge back from my space elbowing his hands down off my collar. By now I was reeling – incensed with his over-the-top invective outburst.

"Please! Calm down... You stand corrected... Sir. Firstly you are a paying guest on our property, secondly your room was tidied as per usual, your things were placed neatly away in the dresser – not exactly a hardship for you to find! And finally there's no excuse for physically intimidating me... you of all people should know better..." I retorted, almost bursting with adrenalin up to my eyeballs.

He glared at me with his flashing eyes, and then raising his voice a couple more octaves, fired-off echoing like a foghorn across the Thames Barrier...

I don't like this, and I don't like that, ranting on and on delirious like a maniac. Haranguing us for what...? It was bizarre...

"What is your problem?" interjected Mike. I thought he was about to deck him, and Barnaby growled, which is such a rarity.

This was getting more ugly by the second; his impromptu attack was no doubt alarming. Nothing on this scale had ever occurred before. And I was sure Bert and Fran, had heard everything at the Pembroke table in the sanctity of the lounge.

"Back off, turn yourself around – pack your bags, and leave, because you know what Mister high and mighty judge? This is totally unacceptable!" I fired-off in riposte, my blood curdling with the *injustice* of it all. How ironic…!

And then… he became even more agitated. I thought the pompous-ass was about to thump me by the way he postured. He inhaled deeply, psyching me out…. stole a glance at Barnaby, then at Mike. Barnaby became more agitated – sensing all the angst… But I held him too.

"Well, an apology is due, is it not…?" Mike beckoned.

I mulled over this antithesis of his profession. Years of passing his heavy sentences in rancour with his unquestioned authority, and that booming voice. I bet he's the type that even treats a game of *Monopoly* as a blood sport…

Crikey! I would not like to be standing in his dock.

The moment was precarious and suddenly in a fit of pique… He did an about-turn, pushing the ledge and brace door back with such ferocity, that its latch cracked the dining room wall, actually indenting the plaster. Then he hastily crossed to the front door, over-turning a chair sending it crashing across the room, a glass smashed to the floor. And he slammed the front door so violently it shook the entire house.

Fortunately his wife had left the table prior to the incident, and the young couple had long since gone for the day, but it was Bert and Fran who were still in the lounge as I'd suspected, that had heard the brunt of the contretemps. And in actual fact poor Fran became very upset – she was in pieces about it.

I consoled her, although she consoled me too, with her supportive words…

Subsequently, the strangest thing happened though... While the judge loaded their car, his wife came to settle up. And she was as nice as pie...

"We've had a lovely stay, I am so sorry we have to leave prematurely due to family commitments, but I have to tell you... Holly Lodge is such a wonderful place... Thank you!"

Bert, Fran, Mike and I stood in the front hall just astounded... And I could tell Mike was bursting to say something.

More than baffled by the whiff of her incongruous comments amidst the heat, I was on the brink of telling the poor woman what I really thought of her husband, but as I looked over at Fran – she emanated an err on the side of *professional* caution to me.

God knows the opportune moment had arisen, preying on my distress of being practically assaulted. Mrs Dread lingered on the doorstep fastening her jacket and tying her neck scarf for what seemed ages. And I really was teetering in my angst, but it would have been inane to cause more upset. So I bid the lady a pleasant goodbye. And she was perhaps, none the wiser of the whole grubby ordeal. Who knows...?

Mike patted me on the shoulder affectionately. Bert and Fran gave me a sympathetic hug and then left for the day. And we continued with our duties.

Amazingly that was the first, and last time anybody got the old heave-ho from the Lodge in view of their wholly deranged attitude, and a Judge to *boot*... End of.

As my old mate Lawrence had predicted, there was more than a lingering whiff in the air of the property market starting to cool for the first time in years; little did we all know how this would pan-out into the worst recession since the 1930s, and indeed in post-war modern times.

We had a very promising viewing late that September, from a couple, already well versed in the hotel trade. After successfully running a Bed and Breakfast business at the famous North Norfolk landmark of the 'Cley Windmill', they were now looking for a new prospect. Because unfortunately, after eight years at the Mill, the owners, parents of the chart-topping singer, James Blunt, had decided to sell-up. Therefore they were concurrently looking for a new property, but this time one that would dual as a new home for them too.

We hit it off immediately with the Bolams on their first viewing. Incidentally, Jeremy Bolam was a revered Master Chef in his own right, having once owned a smart London restaurant. So Holly Lodge could prove to be an ideal prospect for them. I'd always felt it would have been an undeniable pity if the Lodge were not to continue in a similar vein, so to pass the property to such capable new owners would at least maintain some continuity. And give me some kind of solace too.

Again a preordained fate played its hand in our destiny, as at the beginning of this whole saga, and now to draw it to an inevitable conclusion. A pattern that seems to repeat itself throughout my life...

Although the first viewing had enticed Jeremy, and his dear Canadian wife, Jill, they still needed to find a buyer for their pretty coastal cottage in Cley, in order to purchase the Lodge.

Some weeks later, literally off a plane from Canada, they stopped by for a second viewing; this time they fell for the place... hook, line and sinker. And then a string of fateful events played out...

After their viewing that day, they popped up to nearby Holt to do some shopping, and subsequently out of the blue, bumped into an old friend from London, whom they hadn't seen in years. They discovered coincidently, that he happened to be looking for a place to buy up on the North Norfolk coast, so they offered to show him their little cottage in Cley. And, *Bob's your Uncle* he bought it on the spot. Cash!

The next morning they made us an offer for the full asking price and dear old Holly Lodge was sold without any further ado. Crucially it's all about timing, and I believe it was *fated* for them, and fated for us too. Boohoo...!

Ironically we have struck up a wonderful friendship with the couple, and we are very gratified that the new owners have kept the standards high, but of course with their own take.

The reward of becoming a Judge for *VisitBritain* for next year's Excellence Awards was the ultimate icing on the cake from the whole Holly Lodge experience, something I never dreamt of ever happening. It was truly an enlightening task, an experience that was of great value to me personally, and which of course I approached with my usual zeal.

I stealthily drove down the drive out of the Lodge at about five that morning, so as not to wake our guests. What with all the stress of selling up this was going to be a challenging new dawn down in London.

I had been booked into the Dolphin Square hotel for a two-night stay, courtesy of *VisitBritain*. The other judges hailed from all spheres of the Travel Industry each with their own expertise to bring to the panel, including notable travel writers, and broadcasters, and of course esteemed officials from the Tourist Board; as well as two previous Gold Award winners, of which I was one.

The first night I attended a really interesting dinner in a private dining room: The Chichester Suite at the hotel, held to acquaint all the judges with one another before Judging Day took place at the 'Government Department of Culture, Media, and Sport' in Cockspur Street, SW1.

I seemed to click instantly with the travel writers enjoying their convivial tales and fascinating banter.

The next day, we all seated ourselves around a courtyard layout of tables in the large meeting room, whilst six independent very experienced specially selected assessors – having spent months anonymously investigating all the regional winners up and down the land – now reported their assessment of each establishment or tourist attraction to us.

A microscopic analysis was presented in the form of a mind-boggling clipboard report of criteria, with photographic evidence, which they carried out with military style precision. The judges would intermittently check into the corresponding websites casting their eyes over these attractions and establishments, whilst digesting these assessments.

Fortunately I had already scrutinised my seventy-page briefing dossier on all the venues, outlining their strengths and weaknesses.

These reports covered: Exteriors – Reception – Public areas – Cleanliness – Bedrooms – Bathrooms – Breakfast – Lunch – Dinner – Accessibility – Guest welcome – Service and Location.

The fifteen-minute presentation on each destination would culminate with the assessor's comments and overview before we could aggressively interrogate him or her about each experience.

I remember a passionate debate ensuing, which at times became quite heated, each of us presenting a particular view based on their evidence, so we could come to a just and fair conclusion for each establishment – culminating in a scoring system out-of-ten for each assessed area in minutiae. We would then file reports on our judging forms recommending Gold, Silver, or Bronze Awards with a written personal comment about each recipient.

We were locked away for an arduous eight hours rigorously making painstaking decisions – sifting through the finer details with immense fervour.

This was such an eye-opener and I could now really evaluate why we'd won our awards for Holly Lodge. It was fascinating to discover why a hotel might be robbed of a Gold... because its cleanliness was not up to scratch, a missed dusty shelf perhaps, the carpet might not have been vacuumed properly in some forgotten corner, hospitality had slipped or the bacon was over cooked etc, etc. A frustrating missed opportunity for any proprietor, I'm sure!

It's this strict criterion that *VisitBritain* make their assessments on, and rightly so! Forming the basis of the quality and standards making for an exemplary benchmark, a standard set to create an outstanding visitor experience at each venue. But, and a very big *But,* it's that certain *Je ne sais quoi*! (That something extra special) that will set you apart from the rest, and make your establishment shine and standout above all the others.

Ironically, 'St Ervan Manor' was up for this much-coveted award yet again, and deservedly so too. How strange that I was now critiquing them... My most worrying competitor back at the ceremony at the British Museum, whom I thought might steal the crown from last year's awards. However in comparing them to the other entrants in the B&B/Guesthouse category, there was no doubt that this time on their outstanding merits, they should win the Gold. For which I was only too happy to oblige them with – when casting my vote.

During the days of judging, I had to keep schtum about our sale, and felt a little fraudulent, even embarrassed when I was confronted with such nice things said about our establishment by the other panellists. It was very difficult behaving furtively with fellow members of the jury, but we were in the final throes of completing the sale.

There is no doubt that the entire judging experience offered me an over-the-counter glance into an exclusive club that fortunately I had the privilege to gain entry to *only* via the success of Holly Lodge.

After I'd fulfilled my commitments and gone back to my hotel room that night... I was in turmoil. What with judging all the residences that day I suddenly had a nostalgic attack of wistful thoughts for the Lodge. Letting go had become a painful ordeal and I was plagued with doubts that night...

Had I really let something so special slip through my fingers yet again? Was this a rerun of when my fashion career was at its apogee, when I walked...?

Oh! I felt terrible... And an overriding emptiness overwhelmed me. I felt *totally* alone in that desolate hotel room... Because even then I still questioned my decision to sell the Lodge. My mind went from pillar to post with these ponderings.

I tossed and turned the entire night. I have always been an epic night dreamer in 3D-HD Technicolor, and now these insecurities played on my mind with grand chicanery.

I saw myself ambling through the bountiful gardens, past the purple buddleia. A myriad of butterflies danced fountain-like above my head. I lay in languor on the jetty amongst the reeds beneath the great Norfolk skyscape. I seemed at one with nature, and at peace with myself. And wondered when I would tell my story. Then, I flashed to the day the house became snowbound. When Mike and I stood transfixed in the Orangery as silent snowflakes fell in angelic abundance all about us; and there for a tangible moment a magical dream was caught in our palms... Suddenly I wasn't sure if I was dreaming anymore because that really did happen! And then...

I observed, a *fly on the wall* view of laughter and banter with dear friends around our beloved monastic table in the refectory that was the true Holly Lodge – snuck away from the contrivance of the hotel.

I awoke in a shivery sweat... Now I could see my sprawling garden, which I had spent years nurturing, and in a funny old way it had become a reflection of my life: controlled, energetic, creative and always colourful beyond the vagaries of the seasons. Meandering paths, leading to surprising twists and turns, sometimes wild, then punctuated by an unexpected intruder: an obstacle just like the real world of course. And the trees, oh yes, bending this way and that, in the capricious breezes to avoid breaking: just like me... A heavenly amalgamation created. And now developed to a wiser maturity beyond its years.

Isn't it really funny how a garden really does reflect a human life?

I lay there exhausted, my emotions spent, I'd be returning to the Lodge in the morning. And I just had to keep sight of my premise for the sale... The bottom line was the sanctity of our relationship. Mike and I could now move onto pastures new, which I was sure would be as rich, and as fertile as we'd ever lived...

CHAPTER 19

LETTING GO

So, here we were immersed in our very last Christmas season at the Lodge. Happy Holidays for our guests continued with business as usual. They had no inkling of our impending departure. We soldiered on...

Even to have informed our ardent regulars would have been a crying shame, because an annual pilgrimage here meant a lot to our loyal clientele.

Christmas at the Lodge had become an art form, and we wanted to go out on a memorable high for all concerned.

Everything had to run as smooth as clockwork so as not to spoil the sentiment of the season. Naturally it tugged at our heartstrings this poignant reminder of almost where it all began. A time of year that is so emotive, and one most will hold dear...

I remember one particular lady so well, but for a most significant reason... She had come over the great Pond, from Nantucket Island to join her friends, our 'Holly Lodgers' as I now called them, whom I likened to habitual swifts, with us once again, while our nest was feathered for its finale.

Esme Johnson, a handsome woman with a feisty, no-nonsense persona, reminiscent of that pioneering spirit that probably first established her ancestors long ago in the verdant pastures of New England had arrived, and was completely unaware of her part she'd play in our destiny. She entered the Lodge sprightly alongside her affable companions – the effervescent Millers.

She spoke with a kind of lax drawl that could sound superfluous with every statement, although one had to listen hard sometimes to interpret the phonetics of her New England intonations. Eerily parallel to the singsong cadence of the Norfolk lingo, which still bemused me at times.

She was tremendous fun though, with her sharp wit imbued with much more than a soupcon of devil-may-care delivery. We adored her free-spirited company right up until Christmas Eve. She'd even invited us over to Nantucket sometime.

The main reason I have mentioned this fine lady is because on that very last morning – the day we closed our doors for good – and waved off our very last guests; she just so happened to be the very last soul to sign-off in our 'Visitors' Book'.

I picked up the vellum bound book and scanned down the buff parchment paper to her handwritten comment. And it simply read...

'A Truly Superb Experience!' Esme Mae Johnson – Nantucket, Massachusetts.

Her kind words rippled through me defining my sentiment *too* about the Lodge. It was almost as if it were a closing epitaph to our six years of life here.

There was many a morning that one of us would anxiously pick up our beloved book to gauge a departing comment from a guest. Their handwritten heartfelt tribute was a lingering testimony of their thoughts on their whole Holly Lodge experience. These words spoke volumes, perhaps above and beyond everything else their sincere sentiment meant the most to us; signed by persons, hailing from all over the country, and indeed from the four corners of the planet.

Thousands and thousands of people have passed through our welcoming doors from every niche of society. Some became good friends; some were part of the transient ebb and flow of our business, but each and everyone one of them added another colourful thread to be woven into the rich tapestry of a **'Truly Superb Experience!'**

Everything was busily cleared away for the very last time. Obviously emotions were running high... and as I carried the stacked tray back to the kitchen, the little china salt pot from the set crashed to the floor and smashed spilling the salt, which some say is bad luck!

I placed the tray down to collect the pieces and brushed the salt into a dustpan, with the realisation that Mike's mother had bought us this fine set of Regency china for the beginning of our journey here, and now she was no longer with us in its conclusion.

An era was ending, and our life was about to change once again, but this time without the comfort of her guiding presence.

"Don't worry, I am sure mother won't mind!"

Mike was loading the dishwasher, and I suddenly wanted to give him a tremendous hug. I was taut with emotion, but daren't ignite his hankering feelings for his dear mum. For sure he'd have loved her there that day. So I held it together.

"Crikey, Mike it's Game Over!" I rinsed some more cups.

"How about that? Hey, who'd have thought it? Best B & B in Britain..." He picked up the napkins, with the linen to go into the wash.

"We've maxed out the points and bonuses, hit the jackpot, with a cacophony of bells ringing, and lights flashing with all that razzamatazz.... I told you we'd do it, that day way back when."

And I chortled as I swept up the crumbs from the surface of the dining table, moped it over, began polishing and then plumped up the chair cushions.

It could have been just another day...

I am thankful that I'd always found time to keep a journal even during our busiest times at the Lodge, an inventory of our life shared caretaking this wondrous place.

I'd sifted through reams of files, many cherished comments from our Visitors' Book, and numerous press cuttings in my scrapbook, to recount my story. Alas soon to become a hazy-grainy dream fading into a past reflection, but oh, such an unforgettable *experience* to be stored forever in the vaults of my mind.

Most of our belongings were by now already packed, but now we could pack up the rest our personal stuff too, in readiness for our departure in the New Year. I'd found a sweet little holiday cottage on Blakeney Harbour for a six month rental so we could take stock, sit out the winter, and sort ourselves out to decide whatever next.

I ferried necessities back and forth as through the years we had accumulated so much in this large house, so downsizing was such a relief now. We'd sold most of the contents of the guest cottages with the business, and off-loaded some key items from the main house too, privately to the Bolams, keen to maintain some semblance of our distinct look.

Unbelievably... the very last day came. It was a grey, chilly morning, early in the New Year...

Mike and Wendy, our cleaning lady, went through the entire place with a fine toothcomb to make sure it was all spick, and span and ready for the new occupants.

In the meantime, I was up at Blakeney, organising our new makeshift home, and helping the removal guys deposit some basic essentials we might need for this holiday cottage by the sea.

"Staying long?" the van driver quizzed me.

"Not sure we'll see!" I replied and headed back to the Lodge with a heavy heart. The past years were spinning through my thoughts...

As I drove up to the door – the dreary winter light overshadowed the house with a pervading sadness and it felt like I'd be saying goodbye to an old friend. And worn down with the routine tedium associated with a move did not help matters either. However, when I came through the hall, and into the hub of the house, I was shocked by the empty hollow void before me.

I welled up... now feeling utterly overwhelmed, but had to try to contain myself.

Naturally Mike and Wendy had done a sterling job putting everything in order this end, ready for the new owners to step into our mantle.

"Well, I guess we're just about ready – just these things to load up now..." Mike tried to be as matter of fact as possible; he knew my emotions would be twisted in knots internally. Although he seemed stoic, I could tell he was simmering too, and just keeping a brave face.

I went upstairs to check all the rooms out, and to fetch Barnaby who'd become one confused dog, disturbed by all the commotion no doubt. Like humans these creatures of habit hate their routines disrupted. Naturally sensing this chaotic time, he just kept out of the way and curled up on his bed.

Somehow, he'd graduated to the single spare bedroom on the landing, not too far from ours, so we could always listen out for him. Imagine, he really had his own nursery...

No wonder... Barnaby, the most pampered whippet this side of the Watford Gap or if you happen to live Stateside a comparable boundary might be the notion of the Mason-Dixon Line, became very reluctant to relinquish his private den. And who'd blame him...

The door to his room was closed and when I entered, he was standing defiantly on the bed. I told him to come... But he just would not have it... He stubbornly refused to leave. He looked at me with his luminous moist eyes. And I stroked and kissed his sweet head.

"Come baby Boo, we have to leave now..."

He was steadfast for another moment, perhaps untrusting to where he might be despatched to... packing always seemed a cue for some kind of departure, and I could tell he was thinking it through. Then with trust in his heart... he leapt from the bed, and picked up his favourite soft toy teddy off the floor and followed me downstairs.

Finally as I reached the dining room, I could stand it no longer and I just let rip, tears streamed profusely. Poor Wendy had never seen me like that before and she started getting very emotional too.

"Don't be ridiculous!" Mike snapped, for he hated tearful farewells. He knew exactly how to handle me, when my feelings were this wired...

I busied myself putting the last items of cookware in the campervan. And then I thought for a transient longing moment... like the day when we'd left the Courtyard and our happy life behind in London...

I really believe we all leave an indelible footprint, which will become inextricably woven into the very fabric of a building that we have loved, and lived a life in, whether happy or sad. No doubt our voices and experiences will be as passing echoes as if frozen in aspic... And in our case, perhaps an echo to languish as a unique faded glory within this masonry...

Wendy hugged us with a tearful goodbye and then she disappeared down the drive. Mike picked up a whimpering, and completely freaked-out Barnaby, and put him into the back of the VW. I shut the doors to our vehicle and returned to close the house down and check for one last time.

I placed a bottle of champers, with a card for the Bolams onto the kitchen counter, next to a fresh bunch of lilies as a warm welcome.

Now the house stood empty once again awaiting its new custodians to fill it with their story. And I thought of the day we had anxiously arrived here all those moons ago, and oh... how disappointed we were with its dour appeal...

But had we done the right thing? Most certainly... Yes! There were no regrets except *maybe* leaving the Lodge, the coming years will tell...

Finally, I peered out through the kitchen windowpanes at a familiar changing backdrop throughout our seasons here... Still winters, where I felt cocooned, budding to life with sweet spring awakenings, then, the hot flush of vibrant summers bursting with surprises, before mellowing into those woody autumns with their heady scents – wafting into my workspace. And I was filled with contentment for a time.

I shivered and wiped my sore wet eyes, and took a very last lingering look on my *labour of love*, a space that was now morphing into the very final moment on the last page of a crucial chapter of my life. And my Mike's too!

One thing for sure though life at the Lodge was more than just a *Brief Encounter,* but an epic romance I'd never forget!

Mike honked the horn and called me to hurry up, he did not want me to linger long for emotion's sake.

I sighed and nodded my head from side to side, stared wistfully into the bare space and simply walked out closing the door behind me on our life at the Lodge forever...

There you have it... The story of how we created arguably one of the best B&B/Guesthouses in the British Isles.

We did not conquer Everest, sail the Seven Seas, invent a cure for cancer or even make a fortune. But what we did achieve was to live-out a fantastical adventure on an exciting roller-coaster journey into a most stunning location. And had the privilege to enjoy a wondrous bucolic way of life in a special corner of North Norfolk on what became our much-beloved ***Samphire Coast***: This is my homage!

Incredible new friends blessed our time here, as we lived out an ambitious dream to staggering results. Whilst ultimately discovering a true sense of self and what really matters at the end of the day... *'Love conquers all'*. We survived, bonding ever stronger, and were now *free* to fast-forward to the next destination turning the page onto more magical adventures together, because hey...! This is not really the end, but just the beginning...

As the old sixties' hippie song by Lobo goes:

'ME AND YOU AND A DOG NAMED** (BARNABY)* ***BOO...'